"Matt Queen has provided us with a comprehensive and clear guide on how to be a winsome witness to Jesus Christ. He engages with the best of classical and contemporary thinkers on the subject. The result is a trustworthy biblical, theological, and practical tour de force. He writes from a rich Southern Baptist context, but this book deserves a wide audience across the spectrum of denominations. As a mainline pastor teaching in an evangelical college, I recommend this book to all who want to learn how and why to share their faith. *Recapturing Evangelism* helped me, it is helping my students, and it will help you."

—**Gregory M. Anderson**, evangelism commission chair,
Council for Christian Colleges and Universities

"Matt Queen exemplifies 'scholarship on fire.' *Recapturing Evangelism* demonstrates Queen's meticulous research of existing evangelism materials, from which he provides practical application for believers today. I read everything Queen writes on evangelism. You should too!"

—**Timothy Beougher**, associate dean and Billy Graham professor
of evangelism, The Southern Baptist Theological Seminary

"*Recapturing Evangelism* is a magnificent work of biblical and theological scholarship, vividly presented by one of Southern Baptist's most passionate, grace-gifted evangelists. After reading this theology of evangelism, which masterfully integrates spiritual, philosophical, and methodological dimensions of the spiritual discipline, scholars, pastors, and those in the pew will exclaim, 'I have recaptured my passion for evangelism!'"

—**Carl J. Bradford**, assistant professor of evangelism,
Southwestern Baptist Theological Seminary

"What are the contemporary issues in evangelism? What are the theological minefields to be aware of? Matt Queen's *Recapturing Evangelism* equips us to answer these questions. By reading this book, you will have a comprehensive foundation of Bible passages and a systematic understanding of relevant categories for evangelism—both in theory and practice. Any serious student of evangelism must read this book."

—**Sam Chan**, author of *Evangelism in a Skeptical World*;
How to Talk about Jesus (*Without Being That Guy*)
and *Topical Preaching in a Complex World*

"Matt Queen's contribution to evangelism scholarship in *Recapturing Evangelism* provides a needed reminder of the gravity of an increasingly unpopular activity. The book moves from the biblical roots of evangelism, through various theologies surrounding the practice, and finally to the application of why and how every Christian ought to evangelize. This work is at once scholarly—researched deeply enough to satisfy any expert in the field—yet accessible—providing instructive anecdotes and strategies understandable by a novice Christian. It would serve equally well as a textbook for seminary courses or a topical study for church small groups."

—**Adam W. Greenway**, president, Southwestern
Baptist Theological Seminary

"While there are many books on the subject of evangelism, *Recapturing Evangelism* is a biblically-grounded and theologically-informed resource that stands out from the others. He combines the study of the Scriptures with the wisdom of evangelists from history and insights of seasoned practitioners today. More than excellent content, however, Matt Queen's passion to reach spiritually lost souls and form them to become fully devoted followers of Jesus, jumps from the pages."

—**David M. Gustafson**, associate professor of evangelism and
missional ministry, Trinity Evangelical Divinity School

"I fear that pastors leading their churches to be evangelistic are often trying to train church members who do not see a need for evangelism in the first place. Ask the members, and they sometimes cannot summarize their own story well. Quiz them, and they cannot clearly explain the gospel. Press them, and they're not all convinced hell is real—or even that good people apart from Jesus are headed there. Matt Queen, one of the most passionate evangelists I know, recognizes that believers need a strong biblical and theological base if we expect them to tell the good news. Dr. Queen has provided this excellent resource to address that need. Read it, and then teach it to your church."

—**Chuck Lawless**, dean of doctoral studies and senior professor of evangelism and missions, Southeastern Baptist Theological Seminary

"Sadly, evangelism has become multiple things to multiple people. As the Church goes into the world, She travels through a fog of confusion regarding this kingdom matter. Much is at stake. Billions are in need of the good news. Matt Queen has provided a means to remove the fog by challenging us to return to the apostolic imagination. *Recapturing Evangelism* is a great book! Queen's scholarly, yet highly practical, work takes us on a journey into present realities while finding guidance from Scripture, history, and contemporary practice as we make disciples of all nations. This work equips us to go with intentionality and urgency and share with gentleness and respect as we proclaim the good news of the Kingdom!"

—**J. D. Payne**, author, missiologist, and professor of Christian ministry, Samford University

"In the book, *Recapturing Evangelism: A Biblical-Theological Approach*, Dr. Matt Queen addresses the essence of evangelism as a theological practice. This is a much needed and timely study for both the local church and academia. I have found that if we do not see evangelism as part of our overall theology, it will most likely be avoided altogether. I very much appreciate Dr. Queen's willingness to deal with the man-made limitations to evangelism that are falsely embraced by many Christian leaders, etc. If you will read this book with an open mind, I am convinced that you will be both challenged and encouraged to join Christ on mission as a multiplying evangelist!"

—**David A. Wheeler**, professor of evangelism and senior executive director of Liberty University Shepherd, Liberty University

RECAPTURING EVANGELISM

RECAPTURING
EVANGELISM

A Biblical-Theological Approach

MATT QUEEN

Foreword by David S. Dockery

ACADEMIC
BRENTWOOD, TENNESSEE

Recapturing Evangelism: A Biblical-Theological Approach

Copyright © 2023 by Matt Queen

Published by B&H Academic
Brentwood, Tennessee

ISBN: 978-1-0877-2335-8

Dewey Decimal Classification: 269.2
Subject Heading: EVANGELISTIC WORK / WITNESSING / CHURCH WORK

Some of the content of this book contains modifications of Matt Queen, *Everyday Evangelism*, 3rd ed. (Fort Worth: Seminary Hill Press, 2019); Matt Queen, *Mobilize to Evangelize: The Pastor and Effective Congregational Evangelism* (Fort Worth: Seminary Hill Press, 2018); and Matt Queen and Alex Sibley, eds., *And You Will Be My Witnesses: 31 Devotionals to Encourage a Spirit of Everyday Evangelism* (Fort Worth: Seminary Hill Press, 2019), with permission from Seminary Hill Press.

The web addresses referenced in this book were live and correct at the time of the book's publication but may be subject to change.

Cover design by Darren Welch Design. Cover images by Bigmouse108/iStock and Ant_art/Shutterstock.

Printed in the United States of America

28 27 26 25 24 23 BHP 1 2 3 4 5 6 7 8 9 10

In honor of my mentor in ministry, the Reverend Jackie Collins—
a man of God, pastor-evangelist, and faithful servant
of Ridgeway Baptist Church of Candler, North Carolina

CONTENTS

FOREWORD

If anything has disappeared from modern thought in the twenty-first century, it is the belief in an eternal heaven and an everlasting hell. Even those who retain some vague idea of heavenly bliss beyond this life are slow to acknowledge the reality of final judgment and condemnation. Modern men and women live with the mindset that there is no heaven, no hell, and therefore no guilt. Much confusion exists concerning the gospel and the need for evangelism in our contemporary context. The church has added to this confusion by primarily focusing on evangelistic methodologies and strategies, as important as these may be, rather than prioritizing an understanding of the meaning, transformational power, and veracity of the message of evangelism, which is the gospel of our Lord Jesus Christ. The book you hold in your hands, by Matt Queen, the L. R. Scarborough Professor of Evangelism at Southwestern Baptist Theological Seminary, thoughtfully addresses these important issues and more.

What has been lost, or at least misplaced in our current context, is the recognition that at the heart of genuine evangelism and outreach must be a firm biblical and theological foundation. Queen rightly begins his thorough treatment of the subject of evangelism at this point. Stressing that biblical and theological foundations undergird the message of the

gospel and the work of evangelism, this contemporary evangelism textbook builds upon and greatly expands the concepts taught by longtime
Southwestern Seminary president L. R. Scarborough in the classic volume *With Christ after the Lost* (Baptist Sunday School Board, 1919).

Queen emphasizes that the message of and commission for the work
of evangelism, which involves the communication of the good news of
God's saving grace in Jesus Christ in word and in deed, is found in the
Bible, God's truthful, inspired, and authoritative written Word (2 Tim
3:16). Furthermore, it is understood that the work of evangelism cannot be done in our human frailty; it requires the empowering of God's
Spirit (Acts 1:8). While the work of evangelism is broad in its scope,
including discipling and teaching others to do all that Jesus commanded
(Matt 28:19), Queen wisely introduces his readers to the work of evangelism with a focus on a theological foundation of the gospel message by
seeking to define evangelism, by articulating the meaning of the gospel,
and by surveying the teachings on this subject in both the Old and New
Testaments.

Queen maintains with conviction that even though men and women
are created in God's image, the entrance of sin into the world has had
great and negative influences upon God's creation, especially for humans
created in God's image. As a result of sin, the image of God, though not
lost, was affected by sin. The role of exercising dominion (Gen 1:28) has
been drastically disturbed by the effects of sin on humans and the curse
on nature (Gen 3). The ability to live in right relationship with God, as
well as with others, with nature, and even with ourselves, has been cor-
rupted. All attempts at righteousness have fallen short (Isa 64:6; Rom
3:23). Humans are ultimately spiritually dead and alienated from God
(Eph 2:1–3). Evangelism is necessary because men and women in every
country and every context, throughout every period of history, are separated and alienated from God.

The message of evangelism is found in the gracious redemption that
God provided in the person of Jesus Christ. It was necessary that Christ
should be both God and man. Only as man could Jesus be a redeemer

for humanity, and only as a sinless man could he fittingly die for others. Yet it was only as God that his life, ministry, and redeeming death could have infinite value and satisfy the wrath of God to deliver others from it. Unless the work of evangelism, the telling of the good news of the gospel, is focused on the person and work of Jesus Christ, it is misguided.

At the heart of the evangelistic message is the amazing news that Christ's death provided for sinners a sinless substitutionary sacrifice that revealed God's love for the world (John 3:16) while satisfying divine justice (Rom 3:21–26). This incomprehensively valuable redemption delivered sinners from enslavement and reconciled and restored believers from estrangement to full fellowship and inheritance in the household of God. The basis of our salvation is totally in God himself and in Christ's atoning, redeeming, and reconciling work on the cross. Because of Christ's accomplishment on the cross, God has chosen to treat sinful men and women who believe the good news of the gospel as children rather than transgressors (2 Cor 5:18–20; Eph 2:12–16; Col 1:20–22). Paul, in 2 Cor 5:14, points us to the motivation for sharing the good news of the gospel in a local context or in a cross-cultural one; it is the love of God made known in Jesus Christ and his death and victorious resurrection.

The Bible maintains that faith is the means by which we receive and appropriate the good news of the gospel. Salvation is a gift of God that cannot be merited by good works (Rom 3:22–24; Eph 2:8–9; Titus 3:5–6). Grace comes to us while we are still in our sins and brings spiritual transformation based on the accomplished work of Jesus Christ. For the recipients of grace, the promise holds that Jesus Christ delivers us from the wrath to come (1 Thess 1:10; 5:9). Those who believe the message of the gospel need not fear future condemnation because believers have been justified by grace through faith (Rom 5:1; 8:1).

The work of evangelism calls for a human response to this good news. When God extends his grace to us, he is the active agent, but he always extends grace through means, such as the preached word, the written Word of God, the sharing of personal testimony, the prayers of other believers, the invitation to respond to grace, and the faith of the respondent. Though faith is more than doctrinal assent, it must include an adherence to the truths made known in Scripture regarding the person and work of Christ, who is the truth, the life, the only way to have relationship with God (John 14:6). In our commitment to Jesus Christ, we acknowledge him as Savior from sin and Lord of our lives (Rom 10:9).

The work of evangelism must be understood within God's overall redemptive work, for God is not just saving individuals, he is saving a people for himself. The plan of salvation includes not only the redemption of individuals, but also the redemption of all creation (Rom 8:18–27; Rev 20:11–15), and the redemption of people from every tribe and language and people and nation (Rev 5:9; 7:9). Queen provides illumination on the reality that the evangelistic message must also reflect awareness of our context, a lesson to be learned from the apostles in the book of Acts (see Acts 2:14–36; 3:11–26; 13:16–41; 17:22–31; 22:6–21; 24:10–21; 26:12–23).

The volume you hold in your hand by Matt Queen is much more than a work on the theology of evangelism, but I am grateful that it is no less than that. Queen recognizes that a firm theological foundation is important for faithful evangelistic proclamation. This volume also carefully explores the spiritual, philosophical, and methodological dimensions of evangelism. Addressing practical matters like the fear and anxiety that many believers experience in attempting to share their faith, Queen, who is a faithful evangelist himself (as I have witnessed on more than one occasion), guides readers toward developing a personal philosophy and approach to evangelism, as enabled by the Holy Spirit.

Recapturing Evangelism also addresses the entailments of evangelism such as communication theory, the place of discipleship and disciple-making, and the significance of the church in this work. Queen exhorts followers of Christ to work harder at closing the gap between our talk about evangelism and the faithful work of evangelism, encouraging our evangelistic efforts to be done for the building up of the church, while emphasizing that proclamation and service must be grounded in a scripturally formed theology. Our evangelistic message must be firmly grounded in the love of God, made known in holy Scripture, while understanding the need for the Holy Spirit's enablement, especially when encountering spiritual opposition (Eph 6:10–17).

This contemporary evangelism textbook is faithful in its message, sensitive in its presentation, and timely in its approach. It will be our prayer that church leaders and students for generations to come will learn from and profit both from Queen's heart and his message. With the author of this fine book, we affirm that our evangelistic proclamation and commitments must be shaped by the truths regarding creation, the fall, and redemption. We join with him in gladly confessing Jesus Christ as Lord, our prophet, priest, and king, who has completely revealed God, reconciled men and women to God, and who now sits enthroned as ruler of God's kingdom and head of his church. In him we place our trust and hope, offering our thanksgiving, praise, and worship for the gift of salvation he has provided for us by grace through faith (Eph 2:8–9). Like the apostle Paul, let us pray for opportunities to proclaim the gospel message with all boldness and without hindrance to a lost and dying world in need of the grace of our Lord Jesus Christ (Acts 28:31).

Soli Deo Gloria
David S. Dockery
President, International Alliance for Christian Education
and Distinguished Professor of Theology,
Southwestern Baptist Theological Seminary

PREFACE

In the contemporary milieu, the intentional practice of evangelism by evangelicals is decreasing.[1] Arguments over the prioritizing of "proclamation vs. justice," "evangelism vs. discipleship," and "old evangelism methods vs. new evangelism methods" dominate their attention, resulting

---

[1] A prime indicator of this phenomenon has been observed since the early twenty-first century within the Southern Baptist Convention, the largest evangelical denomination in the United States. Charles S. Kelley Jr. has documented this situation in "The Dilemma of Decline: Southern Baptists Face a New Reality." Since 2009 Southern Baptist congregations have reported a decline in their number of annual baptisms. Specifically, Southern Baptists reported 349,737 baptisms in 2009, a number that has consistently dropped except in 2011 when they reported an increase of 2,333 over 2010, as well as in 2021 with an increase of 31,541 over 2020, when reported baptisms hit a one-hundred-year low due to the COVID-19 pandemic.

This trend is even more pronounced in the majority of other Protestant denominations. In fact, mainline denominations have been declining for decades, see Roger Finke and Rodney Stark, *The Churching of America 1776–2005: Winners and Losers in Our Religious Economy* (New Brunswick, NJ: Rutgers University, 2006), 235–83; and Ed Stetzer, "If It Doesn't Stem Its Decline, Mainline Protestantism Has Just 23 Easters Left," *Washington Post*, April 28, 2017, https://www.washingtonpost.com/news/acts-of-faith/wp/2017/04/28/if-it-doesnt-stem-its-decline-mainline-protestantism-has-just-23-easters-left/.

in more talk *about* evangelism and less telling *of* the gospel. Richard R. Osmer confirms this decline in evangelism:

> Many Christian denominations or communions today do not practice evangelism. . . . The problem with this situation is the neglect of evangelism altogether. Yet this is the reality in many mainline congregations today. Increasingly, it also is the reality of evangelical congregations whose members believe they should evangelize but do not.
>
> Moreover, evangelical leaders are beginning to raise questions about evangelism as conversionism, especially the traditional methods associated with instantaneous conversions.[2]

He asserts concerning this phenomenon that "[o]ld-timers may be complaining that people are less willing to share their faith today than in the past or that altar calls are no longer the norm or that door-to-door evangelism has declined, but many leaders realize these methods no longer work, especially with young people."[3] With all due respect to these leaders Professor Osmer invokes, the decline in today's evangelism is not due to the fact that intentional evangelism does not work in this era as it did in the past; rather it is because believers do not work evangelism as they have in the past.

This volume aims to present a thoroughly biblical philosophy and practice of personal and corporate evangelism to advance Great Commission disciple-making in the twenty-first century. It will link to evangelicals' evangelistic heritage by drawing from past voices, as well as interact with present voices to address contemporary issues in evangelism. As the ninth occupant of the world's first academic chair of evangelism—the L. R. Scarborough Chair of Evangelism ("Chair of Fire")—I want to contribute a text consistent with the Southwestern Baptist Theological

---

[2] Richard R. Osmer, *The Invitation: A Theology of Evangelism* (Grand Rapids: Eerdmans, 2021), 11.

[3] Osmer, 11.

Seminary tradition. Along with Scarborough's *With Christ After the Lost*, E. D. Head's revision of that same book, and C. E. Autrey's *Basic Evangelism*, this textbook intends to offer a biblically comprehensive, theologically applicable, personally and congregationally reproducible, and intentionally focused treatment of evangelism.

The following three sections shape the content of this book: foundations for evangelism, issues in evangelism, and implications for evangelism.

Part 1: Foundations for Evangelism. This part introduces the biblical and theological foundations that undergird the practice of evangelism and the message of the gospel. It includes chapters that define evangelism, investigate the foreshadowing and forecasting of evangelism in the Old Testament, survey evangelistic practices in the New Testament, and discuss the meaning and concepts related to the gospel.

Part 2: Issues in Evangelism. This segment explores the spiritual, philosophical, and methodological dimensions of evangelism. It will discuss spiritual issues, including the roles of the Holy Spirit, prayer, and overcoming fear in evangelism; philosophical questions that assist believers in forming their own personal philosophy of evangelism; and methodological and strategic approaches to evangelism.

Part 3: Implications for Evangelism. The concluding section of the book examines evangelism and its relationships with communication theory, the local church, and disciple-making. Topics include the verbal aspects of communicating the gospel to unbelievers, suggestions and best practices for mobilizing congregations in evangelism, and proposals concerning the relationship between evangelism and discipleship to define the role of evangelism in effective Great Commission disciple-making.

The book will use an inspirational voice at times and an instructive tone at others. The inspirational voice intends to avoid monotony and motivate readers to evangelize. The instructive tone proves necessary when training readers in evangelistic methodology and best practices, while also acquainting them with underlying issues, theories, and ideologies that either threaten or reinforce a biblical philosophy and practice of evangelism.

I did not write this textbook with the intent of it becoming the final word on everything concerning evangelism. Although it cites and interacts with authorities in evangelism, not even their propositions are conclusive on all evangelism matters. The Bible alone serves as the final and authoritative Word for informing and shaping every believer's evangelistic philosophies and practices. As I learned from my missions professor during my first semester of seminary, "When it comes to evangelizing, think outside the box, yes, but not outside the Book!" Accordingly, this primer on evangelism seeks to recapture, articulate, and advance the kind of evangelism that is by the Book.

—Matt Queen
Professor and L. R. Scarborough Chair
of Evangelism ("Chair of Fire")
Roy J. Fish School of Evangelism and Missions
Southwestern Baptist Theological Seminary
Fort Worth, Texas

ACKNOWLEDGMENTS

Although I am credited as this book's author, it would never have been possible to write it without the help and support of so many other people in my life. First, I would like to thank my God—the Father, Son, and Spirit—for creating, calling, equipping, sustaining, and motivating me to write this book. I ascribe all glory to him.

Second, I am deeply indebted to my wife, Hope, and my two daughters, Madison and Matia, all three of whom graciously afforded me time to write and consistently prayed for me so that I could complete this project. Their willing sacrifice is as much an investment in this book as the time and effort I spent writing it. I have no greater supporters and encouragers.

I would also like to thank my parents for ensuring I heard the gospel from an early age and encouraging me to believe it. It was after my conversion that my father first and most significantly instilled within me the responsibility to evangelize.

I am sincerely grateful for the generosity and support of the administration, faculty, staff, and students of Southwestern Baptist Theological Seminary. Specifically, I thank President Adam Greenway, Interim Provost David Dockery, and Dean John Massey. These three men, along with the seminary's board of trustees, graciously granted me a yearlong sabbatical to research and write this contemporary evangelism textbook in the spirit of the Southwestern tradition. I offer special thanks to Dr. Dockery for writing the foreword of this book, which itself is an indispensable theology of evangelism. My faculty colleagues in the Roy J. Fish School of Evangelism and Missions—Carl Bradford, Travis Kerns, and Dean Sieberhagen—were constant sources of inspiration and support. Jessika Sams and Lee Hyatt, administrative assistants in the Fish School, undertook many additional duties during the course of my sabbatical. Moreover, Jessika assisted me by organizing the bibliographic sources for the book. W. Madison Grace II, a colleague in the School of Theology, reviewed and advised me in summarizing a theology of the gospel. Chris Taylor helped me with the transliteration of biblical terms. Craig Kubic and the A. Webb Roberts Library staff not only provided me a study carrel in which I researched and wrote this volume, but they also assisted me in locating and securing vital resources in the seminary's archives and from other libraries. Chris Barrick and Southwestern's IT department provided me with essential computer equipment that was necessary for me to complete this project.

I would like to express appreciation to B&H Academic for publishing this book. Jim Baird, Madison Trammel, Audrey Greeson, Renée Chavez, and especially Michael McEwen provided invaluable counsel and assistance throughout this endeavor from beginning to completion. I am sincerely honored to be counted among the fraternity of those who comprise the B&H Author's Circle.

I am thankful for my church—Lane Prairie Baptist Church of Joshua, Texas. Its lead pastor, Ricky Fuchs, ministry staff, deacons, and members have upheld me in their prayers. Many of them offered timely exhortations that sustained me as I wrote.

Three individuals texted or called me weekly to assure me of their prayers on my behalf as I was writing. I can never thank my mother-in-love, Elizabeth Walters; Mrs. Sandy Smith; and my former pastor, Jerry Clements, enough for their consistent intercession for me to complete this volume. I also want to express my appreciation to Doug and Jennifer

Harmon for their prayers and for providing me a writing retreat so I could complete this project.

A team of current and past doctoral students took time out of their busy schedules to read the manuscript, offer helpful feedback and suggestions, and send texts and emails that motivated me to finish. Thank you, Tony Wolfe, Jenny Kim, Bruce Gale, Brandon Kiesling, Jennifer Rosania, Seth Polk, Anthony Svajda, Matt Henslee, Jonathan Baldwin, Daniel Dickard, James Pritchard, Beau Brewer, and Anna Daub. Your collective and personal input was invaluable to me.

Last, but certainly not least, I thank my seminary evangelism professor—Danny Forshee. In his class at Southeastern Baptist Theological Seminary not only did I first hear about the "Chair of Fire" and Southwestern Seminary's tradition and spirit of evangelism, but I also met my wife. He provided me an opportunity to serve as his graduate assistant, which afforded me a door into the academy. To this day, he continues to teach and sharpen me in my evangelism. Thank you, Dr. Forshee, for your interest and investment in me. Because of your teaching and example, I daily endeavor to be *with Christ after the lost*.

Part 1

Foundations for Evangelism

1

Contemporary Misconceptions
of Evangelism

Most, if not all, Christians view evangelism favorably, but they do not all share the same commitment to it. Some believers like evangelism as long as they own no responsibility to practice it. Other Christians express full-throated support for it—if other people are doing it. Still, a small contingent of believers cherish evangelism and share their faith.

How can one particular word—*evangelism*—be almost universally and favorably affirmed by Christians, yet possess so many different meanings and elicit numerous kinds of responses? For the most part, believers' conception and understanding of what is meant by "evangelism" stimulate these and other types of responsive actions. Some constrict evangelism into a particular method, either that they cannot envision themselves doing—like preaching in a pulpit—or against which they have a prejudice—such as evangelizing door-to-door or preaching with a bullhorn on a street corner. Others believe their participation in events and efforts that meet others' physical needs qualifies as evangelism. And growing numbers of believers have adopted the idea that evangelization is optional and not a required Christian duty. This chapter surveys the most common misnomers attributed to evangelism and provides a biblical corrective to each of them.

Misnomers about Evangelism

Generally speaking, believers do not evangelize for one of at least three reasons. First, fears associated with evangelism, notably the fears of failure and rejection, prevent some believers from evangelizing.[1] Second, believers sometimes do not share the gospel because of their apathy, and thus their own personal rebellion against the Lord, toward obeying the Great Commission.[2] Last, some believers involve themselves either in misguided alternatives to biblical evangelism that prove harmful to the evangelistic enterprise, or in admirable spiritual activities that confuse evangelism with other Christian functions. These issues require a differentiation between evangelism's meaning and the common misconceptions attributed to it. The following sections refute some of the most common misperceptions people have confused with evangelism.[3]

---

[1] Correctives to the evangelistic inhibitor of fear will be discussed in the section "Fear and Evangelism" in chapter 5.

[2] Correctives concerning disobedience in evangelizing will be offered in chapter 3, in the section "Biblical Motivations for Evangelism."

[3] Authors of prominent textbooks and books on evangelism have identified general misconceptions about evangelism, in order to define evangelism biblically. For examples, see George E. Sweazey, *Effective Evangelism: The Greatest Work in the World* (New York: Harper & Brothers, 1953), 21–22; C. E. Autrey, *Basic Evangelism* (Grand Rapids: Zondervan, 1959), 26–30; Mark Dever, *The Gospel and Personal Evangelism* (Wheaton, IL: Crossway, 2007), 69–82; and Dave Earley and David Wheeler, *Evangelism Is . . . : How to Share Jesus with Passion and Confidence* (Nashville: B&H Academic, 2010), vi–ix.

Evangelism Is a Spiritual Gift

The belief that the Holy Spirit bestows a "gift of evangelism" upon a select, exclusive group of believers to carry out the work of evangelism has gained increasing acceptance today. This misconception of evangelism advances a narrative that only certain people can, or should, evangelize. Advocates of this position have convinced themselves that those with "the gift of evangelism" have the sole responsibility to evangelize, or that spiritually gifted evangelists possess some enhanced ability to do so. Some may accept they have a responsibility to fulfill the Great Commission through evangelism but believe that because they do not have "the gift of evangelism" they can practice it more passively and less frequently than those who possess it.

These positions fail to align with the New Testament's teaching about evangelism. First, the Bible never mentions "a gift of evangelism." Paul does identify grace-gifted *evangelists* (Eph 4:11), whom he explains equip the saints in local churches for ministry along with the grace-gifted apostles, prophets, pastors, and teachers (Eph 4:12–13).[4] In Paul's Ephesian paradigm of grace-gifted functionality, all believers are responsible to be

---

[4] Generally Christians refer to grace-gifts as *spiritual gifts*, although the phrase, *charisma pneumatikon* [spiritual gift], is present only once in the New Testament (i.e., Rom 1:11). In 1 Corinthians Paul used the Greek word translated as *spiritual* [sans *charisma*] twice within the context of his explanation about these kinds of gifts. He used cognates of *pneumatikos*, specifically *pneumatikōn* in 1 Cor 12:1 and *pneumatika* in 1 Cor 14:1, to discuss the gifts. Nevertheless, Bible translations (e.g., KJV, NKJV, NIV, NASB, and ESV) that use the wording *spiritual gifts* or *gifts of the Spirit*, add the word *gifts*, although it is not present in the Greek. Mark Taylor has explained reasons why these forms of *pneumatikos* are better translated as *spiritual things* or *spiritual people*, see *1 Corinthians*, New American Commentary, vol. 28 (Nashville: B&H, 2014), 279.

Both Paul and Peter generally and consistently use cognates of *charisma* to refer to the gifts (i.e., *charismatōn* in 1 Cor 12:4; *charismata* in 1 Cor 12:28, 30 and Rom 12:6; *charis* and *dōreas* in Eph 4:7, while Peter uses *charisma* in 1 Pet 4:10). For these reasons the terminology of *grace-gifts* is preferred and will be

equipped for ministry by those who are endowed with these functional grace-gifts, which includes being equipped by grace-gifted evangelists to evangelize. In other words, Christ has not gifted churches with evangelists so that they evangelize for the churches. Instead, he has given churches evangelists so that they might model evangelism and encourage, equip, train, and mobilize their members to practice it. In the contemporary era, Christ continues to equip believers for ministry through grace-gifted evangelists and pastor-teachers.

Additionally, the misconception of "a spiritual gift of evangelism" occurs because believers confuse the New Testament's use of evangelists as a synonym for evangelism. In fact, the noun *evangelism* appears nowhere in the Scriptures, whereas the noun *euangelistēs*, or *evangelist(s)*, appears three times (e.g., Acts 21:8; Eph 4:11; and 2 Tim 4:5). This does not mean that evangelism is not extant in the Bible; rather evangelism permeates the New Testament in its verbal form—*euangelizō*, or *proclaim (preach) the gospel* (i.e., Luke 4:43; 9:6; 20:1; Acts 8:35; 13:32; 14:7; 1 Cor 1:17; 9:16, 18; Gal 1:8b; and Eph 2:17; 3:8).

Second, the evangelistic enterprise of the church cannot advance through the evangelism practiced by "specially gifted evangelists" alone because God has ordained that all believers evangelize the entire world. If, in fact, only a few believers were endowed with "the spiritual gift of evangelism," they would never have the breadth of access to evangelize as many unbelievers in their sphere of influence as do all believers around the world. Nowhere in the Gospels does Christ appoint only "spiritually gifted evangelists" to fulfill the Great Commission on their own. If he had, not all of those first disciples who received the Great Commission would have evangelized others or encouraged the disciples they made to evangelize—but they did (e.g., Acts 4:29–31; 8:4)! Furthermore, if the task of world evangelization falls only upon those with "a spiritual gift

---

used when discussing them, due to its precision with the wording used by the New Testament's authors when describing and explaining these gifts.

of evangelism," then it follows that Jesus's promise to be with his people always (Matt 28:20) also applies only to evangelists.[5]

Third, if evangelism were a spiritual gift, believers could claim that other additional spiritual gifts exist outside of those identified in the New Testament. The inventory of the gifts in the New Testament is found in Rom 12:4–8; 1 Cor 12:1–31; Eph 4:7, 11–13; and 1 Pet 4:10–11. These are the spiritual grace-gifts in the New Testament: a word of wisdom, a word of knowledge, faith, healing, effecting of miracles, prophecy, distinguishing of spirits, speaking in tongues, interpreting tongues, administration, service, exhortation, giving, leadership, mercy, apostles, prophets, evangelists, pastors, and teachers. This list verifies, as mentioned earlier, that the Bible never references "a gift of evangelism." Evangelists are listed, but as explained earlier (1) evangelists exercise their grace-giftedness by equipping believers not evangelizing unbelievers and (2) evangelism and evangelists are two different concepts. If the Holy Spirit does endow some believers with "a gift of evangelism," then it follows that additional grace-gifts of the Spirit exist outside those provided in Scripture. How can the existence of additional gifts not mentioned in Scripture be verified? What prevents people from asserting "a gift of reading the Bible" or "a gift of prayer" as a reason why they do not have the responsibility to read the Bible or pray either consistently or at all? Assigning or identifying grace-gifts not identified in the New Testament would be subjective and fail to obtain a common consensus.

Last, evangelism is not a spiritual gift because the primary beneficiary of spiritual gifts is the church, not the unchurched. The New Testament's

---

[5] This reasoning echoes William Carey's response to critiques John Ryland Sr. raised concerning Carey's interpretation of the Great Commission in Matthew 28. Carey argued, "If the command of Christ to teach all nations extend only to the apostles, then, doubtless, the promise of the divine presence in this work must be so limited; but this is worded in such a manner as expressly precludes such an idea, 'Lo, I am with you always, to the end of the world.'" Carey, *An Enquiry into the Obligations of Christians to Use Means for the Conversion of the Heathens* (Leicester, UK: n.p., 1792), 9.

inventory and explanation of spiritual grace-gifts demonstrate that the purpose of every spiritual gift is to unite diversely gifted believers in the body of Christ (Rom 12:5), to benefit the common good of the body (1 Cor 12:7), to equip the saints for the work of ministry (Eph 4:12), and to serve one another (1 Pet 4:10). All grace-gifts are given primarily to benefit the body of Christ, not unbelievers. Ephesians 4 states that Christ gave evangelists to equip the saints, not to be the only saints to evangelize sinners. Rather than do all the work of evangelism for the saints, grace-gifted evangelists equip, encourage, train, and teach the saints for their perfecting in evangelistic ministry.

Instead of describing "a spiritual gift of evangelism" bestowed upon a select few, the book of Acts presents evangelism as a spiritual discipline all believers in the early churches practiced intentionally and consistently. In his seminal history of evangelism in the early church, Michael Green observed this phenomenon among first-century believers: "It was axiomatic that every Christian was called to be a witness to Christ, not only by life but by lip."[6] He explains:

> The very disciples themselves were, significantly, laymen, devoid of formal theological or rhetorical training. Christianity was from its inception a lay movement, and so it continued for a remarkably long time. . . . They were evangelists, just as much as any apostle was. . . . [Their spreading of the good news] must often have been not formal preaching, but the informal chattering to friends and chance acquaintances, in homes . . . on walks, and around market stalls. They went everywhere gossiping the gospel; they did it naturally, enthusiastically, and with the conviction of those who are not paid to say that sort of thing. Consequently, they were taken seriously, and the movement spread, notably among the lower classes.[7]

---

[6] Michael Green, *Evangelism in the Early Church*, rev. ed (Grand Rapids: Eerdmans, 2003), 246.

[7] Green, 243.

Elton Trueblood translated this first-century reality into a principle for the contemporary era. He declares, "A person cannot be a Christian and avoid being a [personal] evangelist. Evangelism is not a professionalized job of a few gifted or trained men but is, instead, the unrelenting responsibility of every person who belongs, even in the most modest way, to the Company of Jesus."[8]

For these reasons, evangelism fails to meet the biblical qualifications and descriptions of a spiritual gift. If evangelism is not a "spiritual gift," can it be considered a "spiritual fruit"? In Gal 5:22–23 Paul identified the virtues of love, joy, peace, patience, kindness, goodness, faithfulness, gentleness, and self-control as spiritual fruit. As in the inventories of spiritual gifts, Paul also excluded evangelism from his list of spiritual fruit. Therefore, it also cannot be categorized as a spiritual fruit. What, then, is evangelism?

Evangelism meets the qualifications of a spiritual discipline. A *spiritual discipline* is a deed commanded by God in the Scriptures that requires a Christian's obedience for the purpose of spiritual growth and intimacy with God. Due to the imperatival commands and obedient expectations associated with them in the Scriptures, activities such as reading and studying the Bible, praying, worshiping, serving, giving, and fasting qualify as spiritual disciplines. As with each of these disciplines, the New Testament authors also instructed and expected believers to practice evangelism. Many of them recounted Jesus's command that his disciples evangelize (cf. Matt 10:7; 28:18–20; *Mark 16:15*; Luke 24:47–48; John 20:21; Acts 1:8).[9] Because it meets the necessary criteria, Christians should consider evangelism as a spiritual discipline.[10]

---

[8] Elton Trueblood, *The Company of the Committed: A Bold and Imaginative Re-thinking of the Strategy of the Church in Contemporary Life* (New York: Harper & Row, 1961), 55.

[9] Mark 16:15 is denoted in italics because many scholars suggest that due to its omission in the majority of the oldest Marcan manuscripts, it likely was not included in the original manuscript of Mark's Gospel.

[10] To distinguish those individuals who are grace-gifted to equip and mobilize churches for evangelism from every Christian who is obligated to evangelize,

Even though evangelism fails to meet the criteria of a spiritual gift, God has given every believer a gift to aid them in their evangelistic endeavors. The 1939 film adaptation of L. Frank Baum's *The Wonderful Wizard of Oz* illustrates this spiritual benefit he affords his children. The film portrays the fantasy tale of Dorothy Gale's journey to the Emerald City to inquire of its Wizard the way home from Oz to Kansas. While on the yellow brick road to the city, she encounters and subsequently enlists a brainless Scarecrow, a hollow-chested Tin Man, and a cowardly Lion. In addition to Dorothy's wish to go home, the Scarecrow desires a thinking brain; the Tin Man, a beating heart; and the Lion, ferocious courage. Arriving at the Emerald City, Dorothy and her band of misfits present themselves before the great and powerful Oz, who knows what they want before they even ask. He agrees to grant their requests, providing they can defeat the Wicked Witch of the West and bring him her broomstick. Motivated by his rewarding offer, Dorothy leads her mindless, heartless, and fearful army to undertake a mission impossible to win without brains, heart, and bravery.

Nevertheless, Dorothy, the Scarecrow, the Tin Man, and the Lion returned triumphantly to the Wizard with the broomstick of the Wicked Witch of the West. The Wizard rewarded the Scarecrow with a "doctor of thinkology" diploma, the Tin Man with a ticking heart clock, and the Cowardly Lion with the Triple Cross Medal of Courage. He explained to them, however, that by virtue of the way they defeated the Wicked Witch, the brainless Scarecrow had been able to think all along, the heartless Tin Man had been able to love all along, and the Cowardly Lion had been courageous all along!

Similarly, many believers have convinced themselves that because they have not been endowed with a "gift of evangelism," they do not possess enough knowledge, love, or courage to share the gospel. But God's people do not require "a gift of evangelism" to make disciples—they

---

I will refer to the former as *grace-gifted evangelist(s)* and the latter as *personal evangelist(s)*.

already have what, more specifically, they need to do so intentionally and consistently. God does endow believers with a gift to evangelize, but it's not "a gift of evangelism"—it's his Holy Spirit!

Evangelism Is "Using Words When Necessary"

Some believers think they practice evangelism on the basis of their moral and upright lifestyles, apart from actually verbalizing the gospel. In describing advocates of this way of thinking, Trueblood says:

> [Some] people [have] decided that while they might continue as believers in Christ, they would never be caught dead talking about it. They determined to be discreet and quiet about their faith, to let their lives speak, if any speaking was required, and to avoid, at all costs, forcing their opinions upon anyone else. They did not want to emulate the people who invaded the privacy of others, because, they said, they did not want to have their own privacy invaded.[11]

Those who espouse evangelism in this way can caricature believers who emphasize gospel proclamation as outdated legalists who care only about a message and disregard the need for accompanying action. Yet while a few Christian evangelists throughout history have elevated proclamation to the detriment of Christian ethic, most evangelistic Christians recognize the importance of both. Furthermore, merely living out the gospel without actually sharing it makes it no less moralistic than legalistic Christianity.

Others believe that the differences Christ has made in believers' lives, without a verbal declaration of the gospel, will raise unbelievers' curiosities, leading them to initiate conversations with believers concerning the gospel. Practitioners of this approach fondly invoke a common misnomer attributed to Francis of Assisi: "Preach the gospel; use words

---

[11] Trueblood, *The Company of the Committed*, 46.

when necessary." Nevertheless, after conducting biographical research on Francis, Mark Galli states:

> Francis of Assisi is said to have said, "Preach the gospel at all times; when necessary, use words." This saying is carted out whenever someone wants to suggest that Christians talk about the gospel too much, and live the gospel too little. Fair enough—that can be a problem. Much of the rhetorical power of the quotation comes from the assumption that Francis not only said it but lived it. The problem is that he did not say it. Nor did he live it.[12]

Duane Litfin also critiques the quote and its attribution to Francis. He asserts, "According to those who know the relevant history well—the Franciscans—Francis never uttered these words. But more important, on its face this dictum represents a significant error. It's simply impossible to preach the gospel without words. The gospel is inherently verbal."[13] The sentiment, "Go, preach the gospel; use words when necessary," is like saying, "Go, feed the hungry; use food when necessary." Food is necessary to feed the hungry; and likewise, words are necessary to preach the gospel.

Those who hold this view correctly promote moral and upright lifestyles, but they have been called to live according to the highest standard of righteousness, that is, holiness (cf. Eph 1:4; 5:27; 1 Pet 1:15–16). They leave out an essential aspect of evangelism: the proclamation of a verbal message. While believers' lifestyles must match the demands of the gospel, they must also perform their duty to the gospel. Personal evangelists proclaim the gospel verbally through vocal means

---

[12] Mark Galli, "Speak the Gospel, Use Deeds When Necessary," May 21, 2009, http://www. christianitytoday.com/ct/2009/mayweb-only/120–42.0.html. Galli also discredited this quote being attributed to Francis in *Francis of Assisi and His World* (Downers Grove, IL: InterVarsity, 2003).

[13] Duane Litfin, "Works and Words: Why You Can't Preach the Gospel with Deeds," May 30, 2012, https://www.christianitytoday.com/ct/2012/may /litfin-gospel-deeds.html.

as well as through written and signed gospel presentations to those who are physically unable to speak and/or hear. Today's Christians, like first-century believers, are called to proclaim the gospel (cf. Acts 10:42; Rom 10:15; 1 Cor 1:17; Gal 1:15–16; Eph 3:8; and 2 Tim 4:1–2), not merely to live holy lives. In fact, holy living that accommodates being less than wholly obedient to all Christ's commands might meet ours or others' standards, but it fails to meet God's. As Trueblood explains, "[T]he living deed is never adequate without the support which the spoken word can provide. This is because no life is ever good enough. The person who says naively, 'I don't preach; I just let my life speak,' is insufferably self-righteous."[14] The reverse is also true. Believers should not merely share the gospel. They must also live their lives in such a way that attests to the righteousness imputed to them through the gospel they have believed and now proclaim.

Christians believe that the gospel works in such a way as to result in conversions. Why, then, would they not also work the gospel into their conversations? Donald Whitney recounts the following precautionary tale for those who downplay the necessity of the gospel's verbal components:

> I heard the story of a man who became a Christian during an evangelistic emphasis in a city in the Pacific Northwest. When the man told his boss about it, his employer responded with: "That's great! I am a Christian and have been praying for you for years!"
>
> But the new believer was crestfallen. "Why didn't you ever tell me you were a Christian? You were the very reason I have not been interested in the gospel all these years."
>
> "How can that be?" the boss wondered. "I have done my very best to live the Christian life around you."
>
> "That's the point," explained the employee. "You lived such a model life without telling me it was Christ who made the

---

[14] Trueblood, *The Company of the Committed*, 53.

difference, I convinced myself that if you could live such a good and happy life without Christ, then I could, too."[15]

As Whitney's story illustrates, failing to provide any verbalization of the gospel while modeling a Christian lifestyle can hinder evangelism. In a similar way, believers who relegate the gospel into conversations only when they determine it essential to do so impede the gospel's advance. Consider the model of the apostles and other first-century believers. They did not "use words when necessary" when they practiced evangelism the New Testament. Words were necessary for personal evangelists in the New Testament! Examples of New Testament evangelism occur in the context of proclamation, not mere demonstration or duty alone. In fact, the New Testament addresses this kind of approach only once, and it refers to a marriage in which a believing wife is married to an unbelieving husband (1 Pet 3:1–2). As such, this passage's specific context and intent is not prescriptive for all believers, that is, for men and women to which this situation does not apply; nor should it be adopted by all believers as a normative evangelistic approach.

Evangelism Is an Opportunity for Which Believers Should Await

Some believers assume they should wait for God to provide them evangelism opportunities. Those who hold this concept of evangelism believe they should be obedient to evangelize; however, their obedience is more passive than proactive in nature. Advocates of this view determine they will wait expectantly for the Holy Spirit to generate the perfect circumstance or situation that will prompt them to evangelize. An example of such an "opportunity" entails believers waiting until unbelievers randomly,

---

[15] Donald S. Whitney, *Spiritual Disciplines for the Christian Life*, rev. and updated ed. (Wheaton, IL: Tyndale House, 2014), 133.

at the Spirit's prompting, ask them about Christianity, the gospel, Jesus, or some other spiritual matter before they share the gospel with them.

The New Testament provides a corrective to those who wait for opportunities to share the gospel. In his charge for Timothy to fulfill his ministry as a grace-gifted evangelist, Paul commanded, "Preach the word; be ready in season and out of season" (2 Tim 4:2a). Most Christians interpret this verse incorrectly in two ways. First, they interpret *kēryxon ton logon* to mean "preach the Bible." But when Paul used the Greek word *logos* in his Epistles, he overwhelmingly meant "the gospel," not "the Scriptures," "the Word of God," or "the Bible." When he had the Scriptures or its derivatives in mind, he used *graphē*. Thomas D. Lea corroborates this understanding:

> Many American Evangelicals use the term "the word of God" as a reference to the words of Scripture. In the Pastorals the term "word," "word of God," or "word of truth" is frequently a reference to the gospel. In the following passages from the Pastorals, this is the usual meaning of the term: 1 Tim 5:17; 2 Tim 1:13; 2:9; 2:15; Titus 1:3; 2:5. The term "gospel" has a wider reference than a mere explanation of the plan of salvation. It refers to the message of salvation along with the truths and moral demands that accompany it and support it.[16]

He also explained the context for "preach" in this passage: "To 'preach' does not imply that an ordained minister is to stand behind a stately pulpit and expound Scripture. [Paul's charge] called Timothy to a public heralding of the gospel message, whether done in a mass meeting or person-to-person. An example of the 'Word' Timothy was to declare is found in 1 Tim 1:15."[17] In this context, the meaning of "preach" is synonymous with the activity of evangelism.

---

[16] Thomas D. Lea and Hayne P. Griffin Jr. *1, 2 Timothy, Titus*, The New American Commentary, vol. 34 (Nashville: B&H, 1992), 242–43.

[17] Lea and Griffin, 243.

Second, Christians typically understand *epistēthi eukairōs akairōs*, translated by a majority of translations as "be ready in season and out of season," to mean that preachers and pastors should "have a sermon ready to preach when you know you are expected to preach one, as well as when you might be unexpectantly invited to preach one." The HCSB best captures the intended meaning of this passage: "Proclaim the message; persist in it whether convenient or not" (2 Tim 4:2). Lea offered a helpful corrective to this common misinterpretation of the phrase:

> Timothy was to stand "prepared in season and out of season" ("press it home on all occasions, convenient or inconvenient," NEB). The command implies that each Christian leader must always be on duty and take advantage of every opportunity for service. Paul urged Timothy to stand by his message. . . . The phrase "in season and out of season" may point either to Timothy or to his listeners. If the former is true, then Paul was saying that Timothy should stay with the task whether or not he felt like it (see 2 Tim 1:6–7). If the latter is true, Paul urged Timothy to declare the truth whether or not his hearers found it a convenient time to listen. In light of Paul's words in vv. 3–4, the latter reference is probably what Paul intended. We should not apply the command so as to violate Jesus's warning in Matt 7:6, but we should realize that the occasion is always "seasonable" for proclaiming the gospel.[18]

Paul's admonition that Timothy preach the gospel whether or not it is convenient should encourage all believers—not only pastors and ministers—opportunities abound for them to proclaim the gospel.

From time to time, God distinctly superintends circumstances at particular places to prompt Christians to evangelize. In such a case the Holy Spirit internally impresses upon a believer that he or she must share the gospel with a specific person. In so doing the Spirit is personally

---

[18] Lea and Griffin, 243.

making an opportunity for the believer to evangelize. Most other times, however, believers should be taking an opportunity to share the gospel. If they find themselves in conversations with others whose standing with God and eternal destination is unknown to them, such an encounter should prompt them to take an opportunity to share the gospel with those people.

Evangelism does not happen incidentally. It occurs intentionally. Intentionality in evangelism is not simply knowing you should evangelize, rather it is constructing a plan to evangelize consistently and executing it. Believers who are not deliberate in evangelizing will ultimately relegate evangelism to nothing more than a good intention. To practice consistent evangelism, it must be planned—whether into daily, weekly, and/or monthly calendared events, or planned obedience in those moments of unscheduled prompting by the Holy Spirit.

Furthermore, evangelism will never occur by accident. It may take place during times and at places believers neither expect nor anticipate, but it will never occur until and unless they actually decide to evangelize. Those who fail to plan time to evangelize will fail to find time to evangelize. Believers will not evangelize consistently if they do not make evangelism a personal priority.

Evangelism planning can take two forms. The first can be referred to as a *corporate evangelism plan*. This type incorporates groups of believers, preferably those who belong to the same church, who schedule evangelism on a recurring basis. Nathan Lino has suggested, "Organized, public evangelism leads to organic, personal evangelism."[19] This corporate evangelism planning promotes accountability, encouragement, and structure. The group of believers should develop a strategy and employ a coordinator to maintain the plan.

---

[19] Nathan Lino, "#70 – Igniting a Genuine Fire for Evangelism," August 3, 2021, https://www.namb.net/podcasts/evangelism-with-johnny-hunt/70-igniting -a-genuine-fire-for-evangelism, 10:12–16.

The second form of evangelism planning is best described as a *personal evangelism plan*. This refers to an individual believer's own strategy to share the gospel persistently. Those who want to implement their own evangelism plan will find it helpful to incorporate a daily evangelistic petition during their quiet time, such as this one: "Dear God, give me opportunities to share the gospel today. When they occur, help me recognize them, and give me the courage and boldness to make the most of each opportunity to be able to share the gospel."

In addition to praying daily for opportunities to share the gospel, believers should adopt a rubric, or guidelines, by which they can easily identify the evangelistic opportunities God will provide them in answer to their prayers. Charles Stewart, a former pastor who has taught applied ministry at Southwestern Baptist Theological Seminary, has suggested a helpful set of guidelines to assist believers in developing their own personal evangelism plan. He has proposed four evangelism guidelines intended to prompt and encourage the intentionally consistent practice of personal evangelism:

1. **The Holy Spirit Guideline**: In whatever circumstances I find myself, when the Holy Spirit prompts me to engage a specific individual in a gospel conversation, I want to do so obediently.

2. **The Five-Minute Guideline**: If the Lord gives me a captive audience with an individual for five or more minutes, I will try to engage that person in a gospel conversation.

3. **The Homestead Guideline**: When the Lord brings a person whom I have not previously met onto my property or into my home, I will try to engage that person in a gospel conversation.

4. **The Detour Guideline**: When the Lord interrupts my daily routine so as to direct me to a place that puts me in contact with someone I would not otherwise have met, I will try to engage that person in a gospel conversation.[20]

---

[20] An earlier version of Stewart's guidelines was introduced in Matt Queen, *Mobilize to Evangelize* (Fort Worth: Seminary Hill, 2018), 67.

The Holy Spirit Guideline is a foundational principle that stimulates the practice of personal evangelism. Specifically, the latter three evangelism guidelines help personal evangelists become more aware and sensitive to the Holy Spirit's prompting. These guidelines are intended to be principles that encourage believers to practice intentional and consistent evangelism, not some form of legalism that imposes self-condemnatory forms of guilt upon them.

The Lord leaves the work of his evangelistic enterprise neither to mere coincidence nor to convenience. He demands obedience. Instead of waiting for just the right opportunity to evangelize, believers should look for and take every opportunity they have to evangelize.

Evangelism Is the Promotion of Inclusivism and/or Universalism[21]

Believers who either tell others they are already God's children or simply believe it to be true constitute an "everyone is okay with God" mentality, or universalism. But as Paul explained in Rom 3:23, "All have sinned and fall short of the glory of God." For this reason, he described all humans as "children under wrath" in Eph 2:3. Identifying unbelievers as God's children not only hinders the work of evangelism; it renders evangelism obsolete. One likely inadvertent example of this approach appears in Steve Smith and Ying Kai's book, *T4T: A Discipleship Re-Revolution*. Smith noted that Kai began evangelistic conversations with unbelievers by telling them, "Congratulations, you are God's child! The problem is that you are lost, but I will show you how to be saved."[22] Kai erred in this introduction to his gospel presentation in two ways—biblically and logically.

First, instead of referring to every human being as God's child, the Bible teaches that all people are God's creation (cf. Gen 1:27). Only

---

[21] C. E. Autrey referred to this approach as "syncretism" in *Basic Evangelism*, 29–30.

[22] Steve Smith with Ying Kai, *T4T: A Discipleship Re-Revolution* (Monument, CO: WIGTake Resources, 2011), 217.

through repentance of sin and faith alone in Jesus Christ can men and women be appropriated as the children of God (cf. John 1:12; Rom 8:16; 9:7–9; and 1 John 3:1). If personal evangelists tell their hearers they are already God's children, then what need would they have to repent and believe?

Second, by affirming his hearers are already God's children before they give him evidence of the fact, Kai's pronouncement, taken to its logical conclusion, promotes a type of "Christian" inclusivism that assumes the salvation of all human beings. John Sanders, an inclusivist himself, described and defined Christian *inclusivism*:

> The unevangelized are saved or lost on the basis of their commitment, or lack thereof, to the God who saves through the work of Jesus. [Inclusivists] believe that appropriation of salvific grace is mediated through general revelation and God's providential workings in human history. Briefly, inclusivists affirm the particularity and finality of salvation only in Christ but deny that knowledge of his work is necessary for salvation. That is to say, they hold that the work of Jesus is ontologically necessary for salvation (no one would be saved without it) but not epistemologically necessary (one need not be aware of the work in order to benefit from it). Or in other words, people can receive the gift of salvation without knowing the giver or the precise nature of the gift.[23]

Failing to evangelize with a firm conviction concerning the exclusivity of Jesus for salvation encourages biblical compromise and will ultimately thwart believers' participation in the evangelistic enterprise. Personal evangelists are not spiritual gurus. Instead, they are God's ambassadors that sound forth his love for the world through Jesus Christ's death, burial, and resurrection, calling upon everyone, everywhere to repent of their sins and believe in Jesus Christ alone for salvation.

---

[23] John Sanders, *No Other Name* (Grand Rapids: Eerdmans, 1992), 131.

A compacted problem relating to the evangelization of adherents to the world's religions lies not only in the way some evangelicals have evangelized them, but also in the fact that they are not evangelizing them at all. For the most part, evangelicals soteriologically identify as exclusivists. In terms of soteriology, Christian *exclusivism* maintains that Jesus Christ, through his death, burial, and resurrection, is the only and exclusive means for the salvation of human beings. Unlike inclusivists, exclusivists affirm both the ontological and epistemological necessity of Jesus and his death, burial, and resurrection to save humans. On the theological and philosophical bases of their exclusivism, as well as their understanding of the imperatival nature of the Great Commission, evangelicals avow both the necessity and their responsibility to evangelize any and every person generally, and particularly to do so with those who have never heard the gospel.

In his study of religious diversity in America, Robert Wuthnow made a surprising, yet disturbing, discovery concerning Christian exclusivists:

> Exclusive Christians' assumptions about God, Jesus, and church restrict the amount of contact they have with non-Christians even as they reinforce the view that only Christianity is true. Yet Christianity also encourages evangelism; indeed, any belief system that is not only true but uniquely true is bound to encourage its followers to let other people know about the truth, especially when their immortal souls depend on it. Telling others the "good news" amounts to much more than merely being sociable, like sharing recipes or gardening tips. Thus, it is less surprising that exclusive Christians believe it is right to try to convert others . . . than that they do not engage more wholeheartedly in such efforts. . . . Since most exclusive Christians know few people of other religions, this strategy effectively minimizes their likelihood of evangelizing many such people.[24]

---

[24] Robert Wuthnow, *America and the Challenges of Religious Diversity* (Princeton, NJ: Princeton University, 2005), 145–46.

This reality has unintentionally yielded a scenario in which some evangelicals are simultaneously exclusivists yet not evangelistic. Such a paradox between orthodoxy and heteropraxy yields believing exclusivists who are practicing universalists—they sincerely believe that no one can be saved apart from hearing about Jesus and believing in him, while they neglect to evangelize, acting as though God will eventually save everyone in the end. To the extent that some evangelicals continue not to evangelize those in other faith traditions, and others include inclusivist language in gospel presentations, the practice of evangelism will be threatened in its duty and doctrine.

Evangelism Is Shaming Others into "Repentance"

People often cower and recoil when Jesus Christ's gospel and the Spirit's holiness confront their sin. As a result, those who hear the gospel and are convicted by the Holy Spirit about their sins will experience some combination of guilt, humiliation, remorse, embarrassment, regret, and even shame. Personal evangelists should anticipate this reaction from unbelievers when they evangelize in the power of the Holy Spirit.

Nevertheless, those who for their own pleasure seek to condemn and shame others when they "evangelize" exemplify a "shaming others" mentality. Practitioners of this approach seek to make listeners feel bad about themselves apart from the conviction of the Holy Spirit. Extreme cases of this attitude include self-proclaimed "evangelists" who berate others without even sharing the gospel with them. Such people weaponize evangelism, violating its intent and victimizing those they castigate.

When evangelism is primarily used as a tool to shame others, those who practice it err in at least two ways. First, they egregiously attempt to deify themselves. Only God can convict sinners of the depravity and futility of their sin. Personal evangelists can, and should, explain how unbelievers' sin offends, and thus alienates them from, God. But only the Holy Spirit can convince them of their transgression against the holy God, as well as their complete inability to remedy it. For personal evangelists to attempt to convict unbelievers of their sin in their own strength and ability is at best an exercise in futility and at worst an attempt at self-deification.

Second, practitioners of this "evangelism" misnomer distort a personal evangelist's role. Instead of preaching against sin, they preach against sinners. Rather than humbly explaining how unbelievers have sinned against God, they seek to humiliate them by weaponizing their sins against them. In lieu of convincing those far from God how their sin offends him, they intend to push sinners even farther away from God by offending them.

Personal evangelists must convey to their listeners that they are unrighteous because they have not believed in Jesus Christ (John 3:18–19, 36). Yet believers must also tell them that Jesus Christ died on the cross for their sins, and if they repent of their sins and believe in him, they can be forgiven and declared righteous. Although sinners must be told that hell awaits them if they do not repent and believe, personal evangelists must tell them in such a way that their listeners realize that they care for their souls and want them to avoid hell by faith in Jesus Christ alone.

An incident that occurred in the summer of 2011 illustrates this point. I was conducting a street survey in another country with faculty and students from Southwestern Seminary. Tabitha, a lady in her twenties, indicated her willingness to answer questions asked by my evangelism partner, a seasoned missionary, and me.[25] She told us she was visiting from another country, so after our interview I asked her, "What brings you to this country?" She replied, "I am on a search to find God." Then she asked me, "Why are you here?" I told her, "I have come from Texas to this country to help people find peace with God."

My answer naturally led my partner and me to share the gospel with Tabitha. We urged her to repent and believe in Jesus as her Lord and

---

[25] In order to protect this woman's identity, I have used "Tabitha" as a pseudonym for her name.

Savior; however, she declined. Normally I would have given her a tract and encouraged her to contact us if she changed her mind, but the Holy Spirit prompted me to continue our conversation. I said, "Tabitha, as you search elsewhere for God, I am compelled to tell you something more." I knew what I had to say next, but verbalizing those words I believed at the time would put this new friendship at risk because my partner and I had really connected with her. My eyes began to water as I told her, "If you go through the rest of your life rejecting the God we have shared with you, basically telling him that you want to live the rest of your existence without him, he will give you exactly what you desire. You will spend an eternity in a place called 'hell,' consciously, hopelessly, and eternally apart from God."

Immediately her body language changed. She looked intently in my eyes and asked, "Matt, are you telling me I am going to hell?" I avoided shaming her and had tried my best not to offend her, but I was sure I had. I knew her forthright question deserved an answer, but I did not want to offend her any further than I convinced myself I already had. Trying to regain some sense of goodwill with her, while also telling her God's truth, I shifted the responsibility for my assertion away from myself and toward God: "Well, Tabitha, that is what the Bible teaches." She solemnly said, "Matt, tell me more about hell. You are the first person to ever tell me about it." I was so shocked by her response that I found myself without words. My partner began to explain hell to her and upon regaining my composure, I joined her in retelling the gospel to Tabitha. Although she did not receive Christ that day, she left with a clear understanding of the seriousness of her sin without feeling as though we had tried to embarrass her. In the same way, personal evangelists must be motivated by genuine concern for unbelievers' souls to compassionately inform them of their unrighteousness and offensiveness to God. Those who "evangelize" in such a way that they take pleasure and gratify themselves by demeaning and belittling sinners neither understand evangelism nor practice it.

Evangelism Is "Winning at All Costs"

Christians sometimes view evangelism in terms of winning or losing. This preconception manifests itself in one of two different ways. First, some Christians view evangelistic conversations as argumentative contests that end with a winner and loser. They assume God's honor is on the line and therefore defend the gospel with their mental prowess.

Believers with this "winning" mindset can sometimes seem more interested in winning arguments than they are in winning souls. In their well-meaning attempts to explain and defend the gospel, they argue their point in hopes that their listeners will concede a loss so they can be declared winners. Mack Stiles has written of this mindset: "Sticking people with the right answers won't guarantee they'll turn to Christ. In fact, the smug answer, however correct, may ensure that a non-Christian will never listen to a Christian again. Christianity is not information transfer."[26] In such a scenario, believers might walk away from an encounter having won an argument, but in the end losing souls due to a pretentious spirit.

The truth of the gospel does not hinge on the cleverness of its presentation. Whether personal evangelists win or lose an argument about the gospel and its claims, they should remain confident in the veracity of the gospel they share, as well as the superiority of the Christian gospel to any other "gospel." Nineteenth-century English C. H. Spurgeon, a Particular Baptist pastor, addressed this "winning at all costs" mentality in one of his sermons:

> I believe the best way of defending the gospel is to spread the gospel. I was addressing a number of students, the other day, upon the apologies for the gospel which are so numerous just now. A great many learned men are defending the gospel; no

---

[26] J. Mack Stiles, *Speaking of Jesus: How to Tell Your Friends the Best News They Will Ever Hear* (Downers Grove, IL: IVP, 1995), 121.

doubt it is a very proper and right thing to do, yet I always notice
that, when there are most books of that kind, it is because the
gospel itself is not being preached. Suppose a number of persons
were to take it into their heads that they had to defend a lion, a
full-grown king of beasts! There he is in the cage, and here come
all the soldiers of the army to fight for him. Well, I should suggest to them, if they would not object, and feel that it was hum-
bling to them, that they should kindly stand back, and open the
door, and let the lion out! I believe that would be the best way of
defending him, for he would take care of himself; and the best
"apology" for the gospel is to let the gospel out.[27]

In other words, the best "defense" when it comes to God and his gospel is
for believers to stay on "offense" without being offensive.

Concerning the second way, other Christians have convinced themselves that they must be able to answer any question or respond to any
objection an unbeliever can pose before they can or should share the
gospel. Many believers fear evangelism, worrying that while they have
complete confidence in what they believe about the gospel, they are not
sufficiently prepared to respond to others' critiques or questions. This kind
of uncertainty arises from a legitimate concern; however, Jesus promised
that the Holy Spirit will provide his disciples the words they need when
they testify about Jesus (cf. Matt 10:19; Mark 13:11; Luke 12:11–12). In
addition, believers need to recognize that they will not always have the
answers because, unlike God who is omniscient, their knowledge and
understanding are limited. Trueblood encourages believers who struggle
with these concerns:

We do not have to wait until we know the whole truth about
anything to make our witness. If we were to wait for this, we
should wait forever. There is a paradox in the fact that we can

---

[27] C. H. Spurgeon, "Christ and His Co-Workers," *Metropolitan Tabernacle
Pulpit*, vol. 42, June 10, 1886.

bear witness to the truth without claiming to be possessors of it. The truth is bigger than our systems, yet we must give testimony to the little that we now see. I must risk my reputation on the point at which I am willing to stand, even though much beyond that point is hazy. Only as we are willing to declare where we *are* are [*sic*] we likely to go beyond this unsatisfactory point. It is in this spirit that testimony is able to reconcile the two moods which seem so deeply opposed: boldness and humility. We can never say, "This I know beyond a shadow of a doubt," for that kind of certainty is not given to finite men. All we can say is that "we are persuaded."[28]

Know-it-alls endear no one. No one will ever be an expert on everything, but this lack of expertise should not hinder believers from sharing their faith. They have not failed if they cannot answer every question. Instead, in humility and honesty, they can admit they do not know, research the issue, seek the counsel of their pastor, and return with more information later. This type of honest answer encourages another meeting, furthering a relational trust that could provide a later opportunity for more gospel-centered conversations.

Although these previous evangelistic concepts of "winning" prove to be problematic, evangelism can be philosophically paired with the concept of "winning"—*soul-winning*.[29] Nevertheless, some believers have expressed concerns about associating evangelism with winning in this way. They cite sincere theological reasons to avoid talking about evangelism in terms of "winning people to Christ," objecting to this language because they believe using it deprives God of full credit for his role in saving people from their sins. They contend that to say Christians "win souls" ascribes unmerited recognition to human agents because they do not win souls; God does. Of course he does; however, the Bible does not

---

[28] Trueblood, *The Company of the Committed*, 66.

[29] A biblical examination and defense of evangelism as *soul-winning* will be presented in the section "Winning a Soul" in chapter 3.

record an instance where God won a soul apart from his Spirit working through and in cooperation with the evangelism of human agents.

What, then, does it mean to "win souls," and can this activity incorporate a human dimension without threatening the tenet that God alone saves souls? C. H. Spurgeon, cited earlier, embraced the word *soul-winning*. In *The Soul-Winner* he explained his understanding of the concept:

> What is the real winning of a soul for God? So far as this is done by instrumentality, what are the processes by which a soul is led to God and to salvation? I take it that one of its main operations consists *in instructing a man that he may know the truth of God*. Instruction by the gospel is the commencement of all real work upon men's minds. . . .
>
> We are sent to evangelize, or to preach the gospel to every creature; and that is not done unless we teach them the great truths of revelation. The gospel is a reasonable system, and it appeals to men's understanding; it is a matter for thought and consideration, and it appeals to the conscience and the reflecting powers. . . . The field of instruction is wide if men are to be made to know the truth which saves. "That the soul be without knowledge, it is not good," and it is ours as the Lord's instruments to make men so to know the truth that they may believe it, and feel its power. We are not to try and save men in the dark, but in the power of the Holy Ghost we are to seek to turn them from darkness to light.[30]

Spurgeon's understanding of soul-winning incorporated a cooperation between the divine and the human agencies involved in evangelism. This cooperative effort in evangelism can correctly and accurately be referred to as *soul-winning*.

---

[30] C. H. Spurgeon, *The Soul-Winner; or, How to Lead Sinners to the Saviour* (New York: Revell, 1895), 14–16, emphasis added.

Personal evangelists should share the gospel with complete confidence in its veracity, regardless of the extent to which they can explain it or answer questions about it. If, in evangelism, convicting, convincing, or regeneration depended solely upon believers' cognitive expertise and their ability to answer questions or respond to objections, perhaps they could consider themselves winners or losers based on outcomes alone. But evangelism depends on God. Therefore, the goal is not winning at all costs, but witnessing no matter the cost.

Evangelism Is a Right to Be Earned

In *Invitation to Evangelism* Tim Beougher referenced the most accurate description of evangelism ever written. He wrote, "Someone once defined evangelism as a conversation between two people, both of whom are nervous."[31] Evangelism can certainly make both the evangelizer and the evangelized nervous. These feelings of anxiety stem from the believers' desire not to offend their hearers, as well as unbelievers' desire to avoid being offended. The intent to avoid offending unbelievers has led to the emergence of a philosophy that maintains personal evangelists must earn permission from unbelievers before they share the gospel with them.

In his classic book *Evangelism and the Sovereignty of God*, J. I. Packer discussed the role of relationships and gaining permission to share the gospel:

> You are not usually justified in choosing the subject of conversation with another till you have already begun to give yourself to him in friendship and established a relationship with him in which he feels that you respect him, are interested in him, and are treating him as a human being and not as some kind of "case." With some people, you may establish such a relationship in five

---

[31] Timothy K. Beougher, *Invitation to Evangelism: Sharing the Gospel with Compassion and Conviction* (Grand Rapids: Kregel Academic, 2021), 198.

minutes, whereas with others it may take months. But the principle remains the same. *The right to talk intimately to another person about the Lord Jesus Christ has to be earned*, and you earn it by convincing him that you are his friend, and that you really care about him.[32]

Packer correctly emphasizes the necessity for sincere care for unbelievers, calling personal evangelists to treat them as humans worthy of respect, not some spiritual project. But requiring believers to convince unbelievers of their concern through friendship before they should, or can, evangelize proves problematic for several reasons.

First, any time the gospel was presented in the New Testament, it occurred without believers first having to gain permission before they shared it. Had New Testament preachers earned the right to proclaim the gospel publicly to the crowds due to a preexisting friendship they shared with each and every one of them? Did personal evangelists in the New Testament wait to share the gospel conversationally with people until they established a friendship with them, or did they almost exclusively share the gospel immediately when they were engaged in conversation with them?

Second, earning the right to evangelize unbelievers sometimes leads Christians to dismiss the instantaneous practice of evangelism as a valid way to exhibit compassionate respect for unbelievers. Some believers have been convinced they must earn the right to evangelize unbelievers, because to evangelize without gaining trust disrespects them and places their own concerns before those of unbelievers. In his second correspondence with the Corinthian church, Paul explained to them that the love of Christ compelled him to evangelize (cf. 2 Cor 5:11–15). Building a friendship and trust certainly are helpful ways for believers to demonstrate their genuine love and respect for unbelievers; however, it is not

---

[32] J. I. Packer, *Evangelism and the Sovereignty of God* (Downers Grove, IL: IVP, 1961), 81, emphasis added.

the only way to do so. Biblically informed evangelism compels believers to love sinners, as Christ did, and to demonstrate it by sharing the good news with them.

While recounting an encounter with a Gideon Bible distributor who evangelized him, atheist Penn Jillette attributed this man's evangelism to a demonstration of his love for Jillette. He asserted, "How much do you have to hate somebody to not [evangelize] them? How much do you have to hate someone to believe that everlasting life is possible and not tell them that?"[33] Believers should exhibit a genuine interest, respect, and compassion for unbelievers in every way they can as soon as they can—which includes sharing God's demonstration of his love through Christ with them.

Last, requiring that personal evangelists earn permission before being heard assumes an unrealistic expectation on the part of unbelievers. In addition to causing enmity with God, human sin and depravity prevents sinners from ever desiring reconciliation with God. This basic anthropological principle raises several questions about unbelievers' ability and willingness to grant believers permission to evangelize them. First, due to their habitual rejection of God and his gospel, is it reasonable for believers to assume unbelievers will come to a point where they will ever want to hear the gospel, no matter how much relational capital believers build with them? Second, if believers should wait to share the gospel until they receive permission from unbelievers to do so, would unbelievers even know they are expected to give it? Last, if believers should wait to earn the right to share the gospel, would that not mean that believers' compliance with the Great Commission was based on unbelievers' consent, rather than their willful obedience to the lordship of Jesus Christ?

The apparent answers to these questions should convince personal evangelists not to understand evangelism as a right they must earn from

---

[33] Penn Jillette, "A Gift of a Bible," 3:28–3:38, 2009, vlog, original post https://www.youtube.com/watch?v=7JHS8adO3hM, deleted; available online: https://www.youtube.com/watch?v=6md638smQd8.

unbelievers before they evangelize them. Instead, evangelism is the right
thing for personal evangelists to do. In the same way that no one earns the
right to become God's child—Jesus bestows it upon all who believe—no
one earns the right to evangelize—Jesus gives it to all who have believed.
Perhaps believers should consider such a "right" in terms of evangelism
from a different perspective. In a personal conversation on June 11, 2014,
missiologist Keith Eitel posited an astute question about believers earning a right to share the gospel. He asked, "While we are waiting on the
'right to be heard,' we must seriously consider, 'Do the lost have a right
to hear the gospel?'"

Evangelism Is a Means to Garner Personal Glory

Some personal evangelists seek attention for the positive results of their
evangelism. They share their faith as an act out of pride, seeking recognition for those who profess faith in Jesus Christ. Scripture, however,
exhorts evangelists not to boast or seek credit for what God does in and
through our evangelism (cf. 1 Cor 1:31; 9:16; 2 Cor 10:12–18; Gal 5:25–
26; 6:13–15).

God alone saves humans who repent and believe in the gospel. The
Father sent his Son to humankind as a demonstration of his love, desiring the salvation of the world. Jesus died on the cross, was buried, and
was raised from the dead to provide the way for people to be saved from
their sins. The Holy Spirit convicts, convinces, and draws sinners so that
they will repent and believe in Christ, while simultaneously regenerating
them. In addition, he emboldens, empowers, and fills believers as they
evangelize unbelievers. So, from start to finish, God alone is responsible
and receives any and all credit for saving human beings.

Believers must not succumb to the temptation of using evangelism
to garner personal glory for themselves for a couple of reasons. First, God
is a jealous God and will not share his glory with anyone (cf. Isa 42:8). If
believers attempt to share in God's glory for the positive results of their
evangelism, they can surely expect God's discipline.

Second, those who quantify their evangelistic success by numbers of unbelievers who positively respond to their gospel invitations also tend to measure their evangelistic failure according to how many reject them. In other words, if they take the credit when someone receives Christ, then they must also take the blame when someone rejects Christ. This type of mentality yields a few complications.

One problem with this mindset is that more people will reject the gospel than will ever accept it, regardless of any believer's personal ability to evangelize. Both the Bible (cf. Matt 13:1–9, 18–23; Mark 4:1–9, 14–20; Luke 8:4–8, 11–15) and personal experience attest to this reality. Over time, the disproportionate ratio of those who accept the gospel versus those who reject it has a greater likelihood to discourage personal evangelists than it does to encourage them.

Also, in order to achieve evangelistic "success," personal evangelists will be tempted to pressure or manipulate their hearers in order to achieve their desired results. Such action on the part of personal evangelists often generates bad will, results in a loss of credibility, and yields false professions from unbelievers. Furthermore, J. I. Packer warned:

> It is not right when we take it on us to do more than God has given us to do. It is not right when we regard ourselves as responsible for securing converts, and look to our own enterprise and techniques to accomplish what only God can accomplish. To do that is to intrude ourselves into the office of the Holy Ghost, and to exalt ourselves as the agents of the new birth. . . . For where we are not consciously relying on God, there we shall inevitably be found relying on ourselves.[34]

Those who practice any kind of manipulative evangelism dismiss the convicting work of the Holy Spirit and, instead, attempt to force their hearers into a decision. They would do well to remember that if they can talk people into making a decision, then others can talk them into making

---

[34] Packer, *Evangelism and the Sovereignty of God*, 29.

the opposite one. Worse yet, manipulators can foster a false assurance of salvation within those who have not actually repented and believed in Christ, if not altogether harden sinners' hearts to the gospel because they believe they are saved, when in reality they are not. For these reasons, instead of taking credit for the results of their evangelism, personal evangelists should give glory to whom it alone is due—the triune God.

DISCUSSION AND REFLECTION QUESTIONS

1. What misunderstandings about evangelism have hindered you from practicing it consistently? What are some of the ways this chapter has given you a new understanding of evangelism?

2. Have you ever considered when God prompts you to evangelize someone that it may be his/her only or last opportunity to hear the gospel? What guideline(s), including but not limited to the Holy Spirit, Five-Minute, Homestead, and/or Detour Guidelines, will you adopt to assist you in becoming an intentionally consistent personal evangelist?

3. Whenever an unbeliever either poses a question or raises an objection you are unable to answer, how will you respond?

4. In what ways can you communicate the unrighteousness of unbelievers' sin without shaming or embarrassing them?

2

Toward an Understanding
of Evangelism

With so many misconceptions circulating, what then is evangelism? Any church or believer desiring to practice consistent and intentional evangelism must understand the meaning. This chapter articulates a comprehensive definition and explains the intended objective of evangelism. It concludes by providing a structural framework of biblical, theological, practical, and philosophical affirmations and denials that will set the parameters for this study's concept of evangelism.

Defining Evangelism

Evangelism is *that Spirit-empowered activity whereby all disciples of Jesus Christ give an intentional, complete, and verbal witness to his life, death, burial, and resurrection, exhorting unbelievers to repent of their sins and place their faith in Christ alone for salvation so that they may become his baptized, obedient disciples.* Explaining each phrase of this definition will provide a fuller context and meaning about what it intends to communicate.

Evangelism is that spirit-empowered activity . . . : Personal evangelists practice biblical evangelism by first recognizing it is Spirit-empowered. Far too many believers practice self-empowered evangelism. Those who evangelize in their own power will get their own results. Those who evangelize in the power of the Spirit of God will see him work in the results. If believers try to muster enough courage to evangelize, they will search in vain to find it. But if they entreat the Holy Spirit to give them boldness to evangelize, he will embolden them to do so in his power. If Christians attempt to find the right words within themselves either to begin a gospel conversation or to answer unbelievers' objections, they will likely not find them. But if they recall Jesus's promise that the Spirit will give his disciples the words they need when they stand before the magistrates (cf. Matt 10:17–20; Mark 13:9–11; Luke 12:12; 21:12–15), will he not also give them the words they need to proclaim Jesus to everyone if they ask him?

. . . whereby all disciples of Jesus Christ . . . : Jesus expects everyone who identifies as his disciple to make disciples. He never delimited the obligation of disciple-making only to a particular segment or group—every disciple bears this responsibility. As Trueblood declares, "The call to witness is a call which men can answer affirmatively or negatively, but one who answers it negatively, however kind and pious he may be, is not in the company of Jesus."[1]

As explained previously, evangelism is a spiritual discipline. Like with the other spiritual disciplines, failing to practice evangelism amounts to an act of spiritual disobedience. L. R. Scarborough, the second president of Southwestern Seminary and inaugural occupant of the first established chair of evangelism in the world, "the Chair of Fire," explains, "God calls all His people to give to and faithfully witness to the gospel, but He calls some to preach it. . . . To fail at this point is for God's people to be sinfully

---

[1] Trueblood, *The Company of the Committed*, 49.

treasonable at the most vital matter in time and eternity."[2] The biblical idea of blood guilt associated with a believer's failure to warn sinners of God's judgment (cf. Ezek 3:16–21; 33:1–11; Acts 18:5–6; 20:17–27) substantiates Scarborough's claim.

Reaching all people requires the evangelistic participation of all disciples. The world cannot and will not be won to faith in Christ by only those who serve as ministers and missionaries. The number of unbelievers in the world exponentially outnumbers the size of the Christian ministerial ranks. To reach as many as possible with the gospel, every disciple—new and mature, young and old, male and female, evangelistically experienced and inexperienced—must be employed into Christ's disciple-making enterprise.

. . . give an intentional, complete, and verbal witness . . . : The exercise of evangelism requires its practitioners to be intentional and deliberate. As mentioned in the previous chapter, while some opportunities to evangelize may come at times when believers do not expect them, evangelism will never, ever occur by accident. Believers must predetermine they will be obedient to share the gospel during specific times they have scheduled in their calendar, as well as those unscheduled times when the Spirit spontaneously prompts them to evangelize another person.

Evangelism also requires personal evangelists to attempt to share a complete presentation of the gospel. They will not be able to present the complete gospel every time; however, they should intend to share as much of the gospel as possible without forcing it upon others. No one has been or ever will be saved by a half or partial gospel. The complete gospel—we are sinners; but God in his love sent Jesus Christ to die for our sins, be buried, and raised on the third day; and those who repent and believe will be saved—must be understood by unbelievers before they can be saved. Personal evangelists should emulate the desire of August Hermann Francke when he writes, "As far as I am concerned, I must

---

[2] L. R. Scarborough, *Christ's Militant Kingdom* (New York: George H. Doran, 1924), 174–75.

preach that should someone hear me only once before he dies, he will
have heard not just a part, but the entire way of salvation and in the
proper way for it to take root in his heart."[3]

By its very nature, evangelism is verbal. As explained previously,
evangelism is not merely "using words when necessary"—using words is
absolutely necessary for evangelism. Whether by vocal, written, or sign
language, evangelism requires a clear articulation of the gospel. Focusing
on the need to communicate the evangelistic message does not negate
the necessity for believers' lives and actions to match their evangelistic
speech. Moral living—on its own merits and apart from verbalizing the
gospel—provides only as much, if not less, an explanation of the gospel
than creation generally reveals the existence of a creator God. Evangelism
necessitates the articulation of God's special revelation from his Word
and about his Son.

People all over the world try to live moral lives. Many people follow
religions or internal moral compasses that encourage general religiosity. They live outwardly moral lives, but do not dare proselytize others.
Some Christians strive to live moral—even holy—lives, but do not verbally share the gospel. Sometimes, these Christians are even considered
pietistic. Both general religiosity and silent pietism have one major flaw:
observing sincere displays of sanctimony cannot save anyone; only hearing the verbal proclamation of the gospel can.

. . . to his life, death, burial, and resurrection, . . . : The life, death,
burial, and resurrection of Jesus Christ form the heart of the gospel. In
1 Cor 15:3–4, Paul summarized the gospel thus: "that Christ died for our
sins according to the Scriptures, that he was buried, that he was raised
on the third day according to the Scriptures." By virtue of his sinless
life and his fulfillment of the Old Testament messianic prophecies, Jesus
is the Christ. Peter and John presented this case when they preached

---

[3] Paulus Scharpff, *History of Evangelism: Three Hundred Years of Evangelism
in Germany, Great Britain, and the United States of America*, trans. Helga Bender
Henry (Grand Rapids: Eerdmans, 1966), 46.

in Solomon's Colonnade (cf. Acts 3:17–26). Most personal evangelists emphasize the death of Christ paying the penalty for our sins when they evangelize, and they should. But in doing so, many of them neglect to mention his burial and resurrection. Their failure to include them is not because they do not believe they happened, but because they assume their listeners already know about them.

More people today in the United States know less about Jesus than they ever have. For that reason, if personal evangelists tell them that Jesus died for their sins without mentioning his resurrection, they likely will assume they are being asked to place faith in a dead man. To prevent unbelievers from misunderstanding this cardinal truth of the gospel, believers must pair Jesus's resurrection from the dead with his death on the cross.

Even greater numbers of personal evangelists omit his burial in their gospel presentations than those who omit his resurrection. Yet, when presenting the gospel, Christ's burial should always be included for at least three reasons. First, the fact that Paul mentioned Christ's burial in his summary of the gospel (1 Cor 15:4a) should convince personal evangelists to follow his example. If doing so was necessary for Paul, it should also be necessary for personal evangelists. Second, Christ's burial in the tomb contradicts hypotheses such as the "Swoon Theory," which teaches that Jesus was not dead when they took him off the cross. Instead, its advocates contend that he unconsciously lay in the tomb and sometime later was revived. Yet extremely few, if any, scholars have been convinced of this theory since the mid-nineteenth century due to David Strauss's analysis of it in *A New Life of Jesus*.[4] Including Jesus's burial when presenting the gospel complements the fact that he actually died on the cross. Last, including the burial event in gospel presentations anticipates, for new believers, their profession of faith through baptism by immersion. After assisting their hearers to repent, believe, and confess their faith in

---

[4] See David Strauss, *A New Life of Jesus*, vol. 1, 2nd ed. (Edinburgh: William and Norgate, 1879), 408–12.

Jesus Christ, personal evangelists who include Christ's burial, along with his death and resurrection, should refer new believers back to it so they can visualize the meaning of their baptism—that they profess faith in Christ who died to appease God's wrath for their sin, who was buried, and who was raised to life on the third day.

. . . **exhorting unbelievers to repent of their sins and believe in Christ alone for salvation . . . :** Personal evangelists do not make genuine disciples by manipulating or forcing unbelievers to follow Jesus. Instead, they must exhort unbelievers to respond to the gospel's appeal, as well as to the Holy Spirit's conviction of their sins, by repenting of their sins and placing their faith for salvation in Christ alone. Likewise, unbelievers cannot become disciples on the basis of an internal, cognitive resolve to affiliate with Christ or a decision to live a moral life. They must repent of their sins and believe solely in Christ's death, burial, and resurrection for the forgiveness of their sins.

Evangelism requires personal evangelists to call for repentance. When exhorting unbelievers to become disciples, many Christians have told them that repentance occurs when they make a spiritual about-face and turn the direction of their lives toward God. This picture is fitting but not complete. It does not adequately explain repentance or how a person achieves it. In the New Testament, repentance is a change of mind. It emphasizes the necessity for a change in the current direction of one's beliefs and behavior. This change does not come from a person's internal resolve, but the total transformation that accompanies the regeneration by the Holy Spirit.

Sam Chan offers this helpful explanation of repentance: "Instead of merely looking inward and regretting the past, [repentance] is looking outward and forward. . . . By being outward and forward looking, *metanoia* produces fruit (Matt. 3:8), knowledge (2 Tim. 2:25), life (Acts 11:18), and salvation (2 Cor. 7:10)."[5] Therefore, when personal evange-

---

[5] Sam Chan, *Evangelism in a Skeptical World: How to Make the Unbelievable News about Jesus More Believable* (Grand Rapids: Zondervan, 2018), 29.

lists exhort unbelievers to repent, they should instruct them to change their way of thinking in terms of who they are (their sins make them unrighteous), who God is (God is holy, perfect, righteous, and loving), what they are unable to do (not only does their sin displease God and invoke his wrath, but even their attempts of appeasement by their good deeds offend him), and how they can be forgiven of their sins in order to receive abundant life (only Jesus's death, burial, and resurrection from the dead can appease God's wrath against their sins).

Repentance is the prerequisite for belief. No one will ever believe with the heart before first repenting with the mind. Sometimes in the New Testament, believers call for repentance when evangelizing (cf. Matt 3:2, 8; 4:17; Mark 1:4; 6:12; Luke 3:3, 8; 5:32; 13:3, 5; Acts 2:38; 3:19; 8:22; 14:15; 17:30; 26:20). At other times, they call for belief (cf. John 3:14–16, 36; 5:24; 6:29, 40, 47; 7:37–39; 8:24; 11:25–26; 12:36a, 44–46; Acts 10:42–43; 13:38–40; 16:31; 26:27). But anytime believers evangelize and call for both, repentance always precedes belief, without exception (cf. Mark 1:14–15; Acts 20:21).

Once unbelievers understand their condition and inability to do anything about it, personal evangelists must explain that only Jesus can save them and exhort them to place their faith in him. Non-Christians do not believe in Jesus for the forgiveness of sins by merely assenting to the historical accuracy of his death, burial, and resurrection. Instead, they must affirm the exclusive means of salvation through Jesus's death, burial, and resurrection and exercise complete trust in him so that they may be forgiven by God in Christ. By doing so, they should acknowledge that he is their Lord and confess him as such (Rom 10:9–10).

. . . so that they may become his baptized, obedient disciples: The Lord commanded his disciples in the Great Commission: "All authority has been given to me in heaven and on earth. Go, therefore, and make disciples of all nations, baptizing them in the name of the Father and of the Son and of the Holy Spirit, teaching them to observe everything I have commanded you. And remember, I am with you always, to the end of the age" (Matt 28:18–20). Evangelism aims to make disciples of Jesus Christ, who, upon hearing and receiving the gospel, are taught obedience to all the commands of Jesus Christ and become members of a local church through believer's baptism in the name of the Father, Son, and Spirit.

Jesus commissioned his disciples to make disciples from every nation in the world. His commission is not a suggestion that believers can choose or not choose to perform—it is an imperative, a command. Terry L. Wilder explains:

> The main verb in the text is the aorist imperative μαθητεύσατε ("make disciples"). Aorist imperatives, in general, convey a sense of urgency and immediacy of action. The main verb μαθητεύσατε is modified by the aorist participle, πορευθέντες; not "as you go," as is frequently explained, but "Go and make disciples." Πορευθέντες is an attendant circumstance participle; that is, the action "go," in some sense, is coordinate [sic] with the action of the finite verb, "make disciples." And as such, the participle takes on imperatival force as well. Further, the action of the participle is "something of a prerequisite before the action of the main verb can occur." That is to say, no making of disciples will take place unless you go: "Go and make disciples!"[6]

To make disciples, personal evangelists must exhort unbelievers to become Jesus's disciples through repentance and faith. Telling unbelievers the gospel without exhorting them to become Christ's disciples falls short of genuine evangelism. J. I. Packer agrees: "Evangelizing includes the endeavour to elicit a response to the truth taught. It is communication with a view to conversion. It is a matter, not merely of informing, but also of inviting. It is an attempt to *gain* (KJV), or *win* (ESV), or *catch* our fellow men for Christ."[7] Evangelists must issue their hearers an invitation to become Christ's disciples.

---

[6] Terry L. Wilder, "A Biblical Theology of Missions and Contextualization," *Southwestern Journal of Theology* 55:1 (Fall 2012): 5.

[7] Packer, *Evangelism and the Sovereignty of God*, 50 (see chap. 1, n. 32).

Believers' baptism by immersion and obedience to all Christ's commands form the criteria that indicates a disciple has been made. Baptism professes believers' (1) faith in the death, burial, and resurrection of Jesus; (2) testimony of their death to sin, burial of their old life, and resurrection to walk in the newness of life in Christ; and (3) hope in the resurrection of the dead. In addition, baptism identifies new disciples with the Father, Son, and Spirit—the triune God.

Baptism requires both a candidate and an administrator. A baptism candidate is a new believer, and the administrator is an individual whom a local church authorizes to baptize new disciples. New disciples' baptisms are a public profession of their faith (1 Pet 3:21) and an ordinance that signifies their incorporation into the membership of a particular church (cf. 1 Cor 12:13). Although the Great Commission does not explicitly associate church membership with baptism, the command to teach obedience to all Christ's commands (Matt 28:20a), as well as the contextual descriptions in Acts and the Epistles (cf. Acts 2:41; 1 Cor 12:13; Eph 4:4–6), infer such an association. As the "Baptist Faith and Message" (2000) states: "Being a church ordinance, [baptism] is prerequisite to the privileges of church membership and to the Lord's Supper."[8]

In addition to baptism, new disciples are to be taught obedience to all the commands of Christ. A commonly accepted and applied misconception about the Great Commission advances that in order to make disciples, new believers merely must be taught all Jesus's instructions. The grammar of the Great Commission certainly mandates that new disciples be taught all Christ's commands; however, they are also to be trained to obey what Jesus taught. No new disciple will keep Christ's commands without having been directed in how to do so. Concerning the making of obedient disciples, Scarborough asserts:

---

[8] "Article VII. Baptism and the Lord's Supper," "Baptist Faith and Message," Southern Baptist Convention, 2000.

True evangelism is more than winning souls to know and accept Christ as Saviour. This is one of its tasks, its first great one. But there follows an important and far-reaching task of conserving regeneration's victory and utilizing the newly-saved soul in promoting Christ's kingdom in effective service. Men are not saved to keep out of hell nor to gain heaven. They are saved to serve. The evangelism that stops at conversion and public profession is lop-sided, wasteful, and indeed hurtful. . . . Modern evangelism finds here its greatest leakage and waste, its weakest place. Much of modern evangelism leaves its spiritual children orphans, homeless and motherless. The churches not being organized for constant and constructive evangelism, let the new "babes in Christ" go without a mother's protecting arms, warm heart and love and food, without culture in soul-strength until they drift and become backsliders and spiritual driftwood. Such neglect of spiritual children is unpardonable and positively sinful. . . . The evangelists usually do not stress some important duties to the new convert: his duty to be baptized and follow Christ in church membership, join up in Christ's service and go to work for Him. A new convert is entitled to know by his spiritual parents all Christ tells him to do.[9]

The God-ordained structure for teaching new disciples to obey Christ's commands, as well as for holding them accountable, is the local church.

A Framework for Understanding Contemporary Evangelism

As this chapter has demonstrated, a comprehensive understanding of contemporary evangelism includes both an exhaustive and explanatory definition of its meaning, as well as a differentiation of it and its misnomers.

---

[9] L. R. Scarborough, *With Christ after the Lost: A Search for Souls* (Nashville: Sunday School Board of the Southern Baptist Convention, 1919), 168–69.

On June 13, 2017, Steve Gaines, then president of the Southern Baptist Convention, appointed an evangelism task force at the convention's 2017 annual meeting to study the state of evangelism within the Southern Baptist Convention. He instructed the group to offer recommendations at the next year's annual meeting that might enhance and strengthen the evangelistic efforts among the convention's entities and cooperating churches. At its 2018 annual meeting, the Southern Baptist Convention adopted the evangelism task force's report and recommendations. The report included a series of twelve affirmations and denials, similar to the nineteen affirmations and denials of the "Chicago Statement on Biblical Inerrancy" (1978). The following articles serve as a comprehensive framework for this volume's understanding of evangelism:

EVANGELISM ARTICLES OF AFFIRMATION AND DENIAL

ARTICLE I.

WE AFFIRM that evangelism is in part "soul-winning," as the New Testament employs the words "winning" and "persuading" with regards to imploring unbelievers in the power of the Holy Spirit to believe in Jesus Christ for their salvation (*cf.*, 1 Cor 9:19–22; 2 Cor 5:11, 20).

WE DENY that evangelism should be employed through means of manipulation, coercion, deceitfulness, or intimidation.

ARTICLE II.

WE AFFIRM that the Scriptures teach that gospel conversations should seek to include both clear presentations of the "good news" of salvation and genuine invitations for all people to receive Jesus Christ as Savior and Lord (*cf.*, Matt 19:16–30; Mark 10:17–22; Acts 1:8; 2:26–39; Rev 22:17).

WE DENY that gospel conversations are merely general talk about spiritual things and that an evangelistic invitation may only be extended by a singular methodological approach.

ARTICLE III.

WE AFFIRM that the heart of the gospel is the death, burial, and resurrection of the God-man, Jesus Christ, for the forgiveness of sins (*cf.*, 1 Cor 15:3–4).

WE DENY that the gospel is a humanly-conceived invention or myth divorced from supernatural activity and actual historical reality.

ARTICLE IV.

WE AFFIRM that salvation is by grace alone, through faith alone, in Christ alone; that it is wrought by the Holy Spirit as people repent of their sins, believe in Jesus Christ, and receive Him by confessing Him as Lord and Savior (*cf.*, John 1:12; 14:6; 16:8–11; Acts 2:37–38; 4:12; Rom 10:9–10; Eph 1:13; 2:8; Titus 3:4–7).

WE DENY that salvation can be achieved in and through a person's own power, initiative, or self-actualization.

ARTICLE V.

WE AFFIRM that evangelism is a spiritual discipline that every believer bears the responsibility to practice in order to be found faithful to our Lord's commands (*cf.*, Ezek 3:16–21; 33:1–11; Acts 18:5–6; 20:17–27).

WE DENY that evangelism is a spiritual gift that the Holy Spirit has endowed to some, but not all, believers, thereby excusing certain Christians from personal evangelistic responsibility.

ARTICLE VI.

WE AFFIRM that our Lord's Great Commission is a biblical mandate to be carried out by all true churches and faithful Christians until Jesus comes again (*cf.*, Matt 28:18–20; Mark 16:15; Luke 24:47–48; John 20:21; Acts 1:8).

WE DENY that the Great Commission was restricted only to the apostles and therefore is not binding upon believers today.

ARTICLE VII.

WE AFFIRM that the Great Commission mandate is for believers to share the gospel verbally with all unbelievers so that they might repent of their sins, trust Jesus Christ as Savior and Lord, be baptized (immersed) as witnesses to the truth of the gospel, and learn to obey all of Christ's commands (Matt 28:18–20).

WE DENY that the gospel is primarily concerned with social justice, political engagement, or secular aims resulting in the call to personal repentance and faith being minimized or ignored.

ARTICLE VIII.

WE AFFIRM that the gospel has societal ramifications, leading believers to engage in the biblical causes of justice and reconciliation (Luke 4:18).

WE DENY that the gospel only addresses personal spirituality and individual behavior.

ARTICLE IX.

WE AFFIRM that evangelism and discipleship are interdependent and together constitute the whole of the biblical disciple-making process (Matt 28:18–20).

WE DENY theological and philosophical lines of argumentation or ministry strategies that seek to separate evangelism and discipleship.

ARTICLE X.

WE AFFIRM that evangelism is a way of life to be learned and practiced, as God has gifted all believers with His indwelling Holy Spirit to enable them to witness boldly by His power (*cf.*, Acts 1:8; 4:8; 4:31).

WE DENY that evangelism is merely a human activity or a church program.

ARTICLE XI.

WE AFFIRM that a sinner's prayer is a biblically appropriate and practically effective method by which lost people can personally receive God's gracious offer of the gospel in repentance and faith (*cf.*, Luke 18:13–14; John 1:12; Rom 10:9–13).

WE DENY that people are saved merely by mouthing the words of a specific prayer.

ARTICLE XII.

WE AFFIRM that God gifts certain individuals to function as evangelists as a gift to the church in order to lead in the harvest and to equip believers for greater effectiveness in personal witnessing and corporate outreach in order to build up the body of Christ (*cf.*, Acts 8:12; 21:8; Eph 4:11).

WE DENY that the ministry of the New Testament evangelist ceased at the conclusion of the apostolic age and therefore is not a valid expression of God's calling and gifting today.[10]

---

[10] "Evangelism Articles of Affirmation and Denial," *Annual of the Southern Baptist Convention* (Nashville: Executive Committee, SBC, 2018), 93–95.

In 2016, I submitted a resolution for that year's Annual Meeting of the Southern Baptist Convention entitled, "On Soul-Winning and Evangelism." The 2016 Committee on Resolutions of the Southern Baptist Convention made minor amendments to my proposal and presented it as "Resolution 4: On Evangelism and Soul-Winning" to the Convention during their report. After approving an amendment to the committee's proposed resolution by Kyle Beverlin, a pastor from Missouri, the convention adopted the resolution. *Annual of the Southern Baptist Convention*, 85–86.

The following seminary professors, pastors, and executive director comprised the 2017–2018 Evangelism Task Force: Steve Gaines, Jeff Iorg, Preston Nix, Robert Matz, Alvin Reid, Jim Shaddix, Adam Greenway, David Allen, Paige Patterson, Jordan Easley, Nick Floyd, Noe Garcia, J. D. Greear, James Merritt, Doug Munton, Bartholomew Orr, Jimmy Scroggins, Jim Richards, and me. The task force appointed Adam Greenway and me to compile an initial draft of the Evangelism Articles for the task force. In doing so, we drew from the 2016 "Resolution 4: On Evangelism and Soul-Winning." After our initial draft of the articles was presented and discussed, they were amended by the task force and then recommended to the Southern Baptist Convention for adoption in Dallas, Texas, at the 2018 annual meeting. The recommendations of the task force, which included the Articles of Affirmation and Denial, were approved unanimously by the convention's messengers.

DISCUSSION AND REFLECTION QUESTIONS

1. In what ways does self-empowered evangelism differ from Spirit-empowered evangelism? Would you describe your own practice of evangelism more in terms of self-empowered or Spirit-empowered?

2. What unintended problems can arise if personal evangelists only share with unbelievers Jesus's death on the cross for their sins and exclude both his burial and resurrection?

3. What are some specific ways you can both exhort and instruct unbelievers to repent of their sins?

4. What are some specific ways you can both exhort and instruct unbelievers to place their faith in Jesus Christ for their salvation?

3

Biblical Foundations
of Evangelism

The Scriptures and their sufficiency serve as the foundation and standard of evangelism for at least three reasons. First, the Bible provides evangelistic examples that inform and describe the practice of evangelism. Second, the New Testament contains both direct and indirect divine imperatives that command Christ's disciples to evangelize. Last, the instructions by which Christians should evangelize are found in the Scriptures.

This chapter begins with a survey of the Old Testament to identify some evangelistic forms and prophecies that foretell New Testament occurrences of gospel proclamation. Second, it classifies the different ways various people practiced evangelism in the New Testament. Third, biblical metaphors for evangelism are discussed. Last, the chapter concludes by presenting biblical motivators that encourage the practice of evangelism.

Episodes Related to Evangelism in the Old Testament

Evangelism appears in the Old Testament in three different forms. First, particular actions and occurrences present in the Old Testament portend, or foreshadow, evangelism as practiced in the New Testament. They closely resemble gospel proclamation, but because they do not specifically or overtly preach Jesus and his life, death, burial, and resurrection, they cannot be considered as evangelism. Second, prophets in the Old Testament divinely foretell specific proclamations of the gospel recorded in the New Testament hundreds of years before they occur. Last, the Old Testament contains just a few episodes of proclamation that, if not categorized as evangelism, at least resemble it. The selected incidents that follow provide a sampling of foreshadowed and foretold forms of evangelism within the Old Testament.

God's Walk in Eden

Genesis 3 recounts the fall of Adam and Eve in the garden. Eve encountered a serpent who tempted her to eat fruit from the tree of the knowledge of good and evil. Both she and her husband ate from it. Immediately, both of them were aware of their nakedness, sin, and disobedience against God. They took fig leaves and fashioned loincloths for themselves. The events that followed in Gen 3:8–21 probably constitute history's first account of evangelism.

Adam and Eve heard the Lord God walking in the garden during the cool of the day. All of a sudden, the husband and his wife hid behind some trees. God asked Adam, "Where are you?" (Gen 3:9b). The Lord did not ask because he could not locate Adam. Instead, his question confronted Adam with his sin and its consequences. Adam and Eve had eaten forbidden fruit from a tree, causing them to dress with the leaves of a tree, and then hide from the Lord God behind some trees. Sin had entangled Adam. It also had created a distance between him and his God.

Adam presented himself before the Lord in fear and confessed that he knew he was naked. When asked if he had eaten from the tree he had been commanded to avoid, Adam blamed Eve, and, in turn, Eve blamed the serpent. God cursed the serpent, and then he punished both the woman and the man.

In Gen 3:15, God told the serpent, "I will put hostility between you and the woman, and between your offspring and her offspring. He will strike your head, and you will strike his heel." This pronouncement is known as the *protoevangelium* or "first gospel." This first occurrence and proclamation of the good news prophesied that a descendant of the woman would conquer the serpent and its offspring. In other words, the Father would send his Son, Jesus Christ, to be born of a virgin. Satan would strike the God-man, because in order to save humankind from their sins he would have to die and be buried. But Christ would strike a blow to Satan's head and defeat him by his glorious resurrection from the dead. Foreshadowing Christ's sacrificial death to cover human sin, God made garments of skin to cover Adam's and Eve's nakedness, indicating he took the life of an innocent animal (Gen 3:21).

God's proclamation of the gospel during his walk in Eden, as well as the events that accompany it, meet the standard criteria of evangelism. The Lord God confronted Adam and Eve with their sin. As a result, they expressed godly fear and sorrow before God. The Lord prophesied the gospel to the serpent and to them, alluding to his Son's death and resurrection as a way to destroy the works of the devil (cf. 1 John 3:8). He took the life of an innocent animal, and with its skin he made clothing to cover Adam's and Eve's nakedness—a consequence of their sin. This episode set the pattern for subsequent forms and practices of evangelism that would follow.

A Kingdom of Priests

Moses met with God on Mount Sinai in Exodus 19. During their meeting, God instructed him to remind the people of Israel how he had delivered them from Egyptian captivity. He then commanded Moses to tell them, "'Now if you will carefully listen to me and keep my covenant, you will be my own possession out of all the peoples, although the whole earth is mine, and you will be my kingdom of priests and my holy nation.' These are the words that you are to say to the Israelites" (Exod 19:5–6).

As part of the terms of this covenant, God expressed that if they obeyed and kept his commandments, they would be his chosen nation— his "own possession." Inasmuch, they would be to him a "kingdom of priests" and his "holy nation." Douglas K. Stuart explains what God intended in their role as a kingdom of priests:

> *Israel's assignment from God involved intermediation.* They were not to be a people unto themselves, enjoying their special relationship with God and paying no attention to the rest of the world. Rather, they were to represent him to the rest of the world and attempt to bring the rest of the world to him. In other words, the challenge to be "a kingdom of priests and a holy nation" represented the responsibility inherent in the original promise to Abraham in Gen 12:2–3: "You will be a blessing. I will bless those who bless you . . . and all peoples on earth will be blessed through you." *Priests stand between God and humans to help bring the humans closer to God and to help dispense God's truth, justice, favor, discipline, and holiness to humans.* Israel was called to such a function. How? The answer is not spelled out in the present context, but it surely was to take place in four ways: (1) *Israel would be an example to the people of other nations, who would see its holy beliefs and actions and be impressed enough to want to know personally the same God the Israelites knew.* (2) *Israel would proclaim the truth of God and invite people from other nations to accept him in faith as shown by confession of belief in him and acceptance of his covenant, as Jethro had already done.* (3) Israel would intercede for the rest of the world by offering acceptable offerings to God (both sacrifices and right behavior) and thus ameliorate the general distance between God and humankind. (4) Israel would keep the promises of God, preserving his word already spoken

and recording his word as it was revealed to them so that once the fullness of time had come, anyone in the whole world could promptly benefit from that great body of divinely revealed truth, that is, the Scriptures.[1]

Israel's intermediary function related to the responsibilities of the Levitical priesthood; however, it was unique and different from the priests' because this role was inclusive of all the tribes of Israel. This kingdom priesthood foreshadowed the evangelistic work and role of believers in the New Testament.

When writing to the exiles across the Roman Empire, Peter drew from Exod 19:6 to exhort and encourage them. He repeated the same titles that God used with Moses, referring to them as a "royal priesthood" and a "holy nation" (1 Pet 2:9). As such, the churches and their members are to function as mediators between God and man. A primary dimension of this mediation would occur through evangelism. Thomas R. Schreiner agrees in his explanation of the connection between the royal priesthood mentioned in Exodus 19 and its use and application here: "The priestly calling of the church is understood from [1 Pet] 2:9 to be evangelistic, a praising of God's name so that people from all over the world will join in worshiping him. . . . The declaration of God's praises includes both worship and evangelism, spreading the good news of God's saving wonders to all peoples."[2]

The Prophecy of God's Spirit Poured upon Sons and Daughters

Joel prophesied about the coming day of the Lord. Although Jerusalem had experienced a plague of locusts, their troubles were far from over. An approaching army from the north threatened them. Fear and despair

---

[1] Douglas K. Stuart, *Exodus*, The New American Commentary (Nashville: B&H, 2006), 423, emphasis added.

[2] Thomas R. Schreiner, *1, 2 Peter, Jude*, The New American Commentary (Nashville: B&H, 2003), 107, 116.

were spreading, and Joel sounded a call for Zion to assemble and hear a word from the Lord. He exhorted them to fear and tremble, but not because of what they had endured with the locusts or the impending military forces that were coming. Instead, they were to fear the coming day of the Lord (see Joel 2:1–11).

Instead of advising them to retreat, Joel called them to repent (2:12–17). By doing so, he foreshadowed the calls of repentance that would be issued by gospel preachers in the New Testament. He explained that if they would repent, God would have pity on them by removing their enemies and restoring them to their former state (2:18–27). He prophesied the coming day of the Lord would be preceded by a pouring out of his Spirit upon his people. God would also display his wondrous signs in the heavens and on earth and save whoever calls on his name. God promised through the prophet:

> After this I will pour out my Spirit on all humanity; then your sons and your daughters will prophesy, your old men will have dreams, and your young men will see visions. I will even pour out my Spirit on the male and female slaves in those days. I will display wonders in the heavens and on the earth: blood, fire, and columns of smoke. The sun will be turned to darkness and the moon to blood before the great and terrible day of the LORD comes. Then everyone who calls on the name of the LORD will be saved, for there will be an escape for those on Mount Zion and in Jerusalem, as the LORD promised, among the survivors the LORD calls. (Joel 2:28–32)

Just as Gen 3:15 foretold the gospel, Joel 2:28–32 prophesied about a specific future occurrence of evangelism: Pentecost.

In Acts 2:1–13, the Holy Spirit filled Jesus's disciples, who had been waiting in an upper room so that they could become his witnesses. On the day of Pentecost, he manifested himself by endowing those he filled with the ability to speak in different tongues. The people in the crowd, who had come for the feast, either were confused or mocked what they saw and heard. Those who were confused asked, "What does this mean?" Others who mocked shouted, "They're drunk on new wine." But Peter answered and informed them that they were not drunk. Instead, he explained, the prophecy of Joel 2:28–32 was being fulfilled in those who spoke in these different languages (Acts 2:14–21). Peter, then, proceeded to preach the gospel to them, and about three thousand were saved and baptized. The prophecy of Joel 2 was fulfilled through proclamation evangelism.

Jonah's Preaching against Nineveh

God wasted no time calling Jonah to preach against Nineveh for the evil offenses they had committed against him (Jonah 1:1–2). Nevertheless, the son of Amittai fled westward, in the opposite direction, to board a ship sailing to Tarshish (1:3). God hurled a great wind and storm upon the sea so that it almost sank the ship (1:4). After his disobedience had been exposed by lots and his confession, Jonah advised the sailors to cast him into the water so that the waves would be stilled (1:7–12). Hesitant, but with no other choice, the men cast the Hebrew runaway overboard, and the sea immediately calmed (1:13–16).

God created a large fish that he appointed to swallow Jonah as he was sinking underneath the water and its waves. The runaway prophet cried out for three days and three nights in the belly of the fish (1:17). His three-day burial at sea foreshadowed Jesus's death, burial, and resurrection. Jesus acknowledged this connection between Jonah and himself in Matthew 12:38–40. God responded to the vow Jonah made within the fish and caused it to vomit him back onto land.

After he hit the ground, the word of the Lord came to Jonah a second time commanding him to deliver the message he had for Nineveh. This time, Jonah obeyed God and traveled toward Assyria. When he arrived at the city, he surmised that it would take just as many days to publish God's message throughout the city as was his detainment in the fish's stomach. Over three days Jonah told the inhabitants of Nineveh, "In forty days Nineveh will be demolished!" (3:4).

Although the book provides no evidence that Jonah called upon them to repent, four indications infer that repentance was implied in God's message that he preached. First, Jonah's message reflected pronouncements by other prophets who expected their hearers to repent. As Southwestern Seminary Old Testament professor Josh Williams has said when lecturing to students, "The Old Testament prophets preached judgment through destruction in order to achieve repentance." Second, God's mercy to (1) send a prophet to warn the Ninevites of the impending judgment upon them and (2) delay his judgment for forty days (plus the three days it took for Jonah to travel throughout the city and preach) makes no sense unless God was extending an opportunity for them to change.

Third, upon hearing Jonah, the people immediately knew to repent and did so. In fact, after Jonah preached, the king of Nineveh issued a command that his citizens repent: "Each must turn from his evil ways and from his wrongdoing. Who knows? God may turn and relent; he may turn from his burning anger so that we will not perish" (3:8b–9). Last, when God saw that they had turned from their evil ways, he turned from his righteous anger and relented from the disaster he had intended to bring upon them (3:10). Why would he respond that way if he did not mean for the people to repent? This episode of preaching that accomplished repentance at least foreshadows the evangelism practiced in the New Testament; however, because of Jonah's time in the fish and the connection Jesus made with it and the gospel, it is more than likely an Old Testament form of evangelism.

The Sending of the Messenger to Prepare the Way of the Lord

Isaiah 40:3; Mal 3:1; and 4:5 predict the first New Testament occurrence of evangelism—the preaching of John the Baptist. Isaiah foretold of a voice crying in the wilderness who would prepare the way of the Lord (Isa 40:3). Malachi's prophecy (3:1a) mirrored Isaiah's mentioning a messenger who is coming to prepare the way of the Lord. In 4:5, he specifically identified this messenger as Elijah the prophet.

In the New Testament, the Gospel writers referred to these three prophecies repeatedly (Matt 3:1–17; 11:1–15; Mark 1:2–8; Luke 3:1–18; 7:18–30; John 1:19–37). Each time, they associated them with John the Baptist. In addition to preaching repentance, John also preached Christ as the Lamb of God, who takes away the sin of the world (John 1:36). This prediction of evangelistic activity, as well as the others surveyed, consummated in the New Testament, suggests that evangelism was not devised by Jesus, his apostles, or Paul in the first century. Instead, it has been the plan of God all along, revealed in the Old Testament, and embedded within the pages of the New Testament.

Evangelistic Practices in the New Testament

The foretelling, foreshadowing, and forms of evangelism in the Old Testament were fulfilled in New Testament accounts of gospel proclamation. In them, prophets, fishermen, disciples, apostles, deacons, evangelists, and the Son of God communicated the gospel through five major methods: preaching, teaching, personal conversations, public defenses, and public, persuasive reasoning. The following summaries represent descriptive examples, not an exhaustive list.

Preaching the Gospel

The predominant form of evangelism in the New Testament is by means of preaching. The Greek words and their derivatives frequently used to describe this activity include *euangelizō*, *kēryssō*, *katangellō*, and *martyreō*. Generally, this form of communicating the gospel took place in public settings among groups or crowds of people. The first person in the New Testament to practice this evangelistic method was John the Baptist. He usually preached in the wilderness near the Jordan River, where he also baptized those who heeded his message of repentance.

Others who practiced this form of evangelism include Jesus, Peter, John, Philip, and Paul. Although this was not the exclusive method by which they all shared the gospel, it was the primary way these and other New Testament individuals used. The settings in which they preached varied; however, frequent sites included mountains, beaches, homes, the temple, the countryside, synagogues, and before tribunals.

An excursus to qualify the translation of *euangelizō* as "preach" instead of "evangelize" is necessary due to early twenty-first century academic discussions and proposals and their relationship to the study of evangelism. Matthew Bates has audaciously posited, "English doesn't have a verb for 'gospel' activity. But in the original Greek of the New Testament, the noun *euangelion* ('gospel,' 'good news') has a corresponding verb, *euangelizō* ('to gospel'). To make it clear [in my writing] where gospel activity is in view, I've translated it 'gospeling.'"[3] However, almost every English Bible translation ever published translates *euangelizō* as "preach."

Thomas Johnston asserts that four English Bible translations have departed from this standard, translating *euangelizō* as "evangelize" instead. He explains:

> Since 1382 two English language Bible translations have one use each of the verb "evangelize": the 1884 English John Darby (Luke 3:18; by the way his French translation used "evangelize" 21 times) and the 1899 English Douais-Rheims (Luke 8:1). However, the 2000 Holman Christian Standard broke ranks from six centuries of virtual censorship of the verb "evangelize" in English Bibles by using the word six times (Acts 8:25, 40; 14:7, 21; 16:10; Rom 15:20).[4]

---

[3] Matthew W. Bates, *The Gospel Precisely: Surprisingly Good News about Jesus Christ the King* (Coppell, TX: Renew, 2021), 23. Bates's selection and use of "gospeling" is a creative product of anthimeria, and as such is a fine word to describe "gospel activity"; however, English does, in fact, have several verbs that describe such action. Common English verbs used to describe gospel activity include "evangelize," "preach," "witness," and "testify."

[4] Thomas P. Johnston, "On Defining 'Evangelizing'" in Alvin Reid, *Evangelism Handbook: Biblical, Spiritual, Intentional, Missional* (Nashville: B&H Academic, 2009), 27.

Years later, he discovered that "the Idiomatic Translation of the New Testament by William Graham MacDonald also used the verb 'evangelize' in 7 of the 55 NT uses of εὐαγγελίζω as 'evangelize.'"[5] All other English Bible translations, as well as all the other New Testament occurrences of *euangelizō* in the former three translations, are rendered, "preach."

In his book *Evangelizology*, Johnston offered reasons he believes it commendable to translate *euangelizō* as "evangelize" in the New Testament, as well as some places in the Old Testament.[6] Among the reasons Johnston preferred *euangelizō* to be translated as "evangelize" instead of "preach" include: "1. 'Preach' confuses [εὐαγγελίζω] with formal preaching (cf. homiletics) . . . 2. 'Preach' has had the tendency for it to be confused with classical rhetoric . . . 3. 'Preach' limits the itinerant nature of the New Testament command and example [and the locations where it took place] . . . 4. 'Preach' necessarily limits in some people's minds who can do this activity—uniquely ordained clergy or unordained and untrained laity . . . [men or women]."[7]

Johnston's concerns are legitimate. Nevertheless, I believe the overwhelming number of English Bible translations are correct in translating *euangelizō* as "preach" rather than "evangelize." First, the Christian Standard Bible, which is a revision of the HCSB, did not retain the translation of *euangelizō* as "evangelize" in Acts 8:25, 40; 14:7, 21; 16:10; and Rom 15:20 and instead translated it "preach." Evidently, the translators were convinced to follow the decision of the other English Bible translations.

Second, translating *euangelizō* as "evangelize" in Gal 1:8–9 would create a significant doctrinal problem. Johnston argued, "Had Paul wanted to use κηρύσσω ("preach") with a separate word delineating the message, he could have done so, as he did in 2 Cor 11:4, which is a parallel passage

---

[5] Thomas P. Johnston, *Evangelizology: A Biblical-Historical Perspective on Evangelism*, vol. 1 (Liberty, MO: Evangelism Unlimited, 2014), 378.

[6] Johnston, 300–304.

[7] Johnston, 300–301.

to Gal 1:8–9."[8] For this reason Johnston has translated Gal 1:8–9: "But when even we ourselves, or an angel from heaven, should evangelize you other than how we evangelized you, may he be excretion. As we have already said, so I say once again, if someone is evangelizing other than what you received, may he be excretion."[9] Yet if someone shares a "gospel" that is in opposition to the gospel Paul preached, can it be considered "evangelism"? I would argue it cannot because a "gospel" in opposition to the one Paul and his companions shared is a false gospel. Those who proclaim a false gospel, be it the Judaizers (whom Paul had in mind in his Galatians' correspondence), Jehovah's Witnesses, or Mormons today, do not evangelize; they preach. For these reasons, and despite some of the unfortunate preconceptions associated with "preach" that Johnston identified, "preach" is preferred when translating *euangelizō*.

Teaching the Gospel

Another way evangelism occurred in the New Testament was through teaching. Teaching evangelism took two forms. The first way involved the New Testament activity attributed to *didaskō*, or "teaching." The gospel of the kingdom and Jesus's resurrection were the common content taught in these episodes. Sometimes the writers used "teaching" as a synonym for sharing the gospel (see Matt 4:23; 11:1; 28:20). At other times, they paired its use with words like *kēryssō* and *martyreō* in evangelistic contexts.

The second form teaching evangelism took was more descriptive. The New Testament attributes the use of this method to Jesus and Paul more than anyone else, although the former practiced it more than the latter. As will be discussed in chapter 10, Jesus's overall method of evangelism by disciple-making the Twelve was more protractive than immediate. Of course, episodes like his call for Peter and Andrew to follow him so he could make them people-fishers, as well as their response to him,

---

[8] Johnston, 301.

[9] Johnston, "On Defining 'Evangelizing,'" 27.

were instantaneous. But he preached the gospel and made disciples of them over the entire course of his ministry.

Although Jesus took around three years to make disciples of the Twelve, they, in turn, practiced a more immediate form of evangelism. Why did they change the timing interval and method of their evangelism and disciple-making from the prolonged format by which they were trained? The most likely answer is their reception of the Spirit. When Jesus sent his Spirit at Pentecost to fill his disciples, the Spirit also worked in conjunction with their preaching to convict those who heard it. His ministry of conviction, which was not in effect until Jesus ascended (cf. John 16:8–11), enabled people who heard the gospel and were convicted of their sins to repent and believe instantaneously, instead of incrementally. In addition, after Jesus's ascension the apostles and his disciples had the complete message of the gospel—that is, his death, burial, resurrection, and exaltation—which they had not fully comprehended from Jesus's teaching (e.g., Matt 16:21–23; Mark 8:31–33; 9:31–32; 10:32b–34; Luke 9:43b–45; 18:31–34; John 13:33, 36–14:6). Those who became Jesus's disciples in response to Peter's sermon and the Spirit's conviction at Pentecost, as well as those who became his disciples later, continued to be taught by the apostles and other believers.

On some occasions in Acts, Paul practiced teaching evangelism. Like Jesus, he not only practiced other forms of evangelism along with this one, but he also practiced those forms more than this one. Paul practiced this kind of evangelism in Antioch, Corinth, and Rome. Upon leaving the Jerusalem council, Paul and Barnabas taught and preached the word of the Lord in Antioch before they commenced on the second missionary journey (Acts 15:35). Luke recorded that while in Corinth "he stayed there a year and a half, teaching the word of God among them" (Acts 18:11). This statement can be easily misinterpreted to mean that Paul taught the Bible to the Corinthians; however, Luke's use of *logos*, or "word," in his Gospel and in Acts overwhelmingly refers to the gospel, not the Bible (or in this particular period of time—the Old Testament). This fact does not mean that Paul did not also teach and explain the Bible to deepen the discipleship of

Crispus, his household, and the Corinthians who upon hearing him preach the gospel believed and were baptized (Acts 18:8). However, Luke intended to emphasize the evangelistic element of Paul's disciple-making, as demonstrated a few verses later when he mentioned the Jews charged Paul with "persuading people to worship God in ways contrary to the law" before Gallio (cf. Acts 18:13). Luke also used *logos* in 18:5, when he described that Paul devoted himself to preaching the "word" by testifying to the Jews that Jesus was the Messiah. In addition, Paul practiced teaching evangelism in Rome when he was under house arrest (Acts 28:30–31).

Personal Conversations about the Gospel

New Testament evangelism also occurred through personal conversations. Many, if not all, of the same people who evangelized through preaching also did so in dialogue with others. Although evangelistic conversations obviously took place in the early first century, recorded experiences of them are not as prominent in the New Testament as those of preaching evangelism.

Some of the more well-known occasions of conversational evangelism are initiated by Jesus, Philip, and Paul. Jesus, for example, evangelized in his conversations with Nicodemus (John 3:1–10), the woman at the well (John 4:7–26), the man born blind (John 9:35–38), and the rich young ruler (Matt 19:16–22; Mark 10:17–22; Luke 18:18–23), to name a few. Philip was directed by the Holy Spirit to have a gospel conversation with the Ethiopian official in the desert (Acts 8:26–39). Paul also conversed with the Philippian jailer about belief in Christ (Acts 16:27–34) and likely engaged in one-on-one discussions with those who visited him under house arrest (Acts 28:30–31).

Public Defenses That Presented the Gospel

Leaders within Judaism viewed Jesus and his gospel as a threat, which often led either to the Sanhedrin or Roman magistrates officiating over tribunals of those who evangelized. When Jesus or his followers made their defenses before these courts, they publicly shared the gospel, but in a more formal way. These presentations appealed to the use of only a few words, formal speech, and sometimes oratory. The New Testament records gospel speeches and defenses being delivered by Jesus, Peter and John, Stephen, and Paul.

In the Gospels Jesus appeared before two tribunals where he gave a witness to the gospel. He testified before Caiaphas and the Council that he was the Christ, the Son of God (Matt 26:62–66; Mark 14:61–65; Luke 22:66–71). When before Pilate, he told him about the truth (John 18:33–38). Rather than presenting the gospel in the form of a speech, Jesus spoke a few poignant statements when his accusers asked him to provide a defense for himself.

Several evangelistic speeches are recorded in Acts. The first two occurrences of this form of evangelism in the book took place by the same people—Peter and John—and before the same group—the Sanhedrin (Acts 4:1–22; 5:17–40). Stephen also practiced this form of evangelism when he defended the gospel by using the Scriptures before the Council (Acts 6:12–7:60).

Paul was also brought before the tribunals to provide a defense for the gospel and his ministry. Before the Jews in Jerusalem, Paul shared the gospel by way of his testimony (Acts 21:39–22:24). When he stood before Felix, he spoke about faith in Jesus Christ and discussed righteousness, self-control, and the judgment to come (Acts 24:24–25). In addition, when appearing before Agrippa and urging him to believe, Paul presented the gospel by testifying about his conversion and quoting the prophets (Acts 26:1–32).

Public, Persuasive Reasoning of the Gospel

The last major evangelistic methodology in the New Testament was the persuasive reasoning of the gospel in public places. This form of evangelism, in some ways, is a conglomeration of the previous four practices. Because it occurred in public places where such discussions were encouraged, it somewhat resembled preaching. Due to the fact that it incorporated instruction and was sometimes practiced for longer intervals of time, it related to teaching. Sometimes these public discussions even turned into conversations on the side. Those who used reason to persuade others to receive the gospel publicly frequently made use of oratorical techniques and rhetoric skills.

Some examples of New Testament evangelism that took the form of public, persuasive reasoning include some of Jesus's multiple engagements with the teachers and the scribes (Matt 9:1–8; 12:22–45; 16:1–4; 22:23–46; Mark 2:1–12; 12:13–40; Luke 20:27–47; John 8:12–59), as well as a few of his interactions with the Jews (John 5:18–47; 6:26–58; 7:14–39; 10:22–39). These occasions also include Paul's preaching about Jesus and his resurrection to the Epicurean and Stoic philosophers in the midst of the Areopagus (Acts 17:22–34), his reasoning with Jews and Gentiles in the Corinthian synagogue (Acts 18:4), and his daily directed discussions in the lecture hall of Tyrannus (Acts 19:9).

Evangelistic Metaphors in the Scriptures

Both the Old and New Testaments use metaphors to convey the practice of evangelism. Although not all of them do so, most of them relate evangelism to common occupations. These analogous jobs include watchmen, fishermen, and seed-sowers. Other correlations made in the Scriptures to describe evangelism relate to activities familiar to those of that day— specifically seeking lost items and persuading people. Whether likened to an occupation or an activity, evangelism according to the Scriptures is not meant to be complicated, as some may perceive it, but rather comprehensible.

Warning to Watchmen

Ezekiel 3:16–21; 33:1–7; Acts 18:6; 20:25–27 refer to believers' responsibility in evangelism. Roy Fish, the well-respected and distinguished professor of evangelism at Southwestern Seminary, explains the biblical metaphor found in God's warning to Ezekiel in such a way and with such clarity that it bears inclusion:

> Out of the imagery of the Old Testament comes the idea for the message. All major cities in the Old Testament world had a watchman stationed atop a tall tower on the wall, where a maximum range of visibility would be his. If an enemy army approached the city, the watchman's duty was to warn the city of an impending attack. If the watchman failed in his duty of warning, and the city was overrun and its citizenry massacred, the watchman would be held responsible. The blood of those who had perished would be on his hands. With this symbolism in mind, God said to the prophet Ezekiel: *"As for you, son of man, I have made you a watchman for the house of Israel. When you hear a word from my mouth, give them a warning from me. If I say to the wicked, 'Wicked one, you will surely die,' but you do not speak out to warn him about his way, that wicked person will die for his iniquity, yet I will hold you responsible for his blood. But if you warn a wicked person to turn from his way and he doesn't turn from it, he will die for his iniquity, but you will have rescued yourself"* (Ezek 33:7–9).

I. The relevance of blood on our hands

Because of the location of the text and the seriousness of its inference, the tendency today is to lay the issue of blood on our hands on a man-made shelf of Old Testament irrelevancy. With the attitude of "what happened before Christ came does not pertain to us," much of contemporary Christianity would reject this principle as outmoded—a thing of the past. This may be a legitimate claim except for the fact that the apostle Paul, inspired by the Holy Spirit, contends that the principle of bloodguilt for negligence is still binding in this Christian age. When he left the city of Ephesus, he boldly stated, *"Therefore I declare to you this day that I am innocent of the blood of all of you, because I did not avoid declaring to you the whole plan of God"* (Acts 20:26–27). The Apostle might have left the city of Ephesus with blood on his hands. But rather, "I am not guilty of blood in Ephesus," he cries. "My hands are clean." According to the New Testament, a failure to discharge a God-given responsibility to speak out means the blood of eternal souls is on our hands. The bloodguilt principle found in the Old Testament is repeated in the New Testament. Its recurrence enforces its ratification in your life and mine.

II. The reality of blood on our hands

Relevance suggests reality, and there is no more frightening reality in the life of any Christian than the reality of being held responsible for the souls of others. That we, by our negligence, can be guilty of a kind of spiritual homicide—that our hands can be stained with blood because of indifference toward those who are lost—what an awesome truth! The reality of blood on our hands rebukes anything short of total commitment to the task of sharing the exciting news of Jesus. The reality of bloodguilt is a reproof to anything short of a life controlled by the Holy Spirit, being in the right place at the right time, playing a part in God's redemptive activity. The reality of bloodguilt is a censure on careless living, sin-obstructed testimonies, and Spirit-grieving habits. It is a constant rebuttal to the kind of cowering fear that causes Christians to shut up when they ought to speak up. But the heart of this message has to do with how the blood may be removed.

III. The removal of blood on our hands

Blood on our hands is a frightening reality. But the blood can be removed. Every preacher of the gospel should seriously consider how. **First, blood can be removed by the cultivation of converts into witnesses.** A slighting of any part of the plan of our Lord can involve us in the bloodguilt of others. There is a part of His plan that generally has suffered sad neglect. This neglected part of His plan is the cultivation of converts into personal witnesses for Christ.

In the fourth chapter of Ephesians, the apostle Paul states clearly that the primary task of the pastor is to mature Christians for the work of the ministry, for the building up of Christ's body. Pastors are to train their people in the work of soul-winning. Jesus said we are not only to make disciples, but we are also to train those who become disciples to make disciples (Matt 28:20). Most of us have regarded the training aspect of the Matthew commission as optional. But the question pastors face is not only, "How many people have I won?" It is also, "How many people have I trained to win others?" It is an indictment against our negligence of the commission of our Lord that only a small percentage of pastors are employing any effective method of training personal witnesses. Thank God if you are actively engaged in winning the lost. But I remind you that if we do not train converts to reach the lost, we are responsible for those who may have been reached through our multiplied ministry.

Second, blood can be removed by consistent concern for lost people. I choose the word "consistent" for a particular reason. Most of us are noticeably inconsistent in our concern. Sometimes we are on fire; other times, we are smoking embers. But one mistake in the area of concern is that many times we let our level of concern determine whether or not we will witness. If we feel concerned, we share with others. If we don't feel a concern, we fail to share. But our efforts in reaching the lost must not be regulated by our feeling of concern. Rather, our efforts are to be regulated by our Lord's feeling of concern for the lost. He is always concerned about them. It is the burden of His heart that should drive us to reach lost people. Not our compassion for sinners but His compassion for sinners must be our motivating factor in witnessing for Him. For this reason, not a love for souls but a love for Christ is the basic condition of effective personal evangelism. If we love Him, His interest will be our consuming interest, and His basic interest toward those who are lost is a redemptive interest.

Third, blood can be removed by a constant commitment to our task. Have you ever considered what failure in consistent witnessing can mean? One missed opportunity can mean one more Christless life and one more Christless grave, which could have been otherwise. On the other hand, consistency in remaining available as a witness delivers us from bloodguilt.

I am far from being what I ought to be as a witness for our Lord. Late one evening, I was exhausted from a teaching session of three hours. I had told the Lord earlier in the day that I was available to Him if He wanted to use me to touch someone's life. It was after midnight when, on an elevator, I ran into Tony. My desire was to get to my room as quickly as possible and get to bed. But the Lord reminded me of my commitment to Him to be available. On the elevator, I sensed the Lord saying to me, "My child, did you really mean it when you told me you were at my disposal? Are you available to me for this situation?"

I responded, "Lord, I am tired. It's almost one o'clock in the morning, and I want to go to bed. And to be honest, Lord, I couldn't care less. But, grudgingly, I make myself available to you."

Tony was reading a newspaper. Before I stepped off the elevator, I took a Billy Graham tract out of my pocket and said to Tony as I stepped off the elevator, "Excuse me, sir, but here is some good news you won't read in today's newspaper."

I shoved the pamphlet into his hand. He took it, turned it over, and saw the name Billy Graham. I didn't know, but the Holy Spirit knew that Tony Maringo, born in Turkey, fluent in eleven languages, worker in the United Nations with Dag Hammershold, had once attended a Billy Graham crusade. At that crusade, God had spoken to his heart about becoming a Christian. He left that crusade service lost, but hungry to know more. When he saw Mr. Graham's name on that pamphlet, the hunger in his heart was revived, and in the early morning, on the fourth floor of that hotel, Tony invited Christ into his heart. I received a phone call from a pastor on Long Island shortly after that, telling me that Tony had come forward in a revival service in his church, confessing Christ as his Savior.

Being consistent in our availability and witness! This is the way to keep blood off of our hands.[10]

Fish's homily on the watchman in Ezekiel conveys the serious responsibility believers have to evangelize. Paul's concept of evangelism incorporated God's warning to watchmen who fail to sound the alert of his coming judgment. He referenced the watchman's bloodguilt in Ezek 3:16–21 and 33:1–7 when he evangelized those who opposed him and the gospel in the Corinthian synagogue (Acts 18:6). Paul also confessed, in his farewell to the Ephesian elders, that he was innocent of the guilt for their blood because he never failed preaching the kingdom and whole plan of God to them (Acts 20:25–27). The biblical metaphor of a watchman's warning teaches that if unbelievers hear the gospel and receive it, God is responsible. If sinners hear it and reject it, then they are responsible. But if the lost never hear the gospel, then believers are responsible.

Fishing for People

Jesus likens evangelism to "fishing for people" (Matt 4:19; 13:47–50; Mark 1:17). The first of those he called to follow him were fishermen by occupation. Jesus naturally correlated activity with which they were familiar to the work they would accomplish if they would follow him.

---

[10] Adapted from Roy Fish, "Blood on Our Hands," in *50 Great Soul-Winning, Motivational Sermons*, ed. Jack R. Smith (Alpharetta, GA: NAMB, 1994), 55–58. © 1994 The North American Mission Board of the Southern Baptist Convention, Inc. f/k/a Home Mission Board, All Rights Reserved. Used with Permission. www.namb.net. Scripture quotations in this sermon have been updated to the Christian Standard Bible and are noted in italics.

The meaning behind this analogy can sometimes be lost upon those in the contemporary era because they associate fishing with a rod, reel, and hook. But the fishing practiced by the first disciples of Jesus yielded more than one fish at a time. They used nets, which enabled them to catch entire schools of fish all at once. In a personal conversation between O. S. Hawkins, Carl Bradford, and me, Hawkins keenly observed: "Most twenty-first-century fishers of men use hooks. First-century fishers of men used nets. Hooks catch fewer fish. Nets catch more fish. Hooks hold bait intended to catch a certain kind of a fish at a time. Nets catch all kinds of fish at one time."

An extension of this common, anachronistic misunderstanding also leads modern believers to envision "people fishing" involves selecting a particular kind of "fish" they want to catch. This misnomer has led to the endorsement or promotion of using only certain kinds of "bait" and going to favorite "holes" when fishing for people. Yet first-century, near Middle Eastern fishermen caught fish with nets, not baited hooks. Instead of anchoring atop a stationary location to fish, they dragged their nets beside or behind the boat as they sailed. Their method caught masses of fish, all at once, and of all different kinds.

The late Adrian Rogers explains, "When we fish for fish we take them out of the beautiful life into death, but when we fish for men we take them out of death into a beautiful life."[11] In addition to describing people fishing, Rogers's statement also alludes to Christ's work in the gospel—he who was sinless and should have lived, willingly died so that those who sin and should die can live. Those who follow Jesus in faith will share the good news of this great exchange with unbelievers. Jesus called to Peter and Andrew, "Follow me . . . and I will make you fish for people" (Matt 4:19). As Charles Alexander, who served as Billy Sunday's, Wilbur Chapman's, and R. A. Torrey's music director, said on many occasions,

---

[11] Adrian Rogers, "Fishers of Men," accessed August 17, 2014, https://www .lightsource.com/ministry/love-worth-finding/articles/fishers-of-men-12822 .html.

"You claim you are following Christ. Are you fishing for men? If you are not fishing, you are not following."[12] The inverse of Alexander's principle is also true—the closer a believer gets in following Christ, the more often that person will likely be fishing for would-be, future followers of Christ.

Sowing Seed

Evangelism seemed to be in mind when Jesus delivered the parable of a sower scattering seed (Matt 13:1–9, 18–23; Mark 4:1–9, 14–20; Luke 8:4–8, 11–15). Using this metaphor can help Christians evaluate their methods of evangelism, as well as their expectations of the results.

In the parable, Jesus likened the gospel, or the "word of the kingdom," to the sower's seed. Scattered by the sower, the seed fell either along the pathway, upon rocky ground, among thorns, or on good soil. Some disagreement exists among commentators about the kinds of responses these four soil types represent. Jesus's explanation of the parable seems to suggest that the three former types of soil indicate people's eventual failure to respond to the gospel's invitation, while the latter soil denotes those who understand and gladly receive the gospel.

God does not expect believers to evangelize only those who are ready to hear it. When preaching Matt 13:3–23, Steven Smith keenly remarked, "It is only when someone is exposed to the seed that they [or you] know what type of soil they are, and if we're not preaching the gospel to people, they [or you] don't have any way to judge who they are."[13] Believing that gospel seed manifests the type of responses people make when they hear the gospel, personal evangelists should base the frequency of their evangelism on their complete confidence in the gospel "seed" rather than their

---

[12] Helen C. Alexander and J. Kennedy MacLean, *Charles M. Alexander: A Romance of Song and Soul-Winning* (Murfreesboro, TN: Sword of the Lord, 1995), 11.

[13] Steven Smith, "The Future of the Gospel," October 13, 2010, http://media.swbts.edu/item/145/the-future-of-the-gospel; video no longer playable.

own personal conjecture about the receiving "soil" (that is, someone's anticipated response).

At times, personal evangelists will doubtless be tempted to base their decisions to evangelize on their own impressions and speculation about people's likelihood to profess or reject Christ at a given moment. They must resist this temptation for at least two reasons. First, Matt 13:1–9, 18–23; Mark 4:1–9, 14–20; and Luke 8:4–8, 11–15 do not substantiate soil-speculative evangelism. The sower-evangelist of these texts scatters the gospel seed indiscriminately and generously, not theoretically or hypothetically. Second, yielding to the temptation of evangelizing only those who appear ready to respond is ultimately an attempt to access omniscience only available to God. Personal evangelists can never know with any amount of certainty how others will respond to the gospel until they provide them with a hearing of the gospel. One of the many ways Scripture attests to Jesus's divinity can be found in his ability to perceive the hearts and minds of others (cf. Matt 9:3–4; Mark 2:6–8; Luke 5:21–22; 24:38; John 1:45–50; 2:24–25; 5:42; 6:61, 64). Only God, not perceptive personal evangelists, possesses the omniscient and intimate knowledge of how anyone, at any time, will respond to a gospel appeal. They can only know how unbelievers with whom they come into contact will respond to the gospel by first sharing it with them, inviting them to receive Christ, and then observing their response.

An evangelism encounter between a woman named Katherine, former Southwestern Seminary evangelism professor Brandon Kiesling, and me best illustrates this point. In 2013, then student Kiesling and I were evangelizing door-to-door a few blocks away from the seminary. As we approached one of our assigned homes to evangelize, we heard the lady who lived there yelling at someone with whom she was speaking by phone. I looked to Kiesling and said, "Do you think we should just go to the next house?" I was completely confident that this lady was in no mood to hear, much less receive, the good news.

"Doc," he replied, "if we do not do it now, we will never know if someone else might do it in the future." Hesitant about the response we would receive, I went with him to the door and knocked. The occupant, still on her phone, abruptly opened the screen door and said, "What do you all want?" I responded with every bit of courage I had, "Hello, ma'am. My name is Matt, and this is Brandon. We are from Southwestern Seminary and have come to tell you how you can have peace with God through Jesus." Immediately, we learned to whom she was talking when she said into the phone, "Mom, I have got to go. There are two men here who want to talk to me about Jesus."

Leaving the screen door wide open, the lady went into a back room and emerged with an open Bible in her hands. She said, "My name is Katherine. I have stopped cussing and smoking. I have married my live-in boyfriend of seven years and started going back to church—but something's missing!" All hesitation left me in that moment, and I replied, "Jesus is missing!" Kiesling then explained the gospel to her using Bill Fay's *Share Jesus Without Fear* script. As Kiesling invited her to receive Christ, tears flowed from her eyes. Standing in her doorway, she began to pray, asking God to forgive her of her sins and expressing her desire to become a Christian. To this day I will never forget how God taught me that I can never know how anyone will ever respond to the gospel until after I actually share the gospel with him or her.

Matthew 13:1–9, 18–23; Mark 4:1–9, 14–20; and Luke 8:4–8, 11–15 remind personal evangelists that sowers scatter seed; they do not inspect soils. Therefore, when sowing the seed of the gospel, they must spend more time proclaiming the gospel of the kingdom than they do evaluating the likelihood of others' responses to it. In other words, they must spend more time proclaiming the seed than they do preparing the soil. Personal evangelists spread seed, and God causes the growth through his Holy Spirit, preparing both the soil and souls.

Seeking Something Lost

The New Testament also portrays evangelism in terms of an individual seeking a lost possession (Matt 18:10–14; Luke 15:1–7, 8–10; 19:10).

Through parables, Christ related evangelism to seeking a coin and a sheep. Although he also included a story about a lost son (Luke 15:11–32), popularly known as the prodigal son, Jesus used that particular parable not so much to illustrate evangelism as to rebuke the Pharisees and teachers of the law for their prejudice against the outcasts of society.[14] A few indications of this claim include (1) the proactive searching by the shepherd and the woman in the first two parables juxtaposed with an inversion that occurs in the last parable as the lost son actually returns to the father, and (2) the similar-sized length and repetitive idea of "rejoicing in heaven" in the first two parables compared to the expanded length and replacement of "joy in heaven" with "anger at the feast" in the last.

Seeking after a lost sheep occurs as a metaphor in Matt 18:10–14 and Luke 15:1–7.[15] In both passages, Jesus employed the parable of a lost sheep when he addressed groups either despised by society or looked upon with suspicion. These groups included children (Matt 18:10), as well as tax collectors and sinners (Luke 15:1–2). The parable introduced a man who lost one sheep among his flock of ninety-nine others. He left the ninety-nine sheep in search of the one that was lost. When he found it, he returned rejoicing.

This parable illustrates the intent behind Jesus's mission and purpose: "For the Son of Man has come to seek and to save the lost," a related clause found in Luke 19:10 to convey Jesus's saving of Zacchaeus. In Luke 15:7 he likened the sheep that was found to a sinner who repented, implying his salvation. As such, Jesus's pairing of "seeking" language

---

[14] It should be noted that the Luke 15 trilogy of parables dealing with a lost sheep, coin, and son all were told by Jesus with the primary purpose to rebuke the teachers who had disdain for the lower members of society who were receiving abundant life through Jesus. Yet the depictions of the man and the woman diligently seeking their lost possessions in Luke 15:1–7, 8–10 carry with them a natural correlation to the work of evangelism.

[15] This paragraph and the next have been adapted from Matt Queen, "Seeking the Lost and Perishing," in *Pastoral Ministry: The Ministry of a Shepherd*, ed. Deron Biles (Nashville: B&H Academic, 2018), 145.

with lost sheep in both Matthew and Luke illustrates the intentional, evangelistic search for those in need of God's salvation, who can receive it only through their repentance.

Jesus also used a parable about a woman diligently searching for a lost coin to illustrate evangelism. Whereas the man had one hundred sheep and lost one of them, the lady in this parable owned ten coins and lost one. The coins in her possession likely represented her dowry or her savings. The value of their sum is estimated close to the amount of ten days' wages.[16] Jesus described the woman's search for her coin with more details than he provided to discuss the man's hunt. She lit a lamp, swept the house, and sought for her coin diligently. As with the first parable, the seeker found the lost item. Again in possession of the coin, the woman invited her friends and neighbors to celebrate with her. While the imagery Jesus used in the parable was used to rebuke the teachers of the law, it also resembled the seeking nature associated with evangelism.

Winning a Soul

The etymology of the phrase *soul-winning* finds its roots in the KJV's, NKJV's, NIV 1984's, and NASB's wording of the last phrase of Prov 11:30: "The fruit of the righteous is a tree of life, And he *that winneth souls is wise*" (KJV); "*who wins souls is wise*" (NKJV); "and he *who wins souls is wise*" (NIV 1984);[17] "And he *who is wise wins souls*" (NASB1995) (emphasis added to delineate the difference in translation wording). The wording of other modern translations differed—some slightly and others considerably. Although the ESV and LEB differ slightly in wording from

---

[16] See Joel B. Green, *The Gospel of Luke*, The New International Commentary of the New Testament (Grand Rapids: Eerdmans, 1997), 576.

[17] *The NIV Study Bible* includes the following explanatory note concerning this phrase: "*Wins souls*. Wins people over to wisdom and righteousness (see Da 12:3; 1 Co 9:19–22; Jas 5:20). However, the Hebrew for this expression is unusual so that its translation is somewhat uncertain," *The NIV Study Bible* (Grand Rapids: Zondervan, 1985), 961.

the KJV/NKJV/NIV 1984/NASB, their translations have retained the language, as well as the idea, that commends as wise those who persuade people, likely the unrighteous, to make a spiritual or moral change in their lives: "whoever captures souls is wise" (ESV)[18] and "he who captures souls is wise" (LEB). In other words, believers who lead people to repent of their sins and place faith in Christ alone are wise.

Due to the unusual nature of this expression in Hebrew, as observed in the study notes in the NIV and ESV study Bibles, as well as an alternative textual tradition surrounding this phrase, the translators of the NRSV and CSB avoided using language that conveyed soul-winning activity in Prov 11:30. The NRSV translated the phrase, "but violence takes lives away." The HCSB, a precursor to the CSB, translated it similarly: "but violence takes lives." Duane A. Garrett advocated for this translation of the phrase over that of the traditional wording. He states:

> Proverbs 11:30 is often taken as commending the evangelizing or enriching of others morally or spiritually. While this is a valid and laudable conviction, the Hebrew probably does not have this meaning. The phrase translated "win souls" is actually a Hebrew idiom that means to "kill," and the interpretation "win souls" is without analogy and therefore suspect. Also, as the NIV has it, the verse deals exclusively with positive behavior, contrary to the pattern of righteous/wicked (or vice versa) found in all the other

---

[18] *The ESV Study Bible* includes the following explanatory note concerning this phrase: "The Hebrew phrase translated **whoever captures souls** is used elsewhere in places where the sense is 'to take life' or 'to kill' (e.g., 1 Sam. 24:11; 1 Kings 19:10, 14; Jonah 4:3). However, this proverb appears to be purposefully playing off the usual sense of the phrase to focus on the effect of **the fruit of the righteous**. The life of the righteous leads not only to blessing for themselves but also provides fruit that 'captures souls' in the sense of leading people out of the path that ends in death. For similar declarations, cf. Dan. 12:3, equating 'those who are wise' to 'those who turn many to righteousness'; see also James 5:20, where the one 'who brings back a sinner from his wandering' will 'save his soul from death,'" *The ESV Study Bible* (Wheaton, IL: Crossway, 2008), 1155.

verses in 11:30–12:2. The pattern is maintained, however, if 11:30b is translated, "But violence takes away lives," as the evidence suggests it should, rather than, "He who wins souls is wise."[19]

The 2017 edition of the CSB departed from the HCSB wording, rendering it "and a wise person captivates people."[20] But in 2020 the translators changed the phrase to read, "but a cunning person takes lives."

Whether or not the latter translation philosophy of Prov 11:30 is correct, the apostle Paul correlated the idea of winning with evangelism. In fact, Paul not only believed in soul-winning, but he also practiced and wrote about it. In 1 Cor 9:19–22a, he described four different groups of people—the Jews, those under the law, those without law, and the weak—and ways that he had endeavored to win them: "Although I am free from all and not anyone's slave, I have made myself a slave to everyone, in order to win more people. To the Jews I became like a Jew, to win

---

[19] Duane A. Garrett, *Proverbs, Ecclesiastes, Song of Songs*, vol. 14, The New American Commentary (Nashville: B&H, 1993), 129. In footnote 238, he explains his reasoning further: "Reading וְלֹקֵחַ נְפָשׁוֹת חָמָס. Alternatively, one could render the line, 'But a violent man is a murderer' with the vocalization חֹמֵס. Several factors weigh against the traditional 'he who wins souls is wise.' First and foremost, לָקַח נֶפֶשׁ elsewhere always means to 'kill' and never to 'win souls' in a positive sense of influencing a person for good (Ps 31:14 [Eng. v. 13]; 1 Sam 24:12 [Eng. v. 11]; 1 Kgs 19:14; Prov 1:19). Second, the emendation from חָכָם to חָמָס involves a minor and common type of scribal error. Third, the emendation is supported by the LXX rendition παρανόμων. Fourth, the reading 'violent' here is echoed by 'brutish' (בָּעַר) in 12:1."

[20] *The CSB Study Bible* (Nashville: B&H, 2017) includes an explanatory note concerning this phrase:

The second part of this verse is difficult. The Hebrew reads literally "the one taking lives is wise." Elsewhere in the Bible the phrase *take a life* is always negative (1:19; 1 Sm 24:11; 1 Kg 19:10, 14; Ps 31:13; Ezk 33:6); it never means "to win a soul." But it does not fit with the rest of Scripture to say that the person who kills people is wise, so there must be another explanation. The CSB interprets *take* to mean "captivate" in this context, so a wise person attracts and holds the attention of people. The LXX implies that the original Hebrew might have read "violence" (*chamas*) instead of "wise" (*chakam*), thus "violence takes lives." (p. 969)

Jews; to those under the law, like one under the law—though I myself am
not under the law—to win those under the law. To those who are without
the law, like one without the law—though I am not without God's law
but under the law of Christ—to win those without the law. To the weak
I became weak, in order to win the weak." Concerning the meaning of
"win" (*kerdainō*), Anthony C. Thiselton explained:

> The missionary background of *winning* disciples for Jesus Christ
> occurs in Matt 18:15, although it derives from the commercial
> background *of gaining an asset* or *making a profit*. Daube shows
> that it was probably a technical term for "winning a proselyte" in
> Judaism, reflecting the Hebrew נשכר (*niskar*, the Niphal of *sakar*,
> *to hire, to gain*). In the light of the metaphor of building materials
> and survival (1 Cor 3:12–15), the permanent and eternal effects
> of this "gain" enhance Paul's notion of what is at issue in volun-
> tary restraint for the greater good.[21]

By "win" he means neither that he simply convinced them nor that he
intellectually triumphed over them. Rather, he meant he led unbelievers
to faith in Christ.

This meaning is understood when Paul continued, "I have become
all things to all people, so that I may by every possible means *save* some"
(1 Cor 9:22b, emphasis added). Notice that by transitioning from *win*
(*kerdēsō*) to *save* (*sōsō*), Paul was establishing a synonymy between both
words. In doing so he was not attributing God's saving ability to himself,
as if any human agent can save another. Instead, he was providing context for the purpose of his winning—he was persuading these groups,
in the power of the Holy Spirit, toward salvation by God in Christ. As

---

[21] Anthony C. Thiselton, *The First Epistle to the Corinthians: A Commentary
on the Greek Text, New International Greek Testament Commentary* (Grand Rapids:
Eerdmans, 2000), 701. In his explanation of the Hebraic roots of *win*, Thiselton
refers to David Daube, "Κερδαίνω as a Missionary Term," *Harvard Theological
Review* 40 (1947): 109–20. On page 109, Daube identifies 1 Pet 3:1 as another
instance of *kerdainō* as *win* in the sense of salvation.

Thiselton explained, "Paul is speaking here [v. 22b] of **winning** converts
. . . he wishes to save some (τινὰς σώσω, i.e., bring some to salvation)."[22]

Paul's evangelism among those living in Corinth, like his evangelism
of Agrippa (cf. Acts 26:25–29), included an element of persuasion. His
use of persuasion in evangelism, however, eschewed the uses of manipulation and self-reliance. As he conveyed in his first correspondence with the
Corinthian church, he sought to win souls as though doing so depended
on him (cf. 1 Cor 9:19–22), while acknowledging that his "speech and
[his] preaching were not with persuasive words of wisdom but with a
demonstration of the Spirit's power, so that [their] faith might not be
based on human wisdom but on God's power" (1 Cor 2:4–5). Though he
was one of the servants through whom they believed, God alone received
the credit and glory for their salvation (cf. 1 Cor 3:4–7).

Biblical Motivations for Evangelism[23]

The glory of God's name serves as the primary motivation for believers' evangelism. As a result of preaching the gospel, Peter and John were
imprisoned and flogged. Yet Luke recorded that they rejoiced over being
treated this way: "Then they went out from the presence of the Sanhedrin,
rejoicing that they were counted worthy to be treated shamefully *on behalf
of the Name*" (Acts 5:41, emphasis added).[24] Their joyful response was not

---

[22] Thiselton, 705.

[23] Classic evangelism textbooks of the past discuss impetuses in evangelism.
They refer to them as motives and/or incentives in evangelism. See Faris Daniel
Whitesell, *Basic New Testament Evangelism* (Grand Rapids: Zondervan, 1949),
177–83; C. E. Matthews, *Every Christian's Job* (Nashville: B&H, 1951), 17–29;
George Sweazey, *Effective Evangelism* (New York: Harper & Brothers, 1953),
26–39; C. E. Autrey, *The Theology of Evangelism* (Nashville: B&H, 1966), 28–38;
Roland Q. Leavell, *Evangelism: Christ's Imperative Commission*, rev. Landrum P.
Leavell II and Harold T. Bryson (Nashville: B&H, 1979), 23–34; and Delos
Miles, *Introduction to Evangelism* (Nashville: B&H, 1983), 111–57.

[24] John Stott referenced Rom 1:5 and 3 John 7, in addition to Acts 5:41, as
evidence that God's glory motivated the apostolic believers. He wrote, "At the

based on their having escaped an even worse punishment; rather it was elicited by the fact that they were counted worthy, through both their preaching and their suffering, to bring glory to God's name.

When asked to identify the scriptural, evangelistic motivation that first comes to their minds, most Christians will say either obedience or love. Nevertheless, John Stott suggested in *Our Guilty Silence* that as "[c]ompelling as the motives of obedience and love are, neither is in fact the strongest evangelistic incentive. . . . The unifying theme [of our worship and witness] is the glory of God and of His Christ, and there is a great need for this to be the supreme incentive of our modern evangelism."[25] Some years later he expanded this idea in his commentary on Romans. He declared, "The highest of all missionary motives is neither obedience to the Great Commission (as important as that is), nor love for sinners who are alienated and perishing (strong as that incentive is, especially when we contemplate the wrath of God . . .), but rather zeal—burning and passionate zeal—for the glory of Jesus Christ."[26] Throughout his book *Let the Nations Be Glad: The Supremacy of God in Missions*, John Piper also argues that God's glory serves as both the means and the end of missions.

Obedience also motivates believers to evangelize.[27] In what is commonly known as the Great Commission, Jesus commanded his disciples,

---

beginning of his letter to the Romans, describing various aspects of the apostleship he has received from Jesus Christ, Paul writes that his mission to all the nations is 'for the sake of his name.' And John refers to certain missionaries who have set out (literally) 'for the sake of the name.' . . . The early Christians, who were proud 'to suffer indignity for the sake of the Name,' [Acts 5:41] were eager to evangelize in the same cause." John R. W. Stott, *Our Guilty Silence* (London: Hodder and Stoughton, 1967), 20.

[25] Stott, 20, 31.

[26] John Stott, *Romans: God's Good News for the World* (Downers Grove: InterVarsity, 1994), 53.

[27] John Hammett claimed that while obedience to the Great Commission should motivate believers' practice of evangelism, as well as other evangelism-related factors within the New Testament, "there is a paucity of commands

"All authority has been given to me in heaven and on earth. Go, therefore, and make disciples of all nations, baptizing them in the name of the
Father and of the Son and of the Holy Spirit, teaching them to observe
everything I have commanded you. And remember, I am with you always,
to the end of the age" (Matt 28:18–20). Concerning this imperative,
believers over the years have been exhorted that Jesus's last command
should be their first concern.[28]

Accounts of his disciples urgently obeying his directive can be found
throughout the pages of the New Testament. The apostles kept this command. When the Sanhedrin ordered Peter and John not to speak or teach
in Jesus's name, they replied, "Whether it's right in the sight of God for
us to listen to you rather than to God, you decide; for we are unable to
stop speaking about what we have seen and heard" (Acts 4:19–20). Soon
thereafter, they again were imprisoned for performing signs and wonders.
An angel of the Lord released them and commanded them to return
to the temple and evangelize. Listening to God instead of their rulers,
the apostles taught about Jesus in the temple courts and were arrested a
third time. When the officials confronted them for not following their
orders, "Peter and the apostles replied, 'We must obey God rather than
people'" (Acts 5:29). On another occasion, Peter explained the reason he
preached the gospel to Cornelius and those in his household by telling

---

relating to evangelism in the New Testament. There is an abundance of descriptions of evangelism; there are principles to draw from examples; and there
are some commands, but surprisingly few." John S. Hammett, "The Great
Commission and Evangelism in the New Testament," *Journal of the American
Society for Church Growth* 10 (Fall 1999): 11. However, he neglected to include
in his research the following references of implied commands to evangelize that
are present within the New Testament: Acts 5:29, 32; 10:42; 13:46–47; Rom
16:25–27; 1 Cor 9:17; Titus 1:3.

[28] Although the Great Commission has been used in this way, not all
Christians throughout history have viewed Matt 28:16–20 as a missional passage; see Daniel L. Akin, Benjamin L. Merkle, and George G. Robinson,
40 Questions about the Great Commission (Grand Rapids: Kregel Academic,
2020), 63–68.

them, "He commanded us to preach to the people and to testify that he is the one appointed by God to be the judge of the living and the dead" (Acts 10:42).

Obedience also motivated Paul's commitment to and the practice of evangelism. When Paul and Barnabas preached the gospel in Antioch, many of those who practiced Judaism were saved. A week later, some of the Jews in the synagogue saw the town's interest in hearing the gospel and began to contradict and insult Paul. "Paul and Barnabas boldly replied, 'It was necessary that the word of God be spoken to you first. Since you reject it and judge yourselves unworthy of eternal life, we are turning to the Gentiles. *For this is what the Lord has commanded us*: "I have made you a light for the Gentiles to bring salvation to the ends of the earth."' When the Gentiles heard this, they rejoiced and honored the word of the Lord, and all who had been appointed to eternal life believed. The word of the Lord spread through the whole region" (Acts 13:46–49, emphasis added). The apostle also references his obedience to and stewardship of Christ's command to proclaim the gospel in correspondences with churches (Rom 16:25–27; 1 Cor 9:16; 2 Cor 5:14–15), as well as with his companions (1 Tim 2:5–7; Titus 1:3).

Love is another evangelistic motivation. In one of his letters to the Corinthian church, Paul identified two emotions that motivated his practice of persuasion in evangelism—the fear of God and the love of Christ. Concerning the latter, he explained, "For the love of Christ compels us, since we have reached this conclusion, that one died for all, and therefore all died. And he died for all so that those who live should no longer live for themselves, but for the one who died for them and was raised" (2 Cor 5:14–15).

Personal evangelists should be motivated by at least three dimensions of love as they share the gospel. First, like Paul, they should be prompted to evangelize because of the love Jesus demonstrated by dying for all. Second, as an expression of their own love for their Savior and Lord, all Christians should tell others about him. Last, because those who love Jesus should also share affection for whomever he loves, believers should exhibit a sincere love for the world by sharing the message of salvation with as many people as possible.

Personal experiences with Christ quicken Christ-followers to evangelize. Those who spend time with Jesus cannot help but spend time telling others about Jesus. The New Testament describes many instances of believers evangelizing because of the time they spent with Jesus. One of the most well-known examples of this motivation took place in John 4. A Samaritan woman encountered Jesus at Jacob's well. Her experience with him, as well as his words, so moved the woman that she quickly left her belongings and went into town to invite the people: "Come, see a man who told me everything I ever did" (John 4:29). Not only did her personal experience with Christ result in her own salvation, but many people believed in him because of what she said, and even more Samaritans believed in him because they, themselves, met him and heard what he had to say (John 4:39–42).

As referenced earlier, because of the things they had seen and heard when they were with him, Peter and John would not be deterred from teaching and preaching Jesus (Acts 4:20). In fact, both of them independently referenced this evangelistic motivator in 2 Pet 1:16 and 1 John 1:1–2. They each told the recipients of their letters that the gospel they shared was based on forensic evidence, of which they had firsthand knowledge and to which they could attest.

Responsibility encourages Christians to share the gospel with others. L. R. Scarborough wrote, "He who professing salvation in Christ refuses to carry the gospel to others by such refusal violates the holiest of trusts and is recreant to the most sacred stewardship."[29] In his letters Paul referred to the stewardship of evangelism entrusted to himself and believers. Concerning his own sense of this duty, he told the Corinthians that he was compelled to preach the gospel (1 Cor 9:16). He then referenced two motivations for evangelism—reward and obligation. He explained, "For if I do this willingly, I have a reward, but if unwillingly, I

---

[29] Scarborough, *Christ's Militant Kingdom*, 174 (see chap. 2, n. 2).

am entrusted with a commission" (1 Cor 9:17). While others in his day preached the gospel willingly for a reward, Paul stated that responsibility, obligation, and stewardship of Christ's command to evangelize motivated his commitment to preach the gospel. He also referenced this steward-ship God entrusted to him when he wrote Titus: "In [God's] own time he has revealed his word in the preaching with which I was entrusted by the command of God our Savior" (Titus 1:3).

Not only did Paul believe he had been entrusted with the responsibil-ity to advance the gospel, but he also believed that responsibility should motivate all believers to evangelize. He reasoned, "How, then, can they call on him they have not believed in? And how can they believe without hearing about him? And how can they hear without a preacher? And how can they preach unless they are sent? . . . So faith comes from what is heard, and what is heard comes through the message about Christ" (Rom 10:14–15a, 17). Paul's logic, simply stated, argued (1) calling on God (2) requires believing in God (3) that necessitates hearing about God, (4) which cannot be done without a preacher of God (5) who is sent out by a local church of God. People will not be saved if believers do not evan-gelize, and those who do not evangelize will bear some sense of responsi-bility for lost people's rejection of God (cf. Ezek 3:16–21; 33:1–11; Acts 18:6; 20:26).

Faith leads believers to bring others to Christ. Mark 2:1–12 tells the story of four men who brought a man who could not walk to Jesus. Because the crowds of people prevented them access to Jesus, who was in a house, the quartet went to great lengths to get the man an audience with Jesus. They carried him to the roof above Jesus and broke through it, likely with their fingers and fists. When they created an opening big enough to lower him to Jesus, Mark says that Jesus saw their faith (Mark 2:5).

Many in that day, including the scribes in attendance, believed the man's sin caused his disability. Nevertheless, the four men believed Jesus could remedy the man's paralysis, whether caused by demerit or defect. As they lowered the paralyzed man to Jesus, he noted their faith as well as the man's. Because of his faith, the Lord forgave him of his sins. And to prove to the aghast scribes that he had God's authority to forgive, he also healed the man.

The Bible clearly teaches that no one can be saved apart from personally exercising saving faith in Jesus Christ. People cannot be saved by someone else's faith on their behalf; they must believe for themselves. Nevertheless, personal evangelists' faith in Jesus's power to save can motivate them to introduce him to those who need his salvation, that they might believe.

Prayer is also used by God to arouse his people to share the good news. Comparing the small number of believers who evangelize with the enormous number of those who need to hear the gospel can be overwhelming. It is enough to cause personal evangelists to worry. In fact, Jesus told his disciples that the ratio of those who were ready to respond to the good news was greater than the number of those who were actually sharing it (Matt 9:37–38; Luke 10:2). He did not encourage them to wring their hands or lay a guilt trip on fellow believers. To see more people join the evangelistic enterprise, they were to "pray to the Lord of the harvest to send out workers into his harvest" (Matt 9:38).

After his ascension, evangelism by those belonging to the church in Jerusalem was met with threats, persecution, and resistance. As mentioned previously, Peter and John were imprisoned for sharing the gospel and later released. When they returned to their fellow believers, Luke says the church prayed in response to the overwhelming situation they faced: "And now, Lord, consider their threats, and grant that your servants may speak your word with all boldness" (Acts 4:29). God answered their prayer by sending an earthquake to shake the place where they met and filling them with the Holy Spirit, whereby they began to share the gospel with boldness (Acts 4:31).

Paul required the prayer of the Ephesians in his evangelism: "Pray also for me, that the message may be given to me when I open my mouth to make known with boldness the mystery of the gospel. For this I am an ambassador in chains. Pray that I might be bold enough to speak about it as I should" (Eph 6:19–20). He also requested that the Colossian church pray for his evangelism: "At the same time, pray also for us that God may open a door to us for the word, to speak the mystery of Christ, for which I am in chains, so that I may make it known as I should" (Col 4:3–4).

Gratitude stimulates those who have been saved to offer the gospel to those who need it. Skevington Wood validated this claim when he explained that converts realize "that each believer is to be a witness and that one of the ways in which he expresses his indebtedness to God is by commending his Savior to men. It is thus that the Gospel spreads."[30] The motivator of thankfulness closely relates to believers' personal experiences with Christ. Anyone who has been forgiven of their sins wants to tell others about him so they too can be forgiven. Personal evangelists can likely recall how the thanksgiving, joy, and excitement of their own conversion experience immediately drove them to tell others about Jesus. The evening I was saved after a church service, I ran out of the building to the parking lot to tell all my friends outside playing tag, "I'm saved! I'm saved! I'm saved! And you can be too!"

One of Jesus's evangelistic encounters involved his casting demons out of a man who roamed a cemetery outside the Sea of Galilee. This account is recorded in Matt 8:28–34; Mark 5:1–20; and Luke 8:26–39. After having Legion exorcised from him, the man sat at Jesus's feet whole, clothed, and in his right mind. The power that Jesus displayed by healing the man caused fear in the residents of that region. They begged him to leave, and he obliged them. Nevertheless, as he was boarding the boat to cross to the other side of the lake, the man pleaded with Jesus to allow him to come along. Jesus denied his request and replied, "Go home to your own people, and report to them how much the Lord has done for you and how he has had mercy on you" (Mark 5:19). Immediately and full

---

[30] A. Skevington Wood, *Evangelism: Its Theology and Practice* (Grand Rapids: Zondervan, 1966), 117–18.

of gratitude, he began telling everyone what Jesus had done for him. As a result of the man's proclamation, when Jesus returned to the region in Mark 6:53–56, crowds of people recognized him and spread who he was throughout all the towns and villages.

The wrath and coming judgment of God should spur Christians to proclaim the gospel. Some may prefer to emphasize God's love over his justice by reciting John 3:16; however, they must not neglect the continuation of John's thought: "but anyone who does not believe is already condemned, because he has not believed in the name of the one and only Son of God" (John 3:18). Unbelievers and their sin are objects of God's holy wrath. The execution of his just wrath is not confined to a future event only. Romans 1:18 says it is already being revealed "against all godlessness and unrighteousness of people."

All people will deal with God's righteous wrath against their sin. His wrath against believers' sins is satisfied through Jesus's death on the cross. On the other hand, his anger against the transgressions of those who never repent and believe will be addressed at the great white throne judgment (Matt 7:21–23; 25:31–36; Rev 20:11–15). God will say to everyone who stands before him at that judgment, "I never knew you. Depart from me, you lawbreakers!" (Matt 7:23). Those who hear him utter those words to them will appease God's holy wrath against their sin by suffering eternally in hell. What a fearful thought, even for those who will not experience it! Any believer who genuinely fears God's wrath and has compassion for those upon whom it rests cannot help but reach them with the gospel, as Jude described by "sav[ing] others by snatching them from the fire" (Jude v. 23).

The fear of the Lord must motivate Christian evangelism. The next chapter will survey numerous fears that impede believers from evangelizing. Unlike them, however, this particular fear should encourage evangelism. In 2 Cor 5:11, Paul wrote, "Therefore, since we know the fear of the Lord, we try to persuade people." Fear of God led Paul to persuade people to believe in Christ.

One verse earlier, Paul informed the Corinthians, "For we must all appear before the judgment seat of Christ, so that each may be repaid for what he has done in the body, whether good or evil" (2 Cor 5:10). Ancient Corinth employed the use of a *bēma*, or judgment seat. Although these raised pedestals were generally used for public proclamations or accommodations, magistrates would also make judicial pronouncements from them. Just as Paul stood before Gallio at Corinth's *bēma* (Acts 18:12–17), he also knew he, along with all believers, will stand one day before the one in heaven in order to give an account for the things done and not done for the Lord. According to 1 Cor 3:12–15, these works will be tested by fire. Some, like gold, silver, and precious stones, will become a precious thing when purified by the fire. Others, like wood, hay, and stubble, will be burned to ash, although those who perform such works will be saved "only as through fire" (1 Cor 3:15). Among these works will include those times we evangelize, as well as those times we do not. The fear accompanied by the realization of this forthcoming judgment should spur us all to evangelize more.

A Motivation to Avoid

The New Testament identifies an evangelistic motivation personal evangelists should avoid—selfish ambition. Leonard Ravenhill offers the following rebuke to selfishly motivated personal evangelists: "[They] who should be fishing for men are now too often fishing for compliments from men."[31] In Phil 1:15–18, Paul wrote, "To be sure, some preach Christ out of envy and rivalry, but others out of good will. These preach out of love, knowing that I am appointed for the defense of the gospel; the others proclaim Christ out of selfish ambition, not sincerely, thinking that they will cause me trouble in my imprisonment. What does it matter?

---

[31] Leonard Ravenill, *Why Revival Tarries* (Minneapolis: Bethany House, 1959), 22.

Only that in every way, whether from false motives or true, Christ is proclaimed, and in this I rejoice." Although Paul rejoiced that the gospel was preached in spite of the less-than-noble motives of his critics, he clearly preferred that Christ be preached out of good will and sincerity over envy, rivalry, and selfish ambition.

Stott warns personal evangelists, "Some evangelism, to be sure, is no better than a thinly disguised form of imperialism, whenever our real ambition is for the honour of our nation, church, organization, or ourselves. Only one imperialism is Christian, however, and that is concern for His Imperial Majesty Jesus Christ, and the glory of his empire or kingdom."[32] Evangelism is not about us. Instead, it concerns God and the lost. As believers evangelize, may they avoid seeking temporary accolades or capturing others' attention in this world, and instead focus on doing everything they can to bring others with them into the new heaven and new earth.

DISCUSSION AND REFLECTION QUESTIONS

1. The following Scriptures relate to evangelism.
   a. Begin by locating and reading each Bible verse in your own Bible. As you read each passage, reflect on the ways it can assist you in your evangelism. Also, consider how you intend to use and apply each one in your personal practice of sharing Christ.
   b. Next, commit these verses to memory.
   c. Last, identify either a believer or an unbeliever to whom you can recite what you have memorized. If you chose a believer, encourage him or her to memorize the verses with you. If you choose an unbeliever, use this exercise to evangelize him or her.

---

[32] Stott, *Romans*, 53.

Ecclesiastes 7:20

Isaiah 53:6

Isaiah 55:6

Ezekiel 3:18–19

Ezekiel 33:11

Daniel 12:3

Matthew 4:19

Matthew 28:16–20

Luke 13:3

Luke 24:47–48

John 1:12

John 5:24

Acts 20:21

Acts 1:8

Acts 3:19

Acts 4:12

Acts 10:42–43

Acts 13:37–39

Acts 16:31

Romans 3:10

Romans 3:23

Romans 5:8

Romans 6:23

Romans 10:9–10

Romans 10:13–15a

Romans 10:17

1 Corinthians 15:3–4

1 Corinthians 9:16

2 Corinthians 5:11

2 Corinthians 5:20–21

2 Corinthians 6:2b

2 Corinthians 7:10

2 Corinthians 13:5

Titus 3:5

Hebrews 9:27

1 Peter 3:18

2 Peter 3:9

1 John 2:2

1 John 5:13

Jude 23

4

Biblical Foundations
of the Gospel

The practice of evangelism rises or falls on the message of the gospel that personal evangelists share. The Bible recounts the gospel's origin, as well as its content. The Old Testament anticipates and embodies, through both prophetic foretelling and forthtelling, the gospel of God. In addition, the New Testament distinctly presents and preserves the meaning and message of the gospel through its narratives, preaching, and epistles. This chapter explores the gospel lexically, hermeneutically, and conceptually to form a biblical foundation for understanding the gospel.

An Old Testament Derivative of the Gospel

Of the numerous prophetic references that announce God's good news about Jesus Christ in the Old Testament, perhaps the most distinct derivative of the gospel concept is the term *bāśār*, which appears thirty times. In its noun form, *bāśār* occurs only six times (i.e., 2 Sam 4:10; 18:20, 22,

25, 27; and 2 Kgs 7:9). Similar to the New Testament's use of *euangelion*, *bāśār* in its noun form means either "news" or "a reward for news."[1] In a strict sense, however, *bāśār* differs with *euangelion* in its common meaning of "good news." Of its six Old Testament occurrences, *bāśār* translates as "good, or glad, news" in only one occurrence (2 Sam 18:27) due to a modifier.[2] Does *bāśār* have a strong correlation with the *euangelion* after all? Millar Burrows contends the answer is no. He claims, "It is quite evident that the Christian use of the noun εὐαγγέλιον is not derived from the Greek Old Testament."[3]

Nevertheless, overwhelming evidence exists to the contrary. First, many times the New Testament uses *euangelion* in religious and theological contexts. John P. Meier asserts one difference between *euangelion* and *bāśār* can be traced to the fact that, "[בְּשֵׂר as a noun] has a secular and not a specifically religious or theological sense."[4] This difference alone does not prevent a derivative connection from being made.

Second, one must consider the connotations from the verbal form of *bāśār* in light of the noun form's minimal appearance in the Old Testament. In fact, while "the Old Testament is quite unpromising as a theological background for the New Testament's use of *euangelion* and more generally for the Christian concept of evangelization, . . . it would be a mistake to restrict [one's] focus in the Old Testament to the noun. More significant for New Testament usage is the Hebrew verb *biśśar*, rendered in the Greek by *euaggelizomai*."[5]

---

[1] John P. Meier, "Gospel in the Old and New Testament," *Mid-Stream* 40, no. 1–2 (January-April 2001): 131.

[2] O. Schilling, "רשׂב," in *Theological Dictionary of Old Testament*, ed. G. Johannes Botterweck and Helmer Ringgren, trans. John T. Willis (1975; repr., Grand Rapids: Eerdmans, 1977), 2:314.

[3] Millar Burrows, "The Origin of the Term 'Gospel,'" *Journal of Biblical Literature* 44, no. 1–2 (1925): 22.

[4] Meier, "Gospel in the Old and New Testament," 131.

[5] Meier, 131.

A closer examination of the theological contexts of *bāśār*'s verb forms, especially those in Isaiah and Nahum, offer a connection between it and *euangelion*. Depending on its verb form, *bāśār* renders such meanings as "to bring good news," "herald of good tidings," "to tell/announce" (in the Piel), and "to receive good news" (in the Hithpael).[6] This approach yields an understanding that both the noun and verb forms denote a good message or good news the majority of the time.[7]

For example, when used in the context of Isa 40:9; 41:27; 52:7; and Nah 1:15, *bāśār* refers to the act of preaching or proclaiming the good tidings of God's salvation. In fact, Joseph Blenkinsopp goes further, "[From Isa 40:9 and 52:7,] early Christians derived both the unique form in which to tell the story of their founder—*euaggelion*, 'good tidings, gospel'—and the essence of his message—the coming of the kingdom of God."[8] Paul Hanson agrees when he attests, "[The gospel/pattern of Isa 52:7] is reformulated by Paul as he applies it to the new gospel of God's act in Jesus Christ (see Rom. 10:14–18)."[9]

As observed in the aforementioned Isaiah passages, *bāśār* conveys the meaning of God's victory over his enemies and his coming to deliver those who are captive. At first, only Zion knows the truth (Isa 40:9; 41:27), but eventually all nations will tell the story (Isa 60:6). The reality of this concept is only and finally met in Christ.[10] Furthermore, this meaning

---

[6] Ludwig Koehler and Walter Baumgartner, eds., "רשׂב," in *The Hebrew and Aramaic Lexicon of the Old Testament*, trans. M. E. J. Richardson, vol. 1 (New York: Brill, 1994), 163–64.

[7] Schilling, "רשׂב," 313.

[8] Joseph Blenkinsopp, *Isaiah 40–55, The Anchor Yale Bible*, vol. 19A (New York: Doubleday, 2002), 344. This is a repeated assertion made by Blenkinsopp on page 186.

[9] Paul D. Hanson, "Isaiah 52:7–10," *Interpretation* 33, no. 4 (October 1979): 390, https://doi.org/10.1177/002096437903300405.

[10] John N. Oswalt, "בָּשַׂר," in *Theological Wordbook of the Old Testament*, ed. R. Laird Harris, Gleason L. Archer, and Bruce K. Waltke (Chicago: Moody, 1980), 1:135.

concerning the Isaiah passages should be conveyed to Nah 1:15 as well. In his examination of its literary parallel, Carl Armerding attested, "Nahum's prophecy [in 1:15] has many affinities with the book of Isaiah . . . which occur verbatim . . . and are without close parallel elsewhere in the OT."[11] A connection between *bāśār* and *euangelion* becomes clearer from these examinations of *bāśār*'s verb forms. These uses of *bāśār* in Isaiah, as well as in Nahum, "form a meaningful background to the New Testament['s] concept of euangelion."[12]

Stephen Hague affirms this connection between the Old and New Testament conception of the gospel message. He explains that the use of *bāśār* conveyed

> the centrality of [such] themes [as] bringing news, proclaiming, and preaching in the NT. . . . To note a selection: *euangelizō*; *kēryssō* (preach, proclaim); *prokēryssō* (preached); *kērygma* (preaching, message); *kēryx* (herald, preacher); *logos* (message, report, preaching); . . . etc. The usage range for some of those terms is broad. This reflects the extensive capacity for communicating information in the NT world. . . . The most notable NT communication is the preaching or proclaiming of the gospel of Jesus Christ. This is without question always good news and is to be brought to all the world. . . . Central to the preaching was the message that Christ, though crucified, was risen from the dead; this is the *kērygma*.[13]

---

[11] Carl E. Armerding, "Obadiah, Nahum, Habakkuk," in *The Expositor's Bible Commentary*, ed. Frank E. Gæbelein, vol. 7 (Grand Rapids: Zondervan, 1985), 453–54.

[12] Jerry W. Lemon, "Luke's Concept of Evangelism as Determined from an Explanation of His Use of Terms for Communicating the Gospel" (PhD diss., Baylor University, 1975), 234.

[13] Stephen T. Hague, "רשׁב," in *The New International Dictionary of Old Testament Theology & Exegesis*, ed. Willem A. VanGemeren (Grand Rapids: Zondervan, 1997), 1:776.

The gospel message is not an exclusive New Testament concept. The Old Testament use of *bāśār* served as the precursor to the New Testament proclamation of the gospel message.

Three Words That Convey the Gospel in the New Testament

The Old Testament's anticipation of the good news found in Jesus Christ was realized in the New Testament. Michael Green has suggested that three Greek roots—*kērygma, euangelion,* and *martyrion*—present the distinct concept of the gospel message in the New Testament. A survey of the lexical meaning of these three Greek roots conceptualizes the gospel in biblical terms that Green proposed—the gospel as *proclamation, good news,* and *witness.*[14]

Kērygma

The New Testament makes use of *kērygma* fewer than ten times as a noun and a little over fifty times as a verb (*kēryssō*).[15] Despite *kērygma*'s minimal appearances in the New Testament, scholars' overwhelming use of this biblical noun in a theological sense proves important to examine. Even though its use is much less frequent in the New Testament than *euangelion,* theologians of the past refer to the content of the gospel by the terminological use of *kērygma.*[16] Likewise, strong evidence exists

---

[14] Michael Green, *Evangelism in the Early Church* (London: Hodder & Stoughton, 1970), 48.

[15] Craig A. Evans says that the nominal cognate occurs six times in the New Testament (Matt 12:41; Luke 11:32; Rom 16:25; 1 Cor 1:21; 2:4; and 15:14), and all refer to the gospel message. Evans, "'Preacher' and 'Preaching': Some Lexical Observations," *Journal of the Evangelical Theological Society* 24, no. 4 (December 1981): 316.

[16] Michael Green exclaims, "[It] is surprising . . . that kerygma has become anglicized as a technical term for the early preaching." Green, *Evangelism in the Early Church,* 58. While the New Testament's use of *euangelion* has a much

that connects *kērygma* with *euangelion*. Each time the New Testament employs *kērygma*, it appears essentially synonymous with *euangelion*.[17]

Along with *kēryssein*, *kērygma* was used outside the New Testament to convey "news," "declaration," "inquiry," "demand," "order," "decree," "command," "proclamation of [a] victor," and "intimation of honours."[18] Lewis Drummond explained, "Something quite profound emerges [when *kērygma* is] used in the New Testament. It implies the proclamation of the gospel is not a mere reciting of theological dogmas; it also speaks of a positive faith response with definite results."[19]

Within the New Testament, *kērygma* incorporates a number of similar meanings. *Kērygma* means "proclamation," "public annunciation," "public inculcation," "preaching," and/or "doctrine."[20] Typically, a *kēryx* ("herald" or "public crier") declares *kērygma*.[21] In the New Testament, Jesus's disciples assume the role as heralds of God and Christ. Of the six times the New Testament employs it, *kērygma* denotes the proclamation of the kingdom of God in the Synoptics and refers to the proclamation

---

broader semantic range than the one used in this study, it seems that a biblical theology of the gospel would reference it as the *euangelic* message rather than the *kerygmatic* message, due to the more prominent presence of *euangelion* over that of *kērygma* in the New Testament. James I. H. McDonald seems to concur with this assessment, see *Kerygma and Didache: The Articulation and Structure of the Earliest Christian Message* (Cambridge: Cambridge University, 1980), 4.

When speaking of a school of interpretation, I will use the translated form (i.e., *kērygma*) rather than the transliterated one (i.e., *kērygma*), as I have here.

[17] Archibald M. Hunter, *The Unity of the New Testament* (London: SCM, 1957), 21.

[18] Gerhard Friedrich, "κήρυγμα," in *Theological Dictionary of the New Testament*, ed. Gerhard Kittel, trans. Geoffrey W. Bromiley (Grand Rapids: Eerdmans, 1965), 3:715.

[19] Lewis Drummond, *The Word of the Cross: A Contemporary Theology of Evangelism* (Nashville: B&H, 1992), 203–4.

[20] Wesley J. Perschbacher, *The New Analytical Greek Lexicon* (Peabody, MA: Hendrickson, 1990), 238.

[21] Joseph H. Thayer, *Thayer's Greek-English Lexicon of the New Testament* (Edinburgh: T&T Clark, 1896; repr., Peabody, MA: Hendrickson, 1997), 346.

concerning Jesus Christ in the Pauline Epistles.[22] Gerhard Friedrich attempts to tie the Synoptic and Pauline meanings together. He explains that "the gospel of Paul is identical with that which Jesus Himself was preaching during His earthly life. . . . Christ Himself speaks in the gospel of Paul. . . . [Paul emphasized] the agreement of his preaching with that of the early Jesus."[23]

Jesus Christ is made known to the world through men's and women's proclamation of the *kērygma*. In 1 Cor 15:14 and Rom 16:25, Paul used *kērygma* in such a way that refers to a "message with a very definite content."[24] Biblically, this term proves essential to understanding the proclaimed message of God's good news to mankind by his people.

Euangelion

The biblical text predominately makes use of the Greek noun *euangelion* some seventy times, many more times than it uses either *kērygma* or *martyrion*. *Euangelion* occurs twelve times in the Gospels and sixty-two times in the rest of the New Testament.[25] The term generally means "good news," or "glad tidings" in the New Testament. The New Testament uses *euangelion* in the context of "God's good news to humans," as well as indicating "details relating to the life and ministry of Jesus."[26] This meaning is derived from combining the Greek adverb *eu* as a prefix, meaning "good," with the noun *angelia*, which means "message," "news," and "announcement."

Euangelion's use in Greek literature outside the New Testament generally refers to "news of victory." An exception arises in the context of

---

[22] Evans, "'Preacher' and 'Preaching': Some Lexical Observations," 316.

[23] Friedrich, "κήρυγμα," 716.

[24] Friedrich, 716.

[25] Evans, "'Preacher' and 'Preaching': Some Lexical Observations," 317.

[26] Walter Bauer, *A Greek-English Lexicon of the New Testament and Other Early Christian Literature*, 3rd ed., rev. and ed. Frederick W. Danker (Chicago: University of Chicago, 2000), 402–3.

the imperial cult when an emperor, whose subjects view him as divine in nature, invokes *euangelion*—ordinances that are celebrated and commands that are sacred writings.[27] Although this meaning closely relates to the way the New Testament uses *euangelion*, certain characteristics cause the New Testament's usage to be uniquely different.

Frank Stagg asserts, "Etymology and pre-Christian usage [of εὐαγγέλιον] may indicate possible New Testament usage, but they do not determine it. In the final analysis, what New Testament writers intend by 'gospel' is to be derived from their own contexts."[28] A couple of interesting characteristics highlight the uniqueness of the New Testament's treatment of *euangelion*. The first of these features relates to *euangelion*'s numerical inflection as a noun. John Meier explains, "[A] striking phenomenon that distinguishes the New Testament's usage of *euaggelion* from that of the Old Testament or Greco-Roman paganism is that the New Testament uses the noun only in the singular." He continues, "In the New Testament, 'gospel' is only and always the content of the good news being proclaimed or the act of proclaiming the good news. This, of course, helps explain why the noun occurs in the New Testament only in the singular."[29]

The second characteristic that distinguishes the New Testament's connotation of *euangelion* has to do with its distinct meaning. Millar Burrows writes, "The Greek term εὐαγγέλιον (neuter singular) is rarely found in the sense of 'good tidings' outside of early Christian literature. We find εὐάγγελος (bringing good tidings) and the verb εὐαγγελίζεσθαι (to bring good tidings), but εὐαγγέλιον in classical Greek means a messenger's reward. In the plural it means a sacrifice for good tidings."[30] In the context of its own distinct usage, the New Testament does not use

---

[27] Gerhard Friedrich, "εὐαγγέλιον," in *Theological Dictionary of the New Testament*, ed. Gerhard Kittel, trans. Geoffrey W. Bromiley (Grand Rapids: Eerdmans, 1965), 2:722–25.

[28] Frank Stagg, "The Gospel in Biblical Usage," *Review & Expositor* 63 (Winter 1966): 7.

[29] Meier, "Gospel in the Old and New Testament," 134.

[30] Burrows, "The Origin of the Term 'Gospel,'" 21.

euangelion to refer to a written document or literary genre. The church fathers began this practice during the second century.[31] This fact does not mean that using "Gospel" to refer to a literary genre contained in the New Testament (i.e., Matthew, Mark, Luke, and John) is unbiblical, only that the New Testament does not use this designation.

Nevertheless, *euangelion* possesses a fuller meaning than just "good news," or "glad tidings" in the New Testament. It embodies specialized content. Thayer observes:

> After the death of Christ [in the Gospels,] the term το εὐαγγέλιον comprises also the preaching of (concerning) Jesus Christ as having suffered death on the cross to procure eternal salvation for [mankind] in the kingdom of God, but as restored to life and exalted to the right hand of God in heaven, [then] to return in majesty to consummate the kingdom of God; so that it may be more briefly defined as *the glad tidings of salvation through Christ; the proclamation of the grace of God manifested and pledged in Christ; the gospel.*[32]

As such, *euangelion* does not denote just any "good news" but a specific message of love, hope, forgiveness, and joy centered upon Jesus.

Wherever the *euangelion* is proclaimed in the New Testament, Becker notes, "It creates faith . . . brings salvation, life . . . and also judgment. . . . It reveals God's righteousness . . . brings the fulfillment of hope . . . intervenes in the lives of men, and creates churches."[33] Millard Erickson believes it to be "apparent when Paul uses [εὐαγγέλιον] as the direct object of a verb of speaking or hearing, [that] he has in view a particular content,

---

[31] For a discussion of *euangelion*'s designation as a gospel by the early church, see Meier, "Gospel in the Old and New Testament," 134 and Friedrich, "εὐαγγέλιον," 735–36.

[32] Thayer, *Thayer's Greek-English Lexicon of the New Testament*, 257.

[33] Ulrich Becker, "Gospel, Evangelize, Evangelist, εὐαγγέλιον" in *The New International Dictionary of New Testament Theology*, ed. Colin Brown, vol. 2 (Grand Rapids: Zondervan, 1971), 111.

a particular body of facts."[34] This term, therefore, serves as the primary biblical reference to understand the basic tenets of the gospel.

Martyrion

Scripture uses *martyrion* as another key word that conveys the basic understanding of the gospel message in the New Testament. *Martyrion* appears twenty times in the New Testament.[35] Although not as frequently in the New Testament as *euangelion*, *martyrion* appears fourteen more times than *kērygma*. This evidence led Francis Glasson to propose that scholars adopt *martyria*, over *kērygma*, when speaking of the gospel.[36] But this notion has been dismissed, probably due to *kērygma's* common acceptance in the field of New Testament studies.

Martyrion appears less frequently in the New Testament than its other, closely related forms (*e.g.*, *martys*, *martyreō*, and *martyria*). Understanding the meanings of these complementary forms proves helpful to understand *martyrion's* own meaning. The New Testament uses the verb *martyreō* primarily as "a legal term and [it] was frequently used in Greek to denote witness to facts and events on the one hand, and to truths vouched for on the other."[37] To be sure, *martyrion* embodies truthful facts and events like its verbal counterpart *martyreō*; however, its content should be understood in a more objective sense than a legal one.

Martyria probably more closely relates to *martyrion* than any of its other forms found in the New Testament, although a notable nuance exists between the two. Perschbacher translates *martyria* as "attestation" and "reputation," whereas *martyrion* can mean "evidence," as well

---

[34] Millard Erickson, *Christian Theology* (Grand Rapids: Baker, 1985), 1062.

[35] Hermann Strathmann, "μάρτυς," in *Theological Dictionary of the New Testament*, ed., Gerhard Kittel, trans. Geoffrey W. Bromiley (Grand Rapids: Eerdmans, 1965), 4:502.

[36] See Thomas Francis Glasson, "Kerygma or Martyria?," *Scottish Journal of Theology* 22 (March 1969): 90–95.

[37] Green, *Evangelism in the Early Church*, 70.

as "solemn declaration."[38] Both *martyrion* and *martyria* connote "testimony" and "witness." Whereas *martyria* typically refers to "making an
active appearance and statement as a witness (μάρτυς) . . . it can take on
the sense of *martyrion*, evidence, as the content of the statement made,
whereas the latter can never [possess] the sense of an action."[39]

This discovery, however, does not discount *martyrion*'s relationship
to a biblical understanding of the gospel. In fact, many times the New
Testament authors use it in the context of either "a proclamation of salvation by the apostles" or "concerning what God has done through Christ
for the salvation of men," more so than their use of *martyria*.[40] Paul's use
of *martyrion* demonstrates an example in that he gives it a specific meaning, "not a matter of a legal document or a piece of evidence or a recollection giving encouragement or a warning; [rather he] uses it in the sense
of the gospel . . . the proclaimed message of salvation in Christ."[41] The
content of *martyrion* when used in such instances, whether intended or
implied, closely relates to an understanding of the gospel message. This
understanding refers to a "testimony bearing on *events* but interpreted by
faith. In other terms, the object of witness is *revealed truth*."[42] As such, the
biblical use of *martyrion*, therefore, assists in understanding the message,
or content, of the gospel.

Three Interpretations of the Apostolic Gospel

In addition to how they have understood the gospel through etymology
and lexical morphology, biblical scholars have expressed varying conceptual

---

[38] Perschbacher, *The New Analytical Greek Lexicon*, 265.

[39] Lothar Coenen, "Witness, Testimony: μαρτυρία," in *The New International
Dictionary of New Testament Theology*, ed. Colin Brown (Grand Rapids:
Zondervan, 1971), 3:1038–39.

[40] Thayer, *Thayer's Greek-English Lexicon of the New Testament*, 391–92.

[41] Coenen, "Witness, Testimony: μαρτυρία," 1043.

[42] Suzanne de Dietrich, "'You Are My Witnesses': A Study of the Church's
Witness," *Interpretation* 8, no. 3 (July 1954): 273.

understandings of the apostolic *kērygma* in hermeneutic terms.[43] Their understandings fall under one of three schools—the British, German, and Anglican schools. In addition to being known as schools, they have also been referred to as views, treatments, or brands.

The British and German schools are historic perspectives that have been accepted throughout the twentieth century until today. Robert A. Bartels provided a basic background of how the two more historic schools, the British and German, received their names:

> With the two major schools of New Testament scholarship wherein the Gospel tradition has been studied during this century, it soon became axiomatic that it was actually the kerygma of the early church which determined either the shape or the outlook of the Gospel tradition, or both. . . . For want of better terms, we shall call the two major schools of scholarship (1) the "German school" and (2) the "British school." The designations, in reality, have nothing to do with nationalities as such, for both schools have followers in Britain and on the Continent as well as on the other side of the Atlantic. The "German school" is so designated because its particular point of view about the Gospel tradition and about the kerygma originated with German scholars. Likewise, the "British school" is so designated because its point of view on both matters is largely the product of British scholarship.[44]

---

[43] For further research, see Harry Poe, *The Gospel and Its Meaning* (Grand Rapids: Zondervan, 1996), 20–44; Matthew Burton Queen, "A Theological Assessment of the Gospel Content in Selected Southern Baptist Sources," (PhD diss., Southeastern Baptist Theological Seminary, 2009), 9–14; and Carl Bradford, "'Schooling' the Gospel: An Investigation of British and German Schools of Kerygmatic Interpretation in the Twentieth and Twenty-First Centuries," (PhD diss., Southwestern Baptist Theological Seminary, 2018).

[44] Robert A. Bartels, *Kerygma or Gospel Tradition—Which Came First?* (Minneapolis: Augsburg, 1961), 4–6. Bartels described these two views in greater detail on pages 6–11.

Lewis Drummond summarized the general, hermeneutical differentiations between the British and German schools when he explained, "The German school has tended to emphasize strongly the existential, experiential elements in proclaiming Christ. . . . The English School, Dodd, Stewart, and others, stresses the historical, objective [content proclaimed]."[45] Throughout the latter half of the twentieth century, conservative evangelicals tended to align more with the views of the British school, whereas liberal and more ecumenical churches matched more with those of the German school.

The Anglican school emerged in the last three decades of the twentieth century and has risen to prominence among evangelicals in the twenty-first century. This school seeks to correct what it views as evangelicalism's overemphasis on the Reformation's doctrine of justification by placing more emphasis on Jesus's exaltation as King in salvation. It gradually emerged out of the British view through Michael Green's critiques of both the British and German arguments about the *kerygma*.[46] Some years later the Anglican school developed out of N. T. Wright's engagement with the *New Perspective on Paul*, and to some extent from Christopher Wright's missional hermeneutic in *The Mission of God*. Scot McKnight's and Matthew Bates's writings on the gospel have popularized this view among evangelicals, as well as those outside evangelicalism. In 2018 Carl Bradford identified this emerging third view, which he designated as the Anglican school due to Green's, the Wrights', and McKnight's identification and affiliation with Anglicanism.[47]

The following chart summarizes the interpretive tenets each school advances in its understanding of the gospel's message and meaning in response to key interpretive questions. A concise description of the

---

[45] Drummond, *The Word of the Cross*, 214.

[46] See Green, *Evangelism in the Early Church*, 60–66. As the section on the *Anglican school* will further explain and document, Green found the British school's insistence on doctrinal formulas to be too rigid, whereas the German school's emphasis on experience over doctrine to be problematic.

[47] See Bradford, "'Schooling' the Gospel."

hermeneutical proposals by representative advocates of the British, German, and Anglican schools will follow. This chart, along with the descriptions of each school, provide a summary of the characteristics and the distinctions between each interpretive school's hermeneutic of the gospel message.

FIGURE 1. Interpretive Tenets of the Three
Kerygmatic Schools of Interpretation

Interpretative Questions	British School	German School	Anglican School
What is the focus of the gospel's proclamation?	The Content of What Is Preached	The Act of Preaching	Unity within What Has Been Proclaimed
What form does the gospel take?	Formulaic/ Patterned	Fragmented	Comprehensive Metanarrative
In what way is Christ viewed and proclaimed?	The Historic Jesus	The Christ of Faith	Christ the King, or Messiah
How is the source material of the gospel interpreted?	Historical-Grammatical	Demythologizing	Canonical
What accounts for the variances in the form of the gospel presentations?	Audience Contextualization	Author Composition	A Cumulative Type of Revelation
Who/What is the primary beneficiary of the gospel?	Individuals	The Church(es)	The Kingdom

The British School of Gospel Interpretation

In the late nineteenth and early twentieth centuries, Martin Dibelius presented what became a seminal formulation of the apostolic message of the gospel, or the *kērygma*. Though he was German and not British, he is credited with the genesis of the so-called, "quest for the historical kerygma."[48] He asserted that throughout Acts, which contained narratives of the apostolic preaching of Jesus,

> there is a . . . well-planned outline whose sections are frequently repeated and only accidently change their order. Thus we have the right to speak of the scheme which the author consciously accepts and which consists of the following: Kerygma or message, scriptural proof, exhortation to repentance. The Kerygma, i.e. the preaching of Jesus Christ, was contained in a few short sentences. What was important was proved out of the Old Testament. Then followed the exhortation to repentance and conversion. . . . [I do] not wish to reveal the variety but the oneness of the Christian preaching.[49]

Although Dibelius observed and suggested a threefold kerygmatic formula—kērygma, scriptural proof, and exhortation to repentance—his proposition neither focused on particular characteristics of Jesus's life nor identified a specific doctrinal content of the gospel.

Instead, Dibelius ascertained that primitive, apostolic preaching concentrated on the message that Jesus had brought salvation rather than an explanation concerning how he brought about salvation. He wrote, "All the observations and conclusions which we can put forward, in fact, prove

---

[48] Harry (Hal) Poe coined this phrase and made this claim about Dibelius in *The Gospel and Its Meaning*, 33.

[49] Martin Dibelius, *From Tradition to Gospel*, trans. Bertram Lee Woolf, Foundations in New Testament Criticism (1971; repr., Cambridge, UK: James Clarke/Lutterworth, 2022), 17.

that the primitive Christian missionaries did not relate the life of Jesus, but proclaimed the salvation which had come about in Jesus Christ."[50] Elsewhere he explained that early Christian preaching ". . . laid emphasis upon what faith longed to hear and upon what was likely to impress and convert unfaith. . . . For it was the purpose of the early Christian preaching both to witness to the faith and to awaken it in others. . . ."[51]

Dibelius's aversion to fixate on the *kērygma*'s specific, formulaic content patterns preserved in Acts, which included Jesus's life, death, burial, and resurrection, resulted from presuppositions influenced by textual criticism. He asserted, "What appears in the Book of Acts is not the verbatim report of actual sermons. All of the 'addresses' in the Book of Acts are much too short ever to have been 'delivered.' On the contrary they represent compositions by the author of the book in which he set forth what he understood to be the message of the apostles."[52] In other words, Dibelius viewed Acts as Luke's personal reflection on what the apostles preached rather than a faithful historical and summative transcript of what they in fact preached. His propositions attracted the attention of scholars in the early-to-mid twentieth century, who entered the quest to understand the *kerygma*—the primitive, apostolic message preached about Jesus Christ.

C. H. Dodd followed Dibelius in 1936 with the publication of a series of lectures he delivered the year before at King's College in London. His book, *The Apostolic Preaching and Its Developments*, became the watershed book about the *kērygma*. Like Dibelius, he observed an outline of the early church's preaching about Jesus in the New Testament. But unlike Dibelius, Dodd perceived specific, event-oriented content that comprised

---

[50] Dibelius, 15.

[51] Martin Dibelius, *The Message of Jesus Christ: The Tradition of the Early Christian Communities*, trans. Fredrick C. Grant (New York: Charles Scribner's Sons, 1939), 128.

[52] Dibelius, 129.

the apostolic *kērygma* and explained how Jesus brought God's salvation to humankind.

The kerygmatic content that Dodd identified in the New Testament took three forms—primitive, Pauline, and Petrine. He summarized the primitive *kērygma* in Mark 1:14–15 in three parts:

1. The time is fulfilled;
2. The kingdom of God has drawn near; and
3. Repent and believe the gospel.[53]

He proposed that fragments of the Pauline *kērygma* could be discerned in the Epistles, but not as a result of practicing textual criticism or demythologizing. Instead, the *kērygma* took a fragmentary form within the Pauline Epistles because he considered their genre as *didache* (teaching that includes theological exposition and ethical instruction) rather than *kērygma* (preaching about the message of Jesus Christ). He then reconstructed the Pauline *kērygma* out of the Epistles' *didache* and proposed the following outline:

1. The prophecies are fulfilled, and the new Age is inaugurated by the coming of Christ.
2. He was born of the seed of David.
3. He died according to the Scriptures, to deliver us out of the present evil age.
4. He was buried.
5. He rose on the third day according to the Scriptures.
6. He is exalted at the right hand of God, as Son of God and Lord of the quick and the dead.
7. He will come again as Judge and Savior of men.[54]

---

[53] C. H. Dodd, *The Apostolic Preaching and Its Developments* (London: Hodder & Stoughton, 1936; repr., Grand Rapids: Baker, 1980), 24, 48.

[54] Dodd, 17.

Last, Dodd proffered the Petrine *kērygma*, which he referred to as the Jerusalem *kērygma*, from Peter's first four speeches in Acts. From them he advanced a sixfold formula of the *kērygma*:

1. The age of fulfillment has dawned.
2. This has taken place through the ministry, death, and resurrection of Jesus.
3. By virtue of the resurrection, Jesus has been exalted to the right hand of God.
4. The Holy Spirit in the Church is the sign of Christ's present power and glory.
5. The Messianic Age will shortly reach its consummation in the return of Christ.
6. The *kerygma* always closes with an appeal for repentance, the offer of forgiveness and of the Holy Spirit, and the promise of "salvation."[55]

Although he referenced all three of these kerygmatic forms in the New Testament, scholars tend to attribute the Petrine or Jerusalem form of the *kērygma* to Dodd exclusively, with very few acknowledging or mentioning the former two forms.

Other scholars aligned themselves with Dodd in forming an event-oriented formula of the *kērygma*. Among them were Roland Allen, A. M. Hunter, Bo Reicke, James Stewart, and Douglas Webster. With the exception of Reicke, who was Swedish, they all were British scholars and thus comprised the British school of kerygmatic interpretation. Unlike Dibelius, they assumed the historical reliability of Acts and rejected its sermons as being Lucan compositions of the Christian message rather than a faithful summary of what the apostles actually preached. The apostolic sermons not only recounted the life and salvific events of the historical Jesus, but they also included a consistent invitation for hearers to repent of their sins and believe in Christ.

---

[55] Dodd, 21–23.

The German School of Gospel Interpretation

Rudolf Bultmann championed a view of the *kērygma* much different than that of Dodd and those associated with the British school, who emphasized event-oriented, kerygmatic formulae. William Baird said that Dodd understood the gospel as "a formula of facts and doctrines about God's action in Christ," whereas Bultmann viewed it as "God's powerful act in which Christ is dynamically present calling men to a decision of faith."[56] Concerning the German school of kerygmatic interpretation, Baird further explained, "Although Bultmann is the best known and most vocal representative of this school, its position is defended from a theological basis by Gogarten and from a philological approach by Friedrich."[57]

Rudolf Bultmann was trained at Tübingen, the epicenter of German higher criticism. Those in his day who practiced biblical, higher criticism investigated the Bible merely as ancient literature to understand the *Sitz im Leben* (that is, the sociological setting) that led to its writing. By its very nature, higher criticism dismissed the Bible's supernatural events as mythical. Although Bultmann interpreted the Bible though the lenses of higher criticism, he also observed the negative effects that hermeneutic was having on the practice of Christianity within the German churches.

To address this consequence, he called upon his contemporaries to demythologize the historical events of Scripture, including belief in the historic Christ. He believed, "If the truth of the New Testament proclamation is to be preserved, the only way is to demythologize it."[58] By

---

[56] William Baird, "What Is the Kerygma? A Study of 1 Corinthians 15:3–8 and Galatians 1:11–17," *Journal of Biblical Literature* 76 (September 1957): 183.

[57] Baird, 183. Baird referenced Friedrich Gogarten, *Demythologizing and History*, trans. N. H. Smith (New York: SCM Press, 1955) and Gerhard Friedrich, κήρυγμα, κηρύσσω, *Theological Dictionary of the New Testament*, ed., Gerhard Kittel, trans. Geoffrey W. Bromiley (Grand Rapids: Eerdmans, 1965), 3:683–716.

[58] Rudolf Bultmann et al., *Kerygma and Myth: A Theological Debate*, 2d ed., eds. Hans Werner Bartsch and Reginald H. Fuller (New York: Harper & Row, 1961), 10.

replacing the supernatural events of the Bible with existential categorizations, he held that the German churches could preserve their belief in an existential Christ of faith, rather than a historical one as those in the British school affirmed.

Bultmann proposed that "theology must undertake the task of stripping the kerygma from its mythical framework, of 'demythologizing' it."[59] The "mythical framework" to which he referred encompassed the views and setting of the community of faith that compiled biblical material that furthered the element of its faith.[60] In other words, scholars would need to strip the mythological content, such as Jesus the God-man, his miracles, his death for sins, etc., attributed in Acts to the early church's preaching about Jesus and his message. Undertaking this task would allow them to recover the extant fragments of the primitive *kērygma*.

By demythologizing the *kērygma*, Bultmann and advocates within the German school that followed took an opposing position to the British school's interpretation of the *kērygma* as event-oriented outlines. As Hal Poe described of Bultmann's and the German school's position, "The idea of a preexistent divine Being appearing on earth as a man, atoning for sin in a sacrificial death, abolishing death, vanquishing demonic forces through a resurrection, and returning to the right hand of God as Lord and King only to return one day soon to complete redemption and judge the world all smacked [to them] of mythology."[61] Like Dibelius, Bultmann emphasized the significance of Christ as salvation itself to the neglect of specific, historic events by which he brought salvation. He explained, "He who formerly had been the *bearer* of the message was

---

[59] Bultmann et al., 3.

[60] For an extensive synopsis of Bultmann's views concerning demythologizing, see Rudolf Bultmann, *Theology of the New Testament*, vol. 1. trans. Kendrick Grobel (New York: Scribner, 1951), and Carl E. Braaten and Roy A. Harrisville, eds. and trans., *Kerygma and History: A Symposium on the Theology of Rudolf Bultmann* (Nashville: Abingdon, 1962).

[61] Poe, *The Gospel and Its Meaning*, 36.

drawn into it and became its essential *content*."[62] Instead of focusing on the biblical content of preaching Christ, Bultmann and his companions preferred to emphasize the act of preaching Christ.

By preaching the existential Christ of faith rather than the historic Jesus of Nazareth, the German school suggested that communities of faith would existentially enter an eschatological reality that would bring them into direct contact with the risen Christ, himself. Bultmann wrote, "Christ meets us in the preaching as one crucified and risen, He meets us in the word of preaching and nowhere else."[63] He continued, "In the word of preaching and there alone we meet the risen Lord. . . . Like the word itself and the apostle [Paul] who proclaims it, so the Church where the preaching of the word is continued and where the believers or 'saints' (i.e., those who have been transferred to eschatological existence) are gathered is part of the eschatological event [of redemption]."[64]

One other way the German school drew upon Dibelius's early work related to how its proponents viewed the composition and genre of Acts. C. F. Evans, another prominent scholar within the German school, proved to be heavily influenced by Bultmann. When surveying the Acts sermons, he viewed the kerygmatic components in the speeches as merely Luke's own literary device.[65] He arrived at this position due to difficulties he had in reconciling the sermons in Acts with their historic and literary contexts. His proposal found consensus with other adherents within the German school, due to their propensity toward de-emphasizing the historical accuracy and value of the events recorded by Luke in Acts, while accentuating the existential nature of the Christian experience that they believed Luke was recording when he wrote Acts.

---

[62] Bultmann, *Theology of the New Testament*, 1:33.

[63] Bultmann, *Kerygma and Myth: A Theological Debate*, 41.

[64] Bultmann, 43.

[65] See C. F. Evans, "The Kerygma," *The Journal of Theological Studies* 7 (April 1956): 25–41.

The Anglican School of Gospel Interpretation

The Anglican school originated out of the British school, and although the former still shares some similarities with the latter, it has taken on its own form and interpretation of the gospel message. Just as the naming of the British and German schools had to do with traditions rather than nationalities, the Anglican school is not classified as such to indicate an official position of Anglicanism, as the view has gained support outside Anglicanism. Instead, it is named such because this view has largely been introduced and popularized by Anglican scholars—specifically Michael Green, N. T. Wright, and Scot McKnight.

Michael Green disagreed with the seemingly forced, formulaic structure of the *kērygma* proposed by Dodd, while also dissenting against Bultmann's emphasis upon the existential element of preaching at the expense of embracing doctrinal assertions. He concluded, "Both positions tend to soft-pedal the evidence which is inconvenient to them, and William Baird is perhaps right in suggesting that both are right in what they affirm and wrong in what they deny: 'Dodd points to the importance of history for the gospel; Bultmann to the importance of the gospel for faith.'"[66] Green determined that the gospel of the early church was "united in its witness to Jesus, varied in its presentation of his relevance to the varied needs of the listeners, and urgent in the demand for decision."[67] His determination about the gospel resonated with evangelicals in the latter half of the twentieth century; however, most of them still associated him with the British school.[68]

After the Lausanne Conference (1974), John Stott wrote *Christian Mission in the Modern World*. In it he addressed the question: "Is there a

---

[66] Green, *Evangelism in the Early Church*, 61. Green quotes from Baird, "What Is the Kerygma?," 191.

[67] Green, 66.

[68] For example, see Drummond, *The Word of the Cross*, 214 and Bradford, "'Schooling' the Gospel," 81.

New Testament gospel?"[69] Within his answer, he referenced his awareness of the dialogue between the German and British schools: "It is well
known that the last-century Tübingen school based much of their interpretation of the New Testament on a supposed fundamental disagreement
between Peter and Paul, and in more recent days the tendency of some
scholars has been to discover a number of viewpoints all to some degree
at variance with each other."[70] His reliance on Dodd in his explanation of
the gospel aligned him with the British school, unlike Green who avoided
being classified either in it or the German school. But Stott's critique of
evangelicals who espoused Free Grace theology inadvertently anticipated
a central theme that would be championed by the forthcoming Anglican
school—the lordship, or kingship, of Jesus Christ. He wrote:

> So the gospel demands are repentance and faith—and (in public)
> baptism. This leads me to mention a controversy in certain evan-
> gelical circles. Some have so determined to maintain the doc-
> trine of justification by faith alone that they have not been able
> to accommodate themselves to the addition of repentance. They
> distinguish sharply between the acceptance of Jesus as Saviour
> and the surrender to him as Lord, and they even promulgate the
> grotesque notion that to insist on surrender in addition to accep-
> tance is to distort the gospel. Well, I honour their conscientious
> desire to protect the gospel from all perversions. And certainly
> justification is by grace alone in Christ alone through faith alone.
> Further, we must be careful never to define faith in such a way as
> to ascribe it any merit. The whole value of faith lies in its object
> (Jesus Christ), not in itself. Nevertheless, saving faith is not an
> 'acceptance of Jesus Christ as Saviour' within a kind of mystical
> vacuum and without any awareness either of the Christ being
> 'accepted' or of the concrete implications of this acceptance.

---

[69] John Stott, *Christian Mission in the Modern World* (Downers Grove, IL:
IVP, 1977), 41–57.

[70] Stott, 41.

Saving faith is a total, penitent and submissive commitment to Christ, and it would have been inconceivable to the apostles that anybody could believe in Jesus as Saviour without submitting to him as Lord. We have already seen that the one exalted to God's right hand is Jesus the Lord and Saviour. We cannot chop this Jesus into bits and then respond to only one of the bits. The object of saving faith is the whole and undivided person of our Lord and Saviour, Jesus Christ.[71]

Stott's reasoning about saving faith in view of Christ's exaltation to God's right hand would be developed substantially different by Matthew Bates four decades later, as the latter would engage more with the soteriology of Reformed rather than Free Grace evangelicals.

In 2012 N. T. Wright began to observe some of the same features about the gospel in the Pauline Epistles as did Dodd while he researched *The Apostolic Preaching and Its Developments*. Yet they arrived at two different conclusions. As mentioned previously, Dodd identified the *kērygma* and *didache* classifications in the New Testament and determined the Pauline Epistles constituted the latter. For this reason, Dodd deduced, Paul's audience was believers; therefore, he addressed *didache* rather than *kērygma*.

Wright, on the other hand, questioned the extent to which, if any, the gospel that Paul preached, which the Reformers claimed to rediscover during the Reformation, was also preserved in the Gospels. Wright was led to posit this question by considering C. S. Lewis's use of gospel in his *History of English Literature in the Sixteenth Century*:

[C. S. Lewis utilized] "the gospel" in the sense of the message: the good news that, because of Jesus's death alone, your sins can be forgiven, and all you have to do is believe it, rather than trying to impress God with doing "good works." "The gospel" in this sense is what the early Reformers believed they had found in

---

[71] Stott, 53–54.

Paul's letters, particularly Romans and Galatians—and particularly Romans 3 and Galatians 2–3.

Now, you can explain that "gospel" in Paul's terms. You can make it more precise fine-tuning the interpretation of this or that verse or technical term. But the point is that you can do all of that without any reference whatever to "the gospels," to the four books that, along with Acts, precede Paul in the New Testament as we have it. . . . [Evangelicals and movements influenced by the Reformation advance the idea that t]his "gospel" consists, normally, of a precise statement of what Jesus achieved in his saving death ("atonement") and a precise statement of how that achievement could be appropriated by the individual ("justification by faith"). Atonement and justification were assumed to be at the heart of "the gospel." But "the gospels"—Matthew, Mark, Luke, and John—appear to have almost nothing to say about those subjects.[72]

In his quest for an answer, Wright explored Bultmann's work that comprised the German School of kerygmatic interpretation but found it lacking an answer to his question. He explained:

For Bultmann and the generations of scholars and students who have been influenced directly or indirectly by his work, the story of Jesus himself formed no part of "New Testament theology"— it was merely the presupposition for such a thing. All that was needed was the fact of Jesus' crucifixion; that was enough. Everything else one needed to know was contained not in his teaching or public career, but in the early church's reflection on the meaning of the cross.

Bultmann therefore read the gospels not as the story of why Jesus lived, not in order to find "the gospel in the gospels" . . . but

---

[72] N. T. Wright, *How God Became King: The Forgotten Story of the Gospels* (New York: HarperOne, 2012), 6.

in order to observe the early Christians expressing their faith by telling and retelling stories that appear to us to be "Jesus stories," but that were, for the most part, "mythological" expressions of early Christian experience projected back onto the fictive screen of the history of Jesus. Bultmann's whole project of form criticism, at least in the way he practiced it, was predicated on the assumption that if you could discover the "forms," the characteristic shapes of the small anecdotes that make up much of the gospel material, you could thereby observe . . . the early church expressing its own faith. That, it was believed, was why the early gospel traditions were passed on: not to remember or celebrate something that *had* happened in the past (i.e., in Jesus' public career), but to celebrate and sustain the continuing life of faith of the early community.

. . . This particular mood, of supposing that the four gospels were not really "about Jesus," let alone "about the gospel," but, instead, "about the early Christian faith," has largely passed. Many scholars now use material from all four gospels, with appropriate critical controls, as evidence for Jesus himself. But the underlying problem has not been addressed.[73]

He also voiced his dissatisfaction with the response of conservative evangelicals to this question. He implicated them, in some respects, as modified neo-Bultmannians:

Here we meet a telling irony. Bultmann's theology has been met, down through the years, with a stubborn and solid "No" from "conservative" quarters. Many "conservative" Christians, in both Europe and America, have been very concerned to stress the authority of the Bible, and so have been horrified by the insistence of Bultmann and his followers on the non-historicity of the gospels. . . . Such "conservatives," then, have stressed the

---

[73] Wright, 21–22.

historicity of the gospels as part of their insistence that "the Bible is true." But when it comes to interpretation and meaning, those same "conservatives" are regularly to be found on exactly the same page as Bultmann, reading most of the stories in the gospels as signposts towards the cross and the faith of the early church. . . . What I observe is this. Faced with a choice between the [Apostles'] creed (some version of it) and the canon of Scripture, . . . the church has unhesitatingly privileged the creed and let the canon fend for itself—which it hasn't always managed to do very successfully. The same is true when, in Protestantism, the great early creeds are implicitly replaced as the "rule of faith" by the various sixteenth- and seventeenth-century formulas that highlight the Reformers' message of "justification by faith."[74]

This stinging rebuke of conservative Christians—more specifically, evangelicals—by Wright formally established what has now been called the Anglican school.

Two additional features have contributed to Wright's influence in the formation of the Anglican school. First, he has incorporated his own proposals of what has now become known as the "New Perspective on Paul" into his propositions about the gospel. The New Perspective on Paul refers to an attempt by scholars to interpret Paul's letters in general, and his idea of justification in particular, from the first-century context of the assimilation of Jews and Gentiles into the new covenant, rather than the understanding of Pauline justification that arose out of the Reformation and has dominated evangelicals' soteriology, as well as their faith and practice.[75]

---

[74] Wright, 22–24.

[75] The seminal idea for the New Perspective on Paul likely began in W. D. Davies, *Torah in the Messianic Age and/or the Age to Come, Journal of Biblical Literature*, vol. 7 (Philadelphia, Society of Biblical Literature, 1952). Previous to N. T. Wright, this view was popularized by Krister Stendahl, *Paul Among Jews and Gentiles* (1976), E. P. Sanders in *Paul and Palestinian Judaism* (1977), and

Second, he has emphasized the role of metanarrative for understanding the meaning and content of the gospel. At times, the gospel's meaning is expressed in relation to the biblical metanarrative throughout the entire canon of Scripture, while at other times it finds expression within a more immediate genre context. For example, Wright interprets Paul's gospel in the context of the Gospels and Acts. Concerning Paul's gospel as he articulated it in 1 Cor 15:3–6, Wright explains:

> [Paul] quotes what seems to be the standard early Christian summary of the good news. This is worth looking at carefully. . . . For something to qualify as news, there has to be (1) an announcement of an event that has happened; (2) a larger context, a backstory, within which this makes sense; (3) a sudden unveiling of the present moment, sitting between the event that *has* happened and the further event that therefore *will* happen. That is how news works. It is certainly how the early Christian good news worked.[76]

Unlike the German school, Wright valued the role of the historical events in conveying the meaning and message of the gospel. But the value he placed on event-oriented, gospel content extended far beyond just the sermon or the epistle in which the *kērygma* was found (which typified the British school), to include the larger context found within the biblical metanarrative.

Influenced by the writings of N. T. Wright, Scot McKnight categorized a tiered gospel within the canon—the "Story of Israel/the Bible"; the "Story of Jesus"; the "Plan of Salvation"; and the "Method of Persuasion"—in his book *The King Jesus Gospel*. He explained that the

James D. G. Dunn, *The New Perspective on Paul* (2005). A helpful review of the development of this school of study is presented by Mark A. Seifrid in his book, *Justification by Faith: The Origin and Development of a Central Pauline Theme*, in the chapter "Salvation in Christ for All as the Essence of Pauline Soteriology: E. P. Sanders and Current Pauline Research," 46–75.

[76] N. T. Wright, *Simply Good News: Why the Gospel Is News and What Makes It Good* (New York: HarperOne, 2015), 23.

foundation of this tiered gospel "is the Story of Israel, upon which the Story of Jesus makes sense. The Plan of Salvation flows out of this Story of Israel/Story of Jesus and the Method of Persuasion flows out of the Plan of Salvation."[77] According to McKnight, the Story of Israel, or the Bible, refers to the redemptive metanarrative contained in the New and Old Testaments that finds its culmination when God establishes his kingdom on earth.[78] He described the Story of Jesus in terms of his birth, life, teachings, signs, death, burial, resurrection, ascension, and exaltation, all of which consummate the Story of Israel.[79] While noting the association between the two, McKnight sharply distinguished the Plan of Salvation from the gospel, proposing that the former comprises the message and resulting effects of salvation drawn from elements or ideas found within the Story of the Bible.[80] Last, he defined the Method of Persuasion as "the specific biblical elements (like God's love and grace and faith) and the bundling of those elements into a rhetorical shape [the evangelistic method(s) by which the gospel is presented]."[81]

Though not an Anglican himself, Matthew Bates extended N. T. Wright's, and specifically, McKnight's proposals about the gospel message. He argued for understanding of *pistis* as *allegiance* in the context of saving faith and the gospel, a proposal that departs from the word's historic and prevalent meaning—*trust*. He proposed:

> *Pistis*, which has traditionally been translated as "faith" in Paul's Letters, is better understood as allegiance when speaking of how the gospel of Jesus unleashes God's power for salvation. . . . My intention is not to flatten the rich multiple meanings and nuances of *pistis* into a bland singleness. Rather it is to claim that, when

---

[77] Scot McKnight, *The King Jesus Gospel: The Original Good News Revisited* (Grand Rapids: Zondervan, 2011), 35.

[78] See McKnight, 35–36.

[79] See McKnight, 36–37.

[80] See McKnight, 37–41.

[81] McKnight, 41.

discussing salvation in generalized terms, *allegiance* is a better overarching English-language term for what Paul intends with his use of the *pistis* word group than the more customary faith, belief, and trust.[82]

Bates's arguments and conclusions seem to be strongly influenced by C. H. Dodd's Petrine kergymatic formula, in addition to Krister Stendahl's, E. P. Sanders's, James D. G. Dunn's, and especially, N. T. Wright's proposals regarding the "New Perspective on Paul."[83] Bates used an event and doctrine-oriented outline to articulate his understanding of the gospel, another factor that evidences that the Anglican school emerged out of the British school. Specifically, his proposal about the gospel's message and meaning relied heavily on Dodd's Petrine and Pauline outlines of the *kērygma*, which he appeared to modify. In doing so, he reinterpreted these two *kērygma* outlines, shifting the emphasis in them from the Holy Spirit and the inauguration of a realized eschaton, which Dodd proposed, to accentuate Christ's kingship in his present kingdom now and the new creation to come. He initially proposed the following eight tenets of the gospel:

Jesus the king

1. preexisted with the Father;
2. took on human flesh, fulfilling God's promises to David;
3. died for sins in accordance with the Scriptures;
4. was buried;
5. was raised on the third day in accordance with the Scriptures;
6. appeared to many;
7. *is seated at the right hand of God as Lord*; and
8. will come again as judge.[84]

---

[82] Matthew Bates, *Salvation by Allegiance Alone: Rethinking Faith, Works, and the Gospel of Jesus Christ the King* (Grand Rapids: Baker, 2017), 78.

[83] See Bates, 52–53, 112–14.

[84] Bates, 52.

He later revised his gospel framework by expanding its original eight core tenets to ten Christological events:

The gospel is that Jesus the king

1. preexisted as God the Son,
2. was sent by the Father,
3. took on human flesh in fulfillment of God's promises to David,
4. died for our sins in accordance with the Scriptures,
5. was buried,
6. was raised on the third day in accordance with the Scriptures,
7. appeared to many witnesses,
8. *is enthroned at the right hand of God as the ruling Christ,*
9. has sent the Holy Spirit to his people to effect his rule, and
10. will come again as final judge to rule.[85]

He italicized Christ's enthronement event to denote special emphasis, because he observed this theme (1) was repeatedly presented throughout the Scriptures as the climax of the gospel and (2) corresponds to what Jesus is doing now in this epoch of the world's history.[86]

In addition to Dodd's influence on how Bates identified the gospel, Stendahl, Sanders, Dunn, and Wright influenced how he interpreted the gospel in light of the doctrine of justification. While discussing the implications for saving faith by interpreting *pistis* as allegiance, as he proposed, Bates addressed how the doctrine of justification, specifically in terms of the New Perspective on Paul, related to his proposition:

Regardless of whether [the] scholarly reassessment [on salvation in Paul's letters by Stendahl, Sanders, Dunn, and Wright] has

---

[85] Matthew Bates, *Gospel Allegiance* (Grand Rapids: Brazos, 2019), 86–87.
[86] See Bates, *Salvation by Allegiance Alone*, 67–72.

correctly described the real position of the Reformers, medieval
Catholicism, or ancient Judaism . . . it is beyond dispute that
this reassessment has had the salutary effect of forcing all serious interpreters of Paul and the New Testament to step out of
habitual ways of reading these texts and to seek to become re-
acclimated. As we move outside the box to reframe, common
sense (as well as inspection of the texts in question) suggests that
it is unlikely that Paul's main goal would be to outline a program
for his ancient Christian readers regarding how to enter into salvation, since Paul indisputably regards his readers as already having decisively entered. . . .

Thus, when we read about "justification" in Paul, which has
traditionally been regarded as denoting the first step of salvation, the moment at which we enter into "right" relationship
with God through Jesus, we ought to begin with at least a modi-
cum of suspicion that Paul's language about justification might
be more flexible than has been encouraged by the traditional
Reformation-inspired systems.[87]

Therefore, Bates and McKnight have attempted to introduce and translate the New Perspective on Paul, particularly as N. T. Wright has con-
ceptualized it, to evangelicals. Their proposals require that evangelicals
reassess and shift their traditional understandings about and implications
concerning the gospel, evangelism, and saving faith. The reception of
these ideas within evangelicalism has been mixed. Greg Gilbert, Will N.
Timmons, and Carl Bradford have provided some particularly helpful
critiques of their conclusions.[88]

---

[87] Bates, 113–14.

[88] See Gilbert, "A T4G 2020 Sermon: What Is and Isn't the Gospel?," April
15, 2020, https://t4g.org/resources/greg-gilbert/what-is-and-isnt-the-gospel,
Timmons, "A Faith Unlike Abraham's: Mathew Bates on Salvation by Allegiance
Alone," *Journal of the Evangelical Theological Society* 61.3 (2018): 595–615; and
Bradford, "'Schooling' the Gospel."

Conceptual Gospel Philosophies

Along with the previous lexical and hermeneutical considerations, a number of conceptualizations of the gospel have arisen since the nineteenth century. They include the *social gospel, liberation gospel, full gospel, prosperity gospel, moralistic therapeutic gospel,* and *justifying gospel.* Their proponents have advanced these concepts after observing some social and/or spiritual deficiency. These "gospel" concepts have emerged in hopes of either addressing or restoring the disenfranchisement resulting from some circumstance of human plight, be it institutionalized or individualized. Each concept that will be discussed, with the exception of the *justifying gospel* propagated by evangelicals during this same period of time, has employed a reader-response, rather than a classic, historic-grammatical or a missional hermeneutic in using the Bible to substantiate and propagate its "good news." In doing so, they have departed from the common, biblical teaching of salvation and the gospel once for all delivered to the saints.

The Social Gospel

The verbiage of *social gospel* began to be used in the late nineteenth century to describe a philosophy and theology that emphasized benevolence to the whole person (i.e., his body and soul), as well as human society as a whole. Early propositions of the social gospel included Adolf Harnack's and Wilhelm Hermann's *Essays on the Social Gospel* (1907) and Harry F. Ward's *Social Evangelism* (1915). The *social gospel* has been commonly associated with the Baptist pastor and theologian Walter Rauschenbusch.

In differentiating his concept of the social gospel from the gospel concept of evangelicals in his day, Rauschenbusch explained: "[The social gospel's] chief interest is concentrated on those manifestations of sin and redemption which lie beyond the individual soul. If our exposition of the superpersonal agents of sin and of the Kingdom of Evil is true, then evidently a salvation confined to the soul and its personal interests is an imperfect and only partly effective salvation."[89]

He viewed the "soul-saving" gospel preached by his fellow evangelicals and Fundamentalists as a doorway to shallow Christianity, at best, and a tool of spiritual deception, at worst. Rauschenbusch sharply defended his social gospel against the attacks of his critics by stating:

> We . . . begin where the old gospel leaves off. . . . We are not disposed to accept the converted souls whom the individualistic evangelism supplies, without looking them over. Some who have been saved and perhaps reconsecrated a number of times are worth no more to the Kingdom of God than they were before. Some become worse through their revival experiences, more self-righteous, more opinionated, more steeped in unrealities and stupid over against the most important things, more devoted to emotions and unresponsive to real duties. We have the highest authority for the fact that men may grow worse by getting religion. Jesus says the Pharisees compassed sea and land to make a proselyte, and after they had him, he was twofold more a child of hell than his converters. To one whose memories run back twenty or thirty years, to Moody's time, the methods now used by some evangelists seem calculated to produce skin-deep changes. Things have simmered down to signing a card, shaking hands, or being introduced to the evangelist. . . . It is time to overhaul our understanding of the kind of change we hope to produce by personal conversion and regeneration. The social gospel furnishes some tests and standards."[90]

He believed the justifying gospel, as it has been called, that was preached by his contemporaries failed to save its converts completely because it led

---

[89] Walter Rauschenbusch, *A Theology for the Social Gospel* (New York: Macmillan, 1919).

[90] Rauschenbusch, 96–97.

them to remain in a sinful state of selfishness. He offered this rebuke of those who preached and believed it:

> At any rate any religious experience in which our fellow-men have no part or thought, does not seem to be a distinctively Christian experience. If sin is selfishness, salvation must be a change which turns a man from self to God and humanity. His sinfulness consisted in a selfish attitude, in which he was at the centre of the universe, and God and all his fellow-men were means to serve his pleasures, increase his wealth, and set off his egotisms. Complete salvation, therefore, would consist in an attitude of love in which he would freely co-ordinate his life with the life of his fellows in obedience to the loving impulses of the spirit of God, thus taking his part in a divine organism of mutual service.[91]

In other words, the social gospel aimed to produce a kind of salvation that led its converts to be more concerned with contributing to the well-being and flourishing of individuals and society than with the salvific benefits afforded them in the justifying gospel, which Rauschenbusch deemed selfish and egotistical—thus sinful.

The Liberation Gospel

The *liberation gospel* reinterprets the salvation of Jesus Christ in terms of liberating disadvantaged and deprived minorities—whether classified as such on the basis of one's ethnic, economic, gender status, or sexual orientation—from racial discrimination or the effects of colonialism, poverty or the effects of capitalism, and patriarchal domination or gender-identification discrimination. The *liberation gospel* is the salvific message of hope advanced by a theological system known as liberation theology. Jim Wallis defines the adjectival descriptor of this gospel system in the following way: "Liberation is God's intention. Liberation

---

[91] Rauschenbusch, 97–98.

from all the spiritual, structural, and ideological shackles which bind and oppress—is the promise of God's salvation in history."[92] Too many forms of the liberation gospel exist to name all its advocates; however, most scholars would identify Gustavo Gutiérrez and James Cone among its chief proponents.

In addition to Christ's death on the cross, Israel's exodus out of Egypt to possess the Promised Land serves as the epochal, biblical event by which liberation proponents interpret their gospel. Gustavo Gutiérrez explains: "The Exodus is the long march towards the promised land in which Israel can establish a free society free from misery and alienation. Throughout the whole process, the religious event is not set apart. It is placed in the context of the entire narrative, or more precisely, it is its deepest meaning. It is the root of the situation. . . . [I]t is in this event that the dislocation introduced by sin is resolved and justice and injustice, oppression and liberation, are determined."[93]

Rather than concentrating on the conversion from sinner to saint as the justifying gospel does, the liberation gospel centers on the conversion away from oneself to relieve the predicament of one's neighbor—particularly one who has been oppressed, exploited, despised, and dominated. Gutiérrez asserts:

A spirituality of liberation will center on a *conversion* to the neighbor, the oppressed person, the exploited social class, the despised ethnic group, the dominated country. . . . To be converted is to commit oneself to the process of liberation of the poor and oppressed, to commit oneself lucidly, realistically, and concretely. It means to commit oneself not only generously, but

---

[92] Jim Wallis, "Liberation and Conformity," in *Mission Trends No. 4: Liberation Theologies*, ed. Gerald H. Anderson and Thomas F. Stransky (New York: Paulist; and Grand Rapids: Eerdmans, 1979), 51.

[93] Gustavo Gutiérrez, *A Theology of Liberation: History, Politics, and Salvation*, trans. and ed. Caridad Inda and John Eagleson (1973; repr., Maryknoll, NY: Orbis, 1988), 89.

also with an analysis of the situation and a strategy of action. To be converted is to know and experience the fact that, contrary to the laws of physics, we can stand straight, according to the Gospel, only when our center of gravity is outside ourselves.[94]

Black liberation theologian James H. Cone translated the liberation gospel's emphasis on "conversion to the neighbor," as espoused by Gutiérrez in Latin America, into the African American context. Referring to the Reformation champion, Martin Luther, Cone exclaims:

> If Luther's statement, "We are Christ to the neighbor," is to be taken seriously, and, if we can believe the New Testament witness which proclaims Jesus as resurrected and thus active even now, then he must be alive in those very men who are struggling in the midst of misery and humiliation. If the gospel is a gospel of liberation for the oppressed, then Jesus is where the oppressed are and continues to work his work of liberation there. Jesus is not safely confined in the first century. He is our contemporary, proclaiming release to the captives and rebelling against all who silently accept the structures of injustice. If he is not in the ghetto, if he is not where men are living at the brink of existence, but is, rather, in the easy life of the suburbs, then the gospel is a lie. The opposite, however, is the case. Christianity is not alien to Black Power; it is Black Power.[95]

Whereas the justifying gospel has primarily focused on the spiritual liberation that Christ offers humans from the bondage of their sin and rebellion against God, the liberation gospel has stressed liberation from the political, ethnic, economic, and/or intolerant bonds of captivity creating an individual's or group's oppressive, exploited, and discriminated plight.

---

[94] Gutiérrez, 118.

[95] James H. Cone, *Black Theology and Black Power* (New York: Harper & Row, 1969; repr., Maryknoll, NY: Orbis, 2018), 43–44.

The Full Gospel

The phrase *full gospel* embodies two different meanings. First, many evangelicals associate it with the four roles of Christ that A. B. Simpson identified in *The Fourfold Gospel*—Christ Our Savior; Christ Our Sanctifier; Christ Our Healer; and Christ Our Coming Lord.[96] Simpson submits that this fourfold, or full, gospel allows believers to experience the fullness and blessings of the gospel in their lives. Other men who advanced a similar version of the full gospel included R. A. Torrey and Andrew Murray.

Nevertheless, the second meaning of *full gospel* comprises the concept in view for the purposes of this discussion. This particular form of the full gospel developed and was propagated by adherents within the Pentecostal tradition. Donald W. Dayton explains that Pentecostals arrived at their understanding of full gospel due to

> a distinct hermeneutic, a distinctively pentecostal manner of appropriating the Scriptures. In contrast to magisterial [otherwise Reformed] Protestantism, which tends to read the New Testament through Pauline eyes, pentecostalism reads the rest of the New Testament through Lukan eyes, especially using lenses provided by the Book of Acts. . . . But to turn from the Pauline texts to the Lukan ones is to shift from . . . didactic to narrative material. Narrative texts are notoriously difficult to interpret theologically. Pentecostalism reads the accounts of Pentecost in Acts and insists that the general pattern of the early church's reception of the Spirit . . . must be replicated in the life of each individual believer. In making this claim, pentecostalism stands in a long tradition of a "subjectivizing hermeneutic."[97]

---

[96] A. B. Simpson, *The Fourfold Gospel* (Harrisburg, PA: Christian Publications, 1925), table of contents.

[97] Donald W. Dayton, "The Limits of Evangelicalism: The Pentecost Tradition," in *The Variety of American Evangelicalism*, ed. Donald W. Dayton and Robert K. Johnston (Downers Grove, IL: IVP, 1991), 42–43.

H. S. Maltby provides an example of this hermeneutic when he references and articulates his thematic iteration of the full gospel (although he used "whole" instead of "full"):

> During the Reformation God used Martin Luther and others to restore to the world the doctrine of justification by faith. Rom. 5:1. Later on the Lord used the Wesleys and others in the great holiness movement to restore the gospel of sanctification by faith. Acts 26:18. Later still he used various ones to restore the gospel of Divine healing by faith (Jas. 5:14, 15) and the *gospel* of Jesus' second coming. Acts 1:11. Now the Lord is using many witnesses in the great Pentecostal movement to restore the gospel of the baptism with the Holy Ghost and fire (Luke 3:16; Acts 1:5) with signs following. Mark 16:17, 18; Acts 2:4; 10:44–46; 19:6; 1:1–28:31. Thank God, we now have preachers of the whole gospel.[98]

In 1948, eight Pentecostal denominational bodies established a cooperative organization they called the Pentecostal Fellowship of North America (PFNA). The PFNA issued the "Statement of Truth," a series of doctrinal affirmations around which they coalesced. Interestingly, with the exception of one article, their statement duplicated the National Association of Evangelicals' (NAE) "Statement of Faith" issued five years earlier. They amended the NAE's "Statement of Faith," adding the following article that they designated as *Article 5*: "We believe that the full gospel includes holiness of heart and life, healing for the body and baptism in the Holy Spirit with the initial evidence of speaking in other tongues as the Spirit gives utterance."[99]

---

[98] H. S. Maltby, *The Reasonableness of Hell: The New Earth, the Pentecostal Movement, Etc.* (Santa Cruz: n.p., 1913), 82–83.

[99] As of October 18, 1994, the PFNA now operates under the name Pentecostal/Charismatic Churches of North America (PCCNA). The organization has renamed its doctrinal statement as "Statement of Faith," available online at https://pccna.org/about_statement.aspx, and the language in the original

This addendum codified the verbiage, *full gospel*, and articulated the doctrinal themes of salvation of sin, divine healing of the body, and Spirit baptism evidenced by speaking in tongues as comprising the overall conceptual understanding of the full gospel. As such, the full gospel teaches that believers become disciples of Jesus through faith in his death, burial, and resurrection. In order for them to receive the full extent of the gospel's benefits, they must experience the Spirit's baptism in subsequent, separate experiences.

The Prosperity Gospel

The *prosperity gospel* distorts salvation into a self-actualized faith-force that obliges God to bestow personal happiness, health, prosperity, and success upon those who wield his Word in order to fulfill their will and attain their own desires. Instead of approaching their own salvation in terms of the undeserved merit of God's grace, proponents of this false gospel are convinced they deserve everything within God's power. Kenneth Copeland, Robert Tilton, Creflo Dollar, Paula White, and Joel Osteen are predominantly associated with the *prosperity gospel*.

This "gospel" has perverted the biblical gospel in multiple ways, not the least of which is in the way it teaches that God's glory and purposes are ultimately supplanted with one's own. In addition, it distorts the salvific concepts of grace and faith taught in the orthodox gospel. Ken L. Sarles observed that instead of speaking about faith in terms of saving faith, advocates of the prosperity gospel believe that faith is a force. He explained their view in this way: "The 'force' of faith is that it 'forces' God to work! God becomes man's servant, waiting to do his bidding—if he has enough faith. When God acts apart from faith, it is considered an example of His grace. But when the 'force of faith' is exerted, God is *required* to

---

Article 5 has now become Article 6. The original "Statement of Truth" (1948) is reproduced in John Thomas Nicol, *Pentecostalism* (New York: Harper & Row, 1966), 4–5.

work. The basis of a believer's relationship to God is turned upside down. Grace is removed and faith is redefined as a human work."[100]

In his promotion of the prosperity gospel, Kenneth Copeland and his colleagues have used language and phrases of historic, Christian vocabulary and have twisted them to suit their own meaning. One example involves Copeland using "born again" and "accept Jesus as your Savior and make Him the Lord of your life" phrases to access blessings and power rather than to initiate a personal relationship with Christ. He wrote, "To prosper spiritually, you must be born again. When you accept Jesus as your Savior and make Him the Lord of your life, your spirit is reborn and brought into fellowship with the Father, the Almighty God. This then puts you in a position to receive from Him *all* the things promised in His Word."[101]

The prosperity gospel also has surpassed its own reader-response hermeneutic to promote its infamous "name it, claim it" life application. In other words, it teaches its adherents to familiarize themselves with the Bible so they can use it as a charm to receive what they desire, with no regard for the authorial intent and textual context of the Scriptures they claim. Copeland explains:

> Your faith is in direct relation to the level of the Word in you. Get your Word level up so that you can believe spiritually, mentally, physically, financially and socially. Thus you will be in the position to handle any problem that comes your way according to the

---

[100] Ken L. Sarles, "A Theological Evaluation of the Prosperity Gospel," *Bibliotheca Sacra* 143 (October–December 1986): 348. In order to verify the audacity of how the prosperity gospel mischaracterizes and maligns the Christian concepts of grace and faith, Sarles quotes Robert Tilton: "There are times when God just heals someone who doesn't have an ounce of faith. . . . That is called grace. Why does He do it? I don't know. . . . But I can guarantee you this: He always will heal on faith." *God's Laws of Success* (Tulsa: Harrison House, 1983), 71.

[101] Kenneth Copeland, *The Laws of Prosperity* (Fort Worth: Kenneth Copeland Publications, 1974), 10.

Word of God. . . . If you know how to use God's ability to receive healing and never use it to help anyone but yourself, then it won't work for you very long. . . . Spread it around! If you know how to believe God financially, start helping the people around you.[102]

As his quote demonstrates Copeland and his peers have encouraged, in convincing fashion, their followers to proselytize this "gospel" to others in their sphere of influence. If, however, their followers fail to see results, they quickly hedge their teaching either by suggesting a lack of faith on the part of the follower or by creating a dependency on the faith teacher for further assistance.

The Moralistic Therapeutic Gospel

The *moralistic therapeutic gospel* is a concept first coined by sociologist Christian Smith in his book *Soul Searching: The Religious and Spiritual Lives of American Teenagers*. Although he identified this belief system as originating among teenagers in the United States, adherents to the *moralistic therapeutic gospel* extend beyond that age or regional demographic. The moralistic therapeutic gospel seems to have emerged particularly from those within the United States who are familiar with the biblical gospel and orthodox Christianity but have rejected a strict adherence to and association with it. In spite of dismissing it, they subconsciously hold to a modified form of Christian deism.

Smith suggests the following tenants of moralistic therapeutic deism, which form its core beliefs:

1. A God exists who created and orders the world and watches over human life on earth.
2. God wants people to be good, nice, and fair to each other, as taught in the Bible and by most world religions.

---

[102] Copeland, 23–24.

3. The central goal of life is to be happy and to feel good about oneself.

4. God does not need to be particularly involved in one's life except when God is needed to resolve a problem.

5. Good people go to heaven when they die.[103]

As this list demonstrates, the moralistic therapeutic gospel promotes the least invasive and most passive form of all the "gospel" concepts. The plight this "gospel" addresses; however, is ambiguous. At its core, this belief system seeks to address its adherents' fear of impeding death or temporary life disturbances. Instead of serving as a firm foundation of faith for its devotees, the moralistic therapeutic gospel operates more in terms of a safety net of hope whenever they convince themselves they need one.

The Justifying Gospel

Of all the "gospel" concepts discussed, the *justifying gospel* most closely aligns with the biblical gospel. On the whole, it is the message that most evangelicals have shared when they have evangelized. By it, believers have advanced a biblically orthodox message of salvation from the Scriptures, reflecting the New Testament's instruction on the gospel. The justifying gospel explains Christ's death on the cross with a penal substitutionary view of the atonement, whereby he satisfied God's wrath against humanity's sins and has provided forgiveness for each person who repents and believes.

While this expression of the gospel most closely mirrors the biblical understanding, some evangelicals' warranted critiques of the aforementioned "gospels" have solely focused upon the gospel's eternal benefits for individual believers. This singular focus upon unbelievers' absolution from personal guilt and their salvation from eternal punishment in hell

---

[103] Christian Smith, *Soul Searching: The Religious and Spiritual Lives of American Teenagers* (New York: Oxford University, 2005), 162–63.

can, and at times has, inadvertently been reduced to a gospel that peddles "eternal hellfire insurance" at the expense of making disciples. Although Jesus's death, burial, and resurrection readily provide these benefits to those who become his disciples, a sole focus on those benefits truncates the gospel. At best it is concerned with glorification at the expense of justification and sanctification; at worst it devolves into the false moralistic therapeutic gospel. In other words, the justifying gospel can sometimes have a tendency to result in: (1) making momentary decisions instead of making lifelong disciples; (2) conceptualizing a profession of faith merely by the words of a sinner's prayer instead of portraying one's faith-witness in the life, death, burial, and resurrection of Christ through believer's baptism; (3) associating with a "non-corporeal church" instead of belonging to and gathering with a local, New Testament church; and 4) being too heavenly minded to be any earthly good.

What Is the Biblical Gospel?

This chapter has surveyed the lexical meanings, hermeneutical approaches, and conceptual understandings of the gospel. So, what is the good news for the purposes of those who want to share it? While each of the philosophies discussed in the previous section emphasize (and in some cases dangerously overemphasize) benefits of the gospel that address human plight, need, or desire, the justifying gospel most closely represents the salvific message proclaimed throughout the history of Christianity. Unlike the other five "gospel" philosophies, its advocates affirm the sufficiency of Scripture and rely on it to express and explain the gospel's meaning and message, interpreting it in alignment with the authorial intent of those who wrote and recorded the *kērygma*.

The biblical gospel originates from the triune God, is preserved in the Holy Scriptures, and is advanced through the disciple-making of his churches. The Scriptures present and sustain the content of the gospel's message (cf. 1 Cor 15:3–4). The fulfillment of the Scriptures' messianic prophecies confirms the veracity of the gospel's message. And the instruction of the Scriptures provides confident assurance in it (cf. 1 John 5:13). The gospel according to the Scriptures is faithfully summarized by Jesus in Mark 1:14–15 and by Paul in 1 Cor 15:3–4.

A concise summary of the biblical gospel declares that everyone has sinned against God; but God loves everyone and has demonstrated his love by sending his Son, Jesus Christ—who is fully God and fully man— to die on the cross to pay the penalty for their sins. He was buried, and three days later, he was raised to life by the power of the Holy Spirit. He ascended to heaven to rule at his Father's right hand. Therefore, God commands everyone to repent of their sins and place their faith in his Son alone by publicly professing the lordship of Jesus Christ through faith-witnessing baptism. This concise summary of the gospel, also referred to as the justifying gospel, incorporates the three persons of the Godhead but emphasizes Jesus Christ.

An expansive summary of the gospel more fully involves the Trinity. The gospel teaches that God created the universe and everything in it. He made the earth by forming and filling it. The crowning achievement of his creation was man and woman. He positioned them in the garden and instructed them not to eat from the fruit of the tree of the knowledge of good and evil. But Adam and Eve disobeyed God's command and sinned against him. As a result, death came into the world, and their posterity inherited a sin nature. Because every person, in time, willfully sins, all are condemned under the wrath of the one and only, holy God revealed in the Scriptures.

According to the Scriptures, God the Father sent his Son, Jesus Christ, to earth to redeem and bring salvation to men and women. Being obedient to the will of the Father, Jesus fulfilled the necessary requirements of righteousness and died on the cross for the sins of men, women, boys, and girls. In doing so, he absorbed God's wrath against humanity's sin. After being buried for three days, Jesus was physically raised from the dead by the power of the Holy Spirit. After his resurrection, he was seen by many eyewitnesses and then ascended to heaven, where he was exalted to God's right hand.

Communication of the gospel occurs when a believer articulates this message in an understandable manner, and the nonbeliever hears and comprehends the gospel. The Holy Spirit convicts nonbelievers of their sin. They respond through repentance and faith alone. Apart from faith in the lordship of Jesus Christ, no one will be saved. The Holy Spirit baptizes, thus indwells, new disciples and transforms them through regeneration by grace alone, through faith alone, and in Christ alone, as they repent and place their faith in Jesus Christ as Lord. They become justified through Christ's righteousness, which is imputed to them.

Having been regenerated and justified, new disciples experience reconciliation with God, as well as a variety of benefits that accompany salvation, such as forgiveness of sins and membership into the body of Christ. New disciples will profess their faith publically through their believer's baptism, which illustrates their identification with Jesus's death, burial, and resurrection. In doing so, they unite with a local, visible New Testament church. They will continuously be sanctified as they await their glorification, when Christ returns physically to judge the living and the dead.

DISCUSSION AND REFLECTION QUESTIONS

1. In what ways do the words that the Old and New Testaments use to convey the gospel contribute to its message and meaning?

2. With which of the three gospel interpretation schools—the British, the German, or the Anglican—do you most closely agree? What features, characteristics, and/or propositions of that school align with your understanding of the gospel? Do any of their tenets concern you? If so, why?

3. Each of the gospel schools had proponents that expressed difficulty finding events from the life of Jesus—other than his death, burial, and resurrection—in Paul's articulation of the gospel. In fact, some of them would go so far as to argue that Jesus and Paul preached different gospels. In what specific ways do the

primitive, Petrine, and Pauline gospel forms share a common set of content that corroborate a unity in the gospel they preached?

4. Select one of the six conceptual gospel philosophies—*social, liberation, full, prosperity, moralistic therapeutic,* or *justifying*—and identify the need or problem it addresses; explain how the biblical gospel differs from it; and locate verses or passages of Scripture that contradict its teachings.

5. How would you summarize the gospel message that you present when you evangelize?

Part 2

Issues in Evangelism

5

Spiritual Issues in Evangelism

Personal evangelists interface with spiritually related issues, including both external and internal dynamics, in their practice of evangelism. This chapter addresses the spiritual nature of prayer, fear, and confidence and how they operate within the practice and discipline of evangelism. Some of these issues, like prayer and confidence, potentially strengthen evangelistic endeavors, while others, like fear, hinder them.

Prayer and Evangelism

Prayer occupies a dominant role in evangelism. Failure to pray in preparation for evangelism potentially forfeits the blessings of God and invites spiritual vulnerability. While evangelism certainly requires prayer, the role of prayer is multifaceted and includes more people than just those who evangelize.

First, personal evangelists should ask God for the boldness to act, the words to speak, and the Spirit-filling they need for their evangelism. Second, they must also pray for others and assist them in prayer. Believers must intercede for the salvation of unbelievers, but also are commanded to pray that God will mobilize other believers to join in the evangelism work. Last, they should be ready to instruct unbelievers who want to become disciples of Jesus in how to confess that "Jesus is Lord" as initial evidence of their internal repentance. Evangelism incorporates prayer for unbelievers, prayer for believers, and prayer by unbelievers.

Prayer for Unbelievers' Salvation

God has honored, and in many instances has answered, the fervent prayers of believers for the salvation of unbelievers. Concerning his own salvation, L. R. Scarborough recounts, "The human beginning of the influence leading to my salvation was in the prayer of my mother in my behalf when I was an infant. She climbed out of bed, having gone down toward the grave that I might live, and crawled on her knees across the floor to my little cradle when I was three weeks of age, and prayed that God would save me in His good time and call me to preach."[1] In fact, research by Thom Rainer and Steve Parr has revealed in recent decades that regardless of their sizes or locations, Southern Baptist churches who report the highest rates of baptisms attribute their evangelistic effectiveness to praying for the salvation of nonbelievers.[2]

Although historical examples and investigative evidence of God's blessing on believers' prayers for the salvation of the lost can be documented, do any biblical precedents exist concerning praying for the salvation of unbelievers to substantiate these examples and evidences? Yes. The Bible gives examples of Jesus and Paul praying for the unsaved. It

---

[1] L. R. Scarborough, "The Evolution of a Cowboy," in *L. R. Scarborough Collection*, 17, Archives, A. Webb Roberts Library, Southwestern Baptist Theological Seminary, Fort Worth, Texas, n.d, 1.

[2] See Thom Rainer, *Effective Evangelistic Churches* (Nashville: B&H, 1996), 67–71, 76–79; and Steve R. Parr et al., *Georgia's Top Evangelistic Churches: Ten Lessons from the Most Effective Churches* (Duluth: Georgia Baptist Convention, 2008), 10–11, 26, 29.

also instructs believers to pray for the salvation of unbelievers through the writings of Paul.

An Example of Jesus Praying for Unbelievers

Christ prayed for the lost. Isaiah foretells his intercession for unbelievers in one of the Suffering Servant passages. He states, "Therefore I will give him the many as a portion, and he will receive the mighty as spoil, because he willingly submitted to death, and was counted among the rebels; yet he bore the sin of many and interceded for the rebels" (Isa 53:12). Luke, in his account of the death of Jesus, confirmed that he interceded on behalf of those who crucified and reviled him. He writes:

> When they arrived at the place called The Skull, they crucified him there, along with the criminals, one on the right and one on the left. Then Jesus said, "Father, forgive them, because they do not know what they are doing." And they divided his clothes and cast lots. The people stood watching, and even the leaders were scoffing: "He saved others; let him save himself if this is God's Messiah, the Chosen One!" The soldiers also mocked him. They came offering him sour wine and said, "If you are the king of the Jews, save yourself!" (Luke 23:33–37)

As Christ suffered for the sins of the world on the cross, he prayed that the sinners who crucified and reviled him would be forgiven. The Bible does not indicate whether all those for whom he prayed actually received the forgiveness he offered them. Nevertheless, one of the crucified criminals, who at first derided him (Matt 27:44), later entreated the Lord. As a result, he was forgiven of his sins and naturalized a citizen of paradise by the Savior who cared enough to pray for him. In addition, perhaps the Roman centurion (and his battalion, cf. Matt 27:53) who guarded Jesus while he was on the cross declared faith in Jesus by calling him "the Son of God" (Matt 27:53; Mark 15:29) and "a righteous man" (Luke 23:47).

An Example of Paul Praying for Unbelievers

Paul also prayed for the salvation of unbelievers. In one example, he interceded for unbelieving Israel. He wrote to the believers in Rome: "Brothers and sisters, my heart's desire and prayer to God concerning [Israel] is for their salvation" (Rom 10:1). Paul's desire for the salvation of his fellow countrymen led him to pray for their salvation. Although not all Israel was saved during his lifetime, he looked forward in faith to a day when the fullness of the Gentiles' salvation would be accomplished and his prayer for Israel to be saved would be answered (Rom 11:26).

The Instruction of Scripture

Finally, Paul implored believers to pray for the salvation of the lost. In 1 Timothy he commanded believers to pray in various ways for all people, kings, and authorities: "First of all, then, I urge that petitions, prayers, intercessions, and thanksgivings be made for everyone, for kings and all those who are in authority, so that we may lead a tranquil and quiet life in all godliness and dignity. This is good, and it pleases God our Savior, who wants everyone to be saved and to come to the knowledge of the truth" (2:1–4). The apostle explained that the prescribed petitions on behalf of "everyone, . . . kings . . . and all those who are in authority" (1) should be practiced in order to live peaceful, godly, and dignified lives and (2) prove good and pleasing to God, desires that everyone be saved. For these reasons, the supplications, prayers, and intercessions required of believers should include a petition for the salvation of all people.

Consider that most, if not all, of the kings and authorities to whom Paul refers were not only nonbelievers, but they had actively oppressed believers. No wonder Paul appeals to the hope of a day when believers could lead godly and reverent lives in peace, free from the threat of persecution. Such a day was possible if the believers in Paul's day would pray that these tyrannical rulers might hear the gospel and believe, thus bringing an end to their oppressiveness.

In addition, Paul claims that praying for the salvation of all men is pleasing and acceptable to God. As Thomas Lea explains, "The relative clause of v. 4 provides the basis for the assertion in v. 3 that prayer for all people is pleasing to God. The goal of the prayers Paul urged is that all people be saved. Intercession for all people pleases the God who desires all to be saved."[3] God desires to see everyone saved and come to the knowledge of the truth, though not all will do so. Therefore, in order to lead godly and reverent lives in peace and to please God with their supplication, prayers, and intercession, believers are instructed to pray for the salvation of all people, great and small.

In a sermon titled "Mary Magdalene," C. H. Spurgeon, speaking of believers' responsibility to plead for the salvation of the lost, preached, "Until the gate of hell is shut upon a man, we must not cease to pray for him. And if we see him hugging the very doorposts of damnation, we must go to the mercy seat and beseech the arm of grace to pluck him from his dangerous position. While there is life there is hope, and although the soul is almost smothered with despair, we must not despair for it, but rather arouse ourselves to awaken the Almighty arm."[4]

On their own merit, historical examples like that of Scarborough's, sermon exhortations such as Spurgeon's, and evidences like those documented by Rainer and Parr provide believers reasons to pray for the salvation of unbelievers. But the example of Jesus, the acknowledgment of Paul, and the instruction of 1 Tim 2:1–4 also reveal to believers their obligation to pray for the salvation of the lost. In fact, until believers plead with God for people's salvation, they will not plead with people to receive God's salvation (cf. 1 Tim 2:1–7).

When believers pray for a lost person who is subsequently saved, skeptics may attribute it to mere coincidence. When churches pray for

---

[3] Lea and Griffin, Jr. *1, 2 Timothy, Titus*, 89 (see chap. 1, n. 16).

[4] C. H. Spurgeon, "Mary Magdalene," Metropolitan Tabernacle Pulpit, vol. 14, January 26, 1868, https://www.spurgeon.org/resource-library/sermons/mary -magdalene/#flipbook.

the salvation of unbelievers by name, and effective evangelistic growth results, cynics might consider it pragmatism. Yet the most appropriate label for believers' prayers for the lost is "biblical."

Prayer for Believers' Evangelism

As they pray for unbelievers, believers also pray for the evangelistic endeavors of other Christians. *The Harvest* tells the real-life, inspired story of a family on a North Dakota farm.[5] The short film opens with a father and his three young sons surveying wheat fields stretching as far as the eye can see. The father explains to these would-be farmer boys, "By the end of the summer, the wheat will be ripened and the harvest will be ready to reap. When the harvest is ready, we must be ready, or we'll lose the whole crop."

A few weeks later the father dies unexpectedly, leaving the looming harvest behind for his grieving wife and three boys. The oldest son remembers his dad saying they would have to be ready when the harvest was ready or they would lose the entire crop. The burden of responsibility bears down on his shoulders, and he doesn't want to let his father's labors go to waste. He can't lose the crop, but even the best efforts of both his brothers and himself will not be enough to prevent it from happening. Their everyday chores are more than enough work for them. The three boys pray that God would send them help. With every day, the weather gets hotter, causing the wheat to ripen sooner than anyone expected. The day suddenly comes when the wheat is ready to be harvested, but the boys simply are not ready for it.

The oldest son wakes up early in the morning, realizing the urgency of the task—how today is just one day closer to the day they will lose the harvest. After dressing, eating, and beginning his morning chores, he

---

[5] Chuck Klein, executive producer, *The Harvest: A Modern Day Parable That Will Touch Your Heart* (Venture Media, 2011), available from https://vimeo.com/146853439.

hears a growing roar and rumbling in the distance. As he looks, he can hardly believe his eyes. Huge combines, one after another, make their way into the harvest fields. It is as if the whole world has come to harvest the crop! Neighboring farmers begin harvesting the wheat in the big northern field until they finish the one in the south. Side by side they move from field to field, leaving a path of the work they have finished behind them.

As the oldest son watches them unload the golden wheat, he remembered his father and how he prayed for help with the harvest after his death. Then he understands—he wasn't alone. These people had work of their own, but they left their own fields to come and help his family. Together they did what no one could do on their own—they brought in an entire harvest in one day. The boys' prayers had been answered! The harvest was finished, the fields were clean, and the wheat was saved!

Jesus used agricultural language too, including a white, wheat-ripened field to represent spiritual truths on various occasions. When sending out his disciples (Matt 9:37–38; Luke 10:2) and responding to their curiosity when he did not eat the food they had brought him (John 4:34–38), our Lord directed their eyes to a ripened, white harvest of weary people ready to believe in him. Laborers would be necessary to reap the spiritual harvest, so Jesus instructed his followers in Matt 9:37–38 and Luke 10:2 to pray that the Lord of the harvest would send them. In John 4:34–38 he commanded them to reap the spiritually ripened field in which others had labored. In light of these passages, consider the following reflections concerning our Lord's commands and the "field" composed of unbelievers.

The Spiritually Ripened Field Awaits Reaping

Jesus described the "harvest" of unbelievers as both "abundant" (Matt 9:37–38; Luke 10:2) and "ready" (John 4:34–38), indicating it was ripe and awaiting reaping. In other words, Jesus told his disciples that numerous unbelievers stand prepared to believe in him and to repent of their sins. Although disciples who labor in a spiritually ripened field do not possess a guarantee to reap a harvest each time, they can be assured that (1) unbelievers across the globe are prepared to believe in Jesus as Savior and Lord right now, and (2) their labors in the field sometimes prepare the crop for future ripening so that in due time others may be able reap it (cf. John 4:38). The work of the Spirit and the labors of past personal evangelists have resulted in today's spiritually ripened field, and today's evangelistic seed-casting cultivates a spiritually ripened field for the future.

The Spiritually Ripened Field Demands Urgency

Jesus's description of the fields being "ready for harvest" (John 4:35) implies a demand for urgency. Even an agricultural novice understands that no field or crop remains ripened indefinitely. Christ's depiction of a whitened harvest reminds evangelistic harvesters that any conversation or encounter they have with an unbeliever potentially could be that person's last opportunity to respond to the gospel call.

Laborers for the Lord of the harvest must not assume spiritually ripened unbelievers are independently or automatically reaped into the Lord's harvest. Any notion that they obtain faith in Christ unconsciously is foreign to the Scriptures. In fact, immediately after Jesus identified the fields as ready for reaping, numerous Samaritans put their faith in Jesus. John records, "Now many Samaritans from that town believed in him because of what the woman said" (4:39). And many more believed because of what he said (v. 41). Note that the Samaritans' salvation did not occur solely on the basis that they were spiritually ripened. Rather, the overwhelming number of Samaritans who believed did so after hearing the testimony of the Samaritan woman, as well as Jesus's word, not automatically on the basis of their own meritorious receptivity. Therefore, harvest workers need to recognize the urgency of the task before them.

Because of life's brevity, numerous unbelievers have limited time remaining to believe the gospel and repent of their sins. The spiritually ripened field will not be the same tomorrow as it is today. With every new day, evangelistic harvesters will observe certain crops lost forever to death. Therefore, laborers for the Lord of the harvest must possess evangelistic urgency each hour of every day.

The Spiritually Ripened Field Receives Reapers through Prayer

In both Matt 9:37–38 and Luke 10:2, Jesus instructed his disciples to pray to the Lord of the harvest for laborers. In particular, Matthew preceded his account of this instruction by mentioning Jesus's deep compassion for helpless and harassed people. Instead of creating anxiety about the situation among his disciples, he prompted them to pray. He informed them that prayerful harvesters are necessary to reap the plenteous fields.

Our Lord left the work of his evangelistic enterprise neither to coincidence nor to convenience; nor did he promote a strategy of lobbying, begging, or shaming others into enlistment. Entrusting the reaping of spiritually ripened fields neither to chance nor to campaigns, the Lord of the harvest commanded his disciples to pray for the mass deployment of evangelistic laborers.

The Spiritually Ripened Field Requires More Than Prayer

Responsibility for harvesting the spiritually ripened field belongs to the believers of Jesus. As previously mentioned, part of the responsibility believers assume is that of praying for the enlistment of harvest laborers. But earnest intercession to the Lord of the harvest requires more than prayer alone. No one will ever pray for evangelistic laborers without also realizing his or her own urgent, evangelistic responsibility to join the endeavor.

Believers should never question whether a prayer to the Lord of the harvest for evangelistic laborers falls outside the rubric of God's will. Likewise, they never need doubt whether the Lord of the harvest will answer such a prayer. Inevitably, the Holy Spirit prompts us to become answers to our own prayers in this regard. Immediately following Jesus's command that his disciples pray for laborers in both Matt 9:37–38 and Luke 10:2, Jesus sent them directly into the fields.

In a different context perhaps some believers have heard someone remark, "Well, all we can do is pray." Usually someone responds this way when the situation or circumstance appears so overwhelming that they feel powerless to act. If believers pray for evangelistic harvesters to be sent into the spiritually ripened fields, they should expect to testify soon after: "Prayer for laborers to enter the spiritually ripened field has prompted us to do all we can do!"

In his book *Send the Light: Lottie Moon's Letters and Other Writings*, Keith Harper includes a letter Lottie Moon wrote on November 4, 1875, to H. A. Tupper, then-executive secretary of the Foreign Mission Board of the Southern Baptist Convention. In it, she made a plea to Southern Baptists of her day about the spiritually ripened field requiring prayer-prompted harvesters:

> "The harvest is plenteous, the laborers are few." . . . What we find missionaries can do in the way of preaching the gospel even in the immediate neighborhood of this city is but as the thousandth part of a drop in the bucket compared with what should be done. I do not pretend to aver that there is any spiritual interest among the people. They literally "sit in darkness & in the shadow of death." The burden of our words to them is the folly and sin of idol worship. We are but doing pioneer work, but breaking up the soil in which we believe others shall sow a bountiful crop. But, as in the natural soil, four or five laborers cannot possibly cultivate a radius of twenty miles, so cannot we, a mission of five people, do more than make a beginning of what should be done. . . . But is there no way to arouse the churches on this subject? We missionaries find it in our hearts to say to them in all humility, "Now then we are ambassadors for Christ; as though God did beseech you by us, we pray you, in Christ's stead," to remember the heathen. We implore you to send us help. Let not these heathen sink

down into eternal death without one opportunity to hear that blessed Gospel which is to you the source of all joy & comfort.[6]

Lottie Moon's words are as true today as the day she wrote them more than one hundred years ago. Though she is dead, she still speaks. Shall we who remain be stirred to enter the global mission field? Shall we who remain sow gospel seed where she and others have broken the soil? Shall we who remain reap the spiritually ripened crop? The Lord of the Harvest awaits our urgent prayers for laborers, and he awaits our exigent, evangelistic labors.

Prayer by Unbelievers as a Response to the Gospel

In his book *The Invitation*, Richard Osmer reflects on several test cases of modern, evangelistic practice. He identified the use of a sinner's prayer in the first test case he referenced. He explains:

> This is a prayer offered by individuals to confess their sins to God and accept the forgiveness offered through the death of Jesus Christ. It represents the first step of a personal relationship with God through Christ. Some believe the sinner's prayer emerged out the [*sic*] widespread use of the mourner's seat and altar call in revivalism. These were popularized by Charles Finney, Dwight Moody, and Billy Sunday. It was not until the 1950s, however, that the sinner's prayer was placed in a standard form in the writings of Bill Bright and Billy Graham.[7]

The use of a sinner's prayer, or to use biblical language—"to call upon the name of the Lord," has been criticized of late.[8] These criticisms generally

---

[6] Lottie Moon, "The H. A. Tupper Letters, November 4, 1875," in *Send the Light: Lottie Moon's Letters and Other Writings*, ed. Keith Harper (Atlanta: Mercer University, 2002), 17.

[7] Osmer, *The Invitation*, 28 (see preface, n. 2).

[8] A few prominent examples of this criticism include William Abraham, *The Logic of Evangelism* (Grand Rapids: Eerdmans, 1989), 141; David P. Gushee,

center around the historicity or the effectiveness of using a sinner's prayer in evangelism. Some, like those whom Osmer references, have believed the historically inaccurate myth that a sinner's prayer originated in the nineteenth century by evangelicals like Finney, Moody, and Sunday. Yet Malcolm Yarnell discovered William Tyndale's "Here foloweth a treates of the pater noster," a prayer that was published in 1526. He has identified this prayer as the first evangelical sinner's prayer published in the English language. Yarnell states, "It is a sinner's prayer with responses from God which displays both conviction of sin under the Law and faith in the Gospel as the means of salvation."[9] Yarnell has traced the prayer to Martin Luther's writings and has demonstrated Luther's influence on Tyndale's sinner's prayer. He explains:

> Tyndale included a prayer intended to lead a sinner into a personal relationship with the almighty God. . . . The preface to the prayer is entirely Tyndale's construction, although it shows a theological dependence on Luther. . . . Luther's *Eine kurze Form* discussed the three things a person must know to be saved: the law (encapsulated in the Ten Commandments), the Gospel (contained in the Apostles' Creed), and prayer (as in the Lord's Prayer). Prayer is likened to a sick person seeking health.[10]

Thom Johnston has extended Yarnell's research by translating Tyndale's sinner's prayer alongside the 1519 French translation of Luther's adaptation of the Lord's Prayer, where he supplied reactive dialogue with the

---

"Jesus and the Sinner's Prayer: What Jesus Says Doesn't Match What We Usually Say," *Christianity Today* (March 2007): 72; and David Platt, *Follow Me* (Carol Stream, IL: Tyndale, 2013), 5–7, 187–91.

[9] Malcolm B. Yarnell III, "The First Evangelical Sinner's Prayer Published in English: William Tyndale's "Here foloweth a treates of the pater noster," *Southwestern Journal of Theology* 47:1 (Fall 2004): 30.

[10] Yarnell, 35.

prayer from selected Old Testament passages.[11] In light of these findings, criticizing the use of a sinner's prayer to assist unbelievers to confess the lordship of Christ based on its being a nineteenth-century innovation is historically inaccurate.

William Abraham also criticized the sinner's prayer out of concern that many people may have uttered the prayer without an authentic conversion:

> Much of modern evangelism . . . is satisfied with half-hearted and very limited initiation into the richness of the reign of God. It is satisfied if the person evangelized . . . has "invited Jesus into his heart," or has "said the sinner's prayer," . . . and the like. Those who have gone through this process will be fortunate if they have laid hold of the real meaning of justification by faith. . . . And they will be very fortunate indeed if they have been linked in an appropriate fashion with a local body of believers in either baptism or confirmation.[12]

Unfortunately, the ratio of how many people have prayed a sinner's prayer to those who have experienced a genuine conversion generally affirms Abraham's critique. Anyone who spends time evangelizing will testify that more people have merely repeated or prayed a sinner's prayer than those who have been genuinely regenerated. Nevertheless, does this phenomenon necessitate jettisoning the use of a sinner's prayer from the practice of evangelism?

Wayne Grudem offers a more charitable assessment:

> What shall we say about the common practice of asking people to pray to receive Christ as their personal Savior and Lord? Since

---

[11] See Thomas Johnston, "Comparing Luther's *Enflamed Dialogue* with Tyndale's *Prayer of the Sinner*," *Midwestern Journal of Theology* 13.2 (2014): 69–79.

[12] Abraham, *The Logic of Evangelism*, 141.

personal faith in Christ must involve an actual decision of the will, it is often very helpful to express that decision in spoken words, and this could very naturally take the form of a prayer to Christ in which we tell him of our sorrow for sin, our commitment to forsake it, and our decision actually to put our trust in him. Such a spoken prayer does not in itself save us, but the attitude of the heart it represents does constitute true conversion, and the decision to speak that prayer can often be the point at which a person truly comes to faith in Christ.[13]

A majority of evangelicals who called on the name of the Lord by using a sinner's prayer would affirm Grudem's assessment of this kind of prayer. The overwhelming New Testament emphases on "calling on the name of the Lord," "confessing, 'Jesus is Lord,'" as well as Christ's disciples suffering persecution for the glory of Christ's name, behooves personal evangelists to retain the use of a sinner's prayer in evangelism, albeit adjusting it to factor in the ways it has resulted in false conversions.

The Scriptures connect both "calling on the name of the Lord" and "confessing, 'Jesus is Lord'" (cf. Joel 2:32; Matt 7:21–22; Acts 2:21; 22:14–16; Rom 10:9–11, 12–13; 1 Cor 1:2; 12:3b; Phil 2:11) with unbelievers' responses to receive the gospel's benefits. So, personal evangelists should instruct unbelievers to confess him verbally as Lord as a part of their response to the gospel. Yet they should not overemphasize the use of a verbal confession of Christ as Lord to the point that it replaces the twofold response to the gospel—repentance and faith.

As discussed previously in the biblical motivations for evangelism, the glory of Christ's name is the preeminent motivation in evangelism. Acts 5:41 recounts the persecution of the apostles for preaching Jesus as the Messiah. This theme of suffering on behalf of Christ and his name is also located in Matt 5:11–12; John 15:20–21; and 1 Pet 4:14–19.

---

[13] Wayne Grudem, *Bible Doctrine: Essential Teachings of the Christian Faith* (Grand Rapids: Zondervan, 1999), 312.

Concerning the relationship between evangelism and the name of Christ, Stott reasons, "We should be 'jealous' (as Scripture sometimes puts it) for the honour of his name—troubled when it remains unknown, hurt when it is ignored, indignant when it is blasphemed, and all the time anxious and determined that it shall be given the honour and glory which are due it."[14] Using Phil 2:9–11, he explained, "For God had 'exalted him to the highest place' and had given him 'the name that is above every name,' in order that 'at the name of Jesus every knee should bow . . . and every tongue confess that Jesus Christ is Lord.' If, therefore, God desires every knee to bow to Jesus and every tongue to confess him, so should we."[15] If believers should evangelize unbelievers "for his name," should they not also call for unbelievers to confess his name as Lord verbally?

Those who have prayed a sinner's prayer for any reason other than as an expression of their repentance and faith have not been regenerated. The vast majority of those who have prayed this kind of prayer without exercising repentance and faith have likely done so by placing their faith in the prayer itself, treating it as some kind of charm or incantation. Therefore, they have displaced faith in Christ as a necessary way to receive Christ.

Personal evangelists, who do not believe that salvation is merited on the basis of a sinner praying a scripted prayer, may find it more helpful to lead unbelievers to become Christ's disciples by guiding them in a sinner's prayer rather than having them repeat one. Using a guide to prompt unbelievers to respond to God in prayer will afford personal evangelists the opportunity to hear what the unbeliever has understood from the gospel presentation and determine if what they say to God is consistent with repentance and faith.

The following two evangelistic encounters demonstrate the benefits of instructing would-be disciples of Jesus to call on the name of the Lord by using prayer prompts as opposed to repeating a script. On the

---

[14] Stott, *Romans*, 53 (see chap. 3, n. 27).

[15] Stott, 53.

first encounter, I had taken an evangelism team from Southwestern to an apartment complex to evangelize. At one of the apartments, we met a lady named Pam. After introducing ourselves we shared the gospel with her, inviting her to receive Christ. She indicated to us that receiving Christ was not only a decision she needed to make, but it was one that she wanted to make. I explained to her, "Pam, if you have changed your mind about your sins to think about them as God thinks about them, and if you believe that Jesus's death, burial, and resurrection is the only thing that can save you, I'd like to invite you to bow your head and close your eyes and have your first conversation with God." She obliged. I continued, "Pam, will you tell God in your own words why you have stopped what you were doing to have this conversation with him?" She began, "Dear Lord, I have sinned against you and I am not happy with my life." I then instructed her, "Pam, will you let God know in your own words what you understand from our conversation is the only way you can be forgiven of your sins?" She continued, "God, I just want to be a better person. I want to please you and I want to make the right choices in life."

Realizing she had not understood the gospel, I stopped providing her any further prayer prompts. I then prayed, asking God to give me the ability to explain the gospel more clearly, as well as have the Holy Spirit help her understand the gospel and how Christ's work, not her own, can forgive her of her sins. We continued the conversation and upon understanding more about the gospel, she declined to receive Christ. Had she repeated a script I had given her, I would not have been able to discern that she was not ready to become a new disciple of Jesus.

Concerning the second encounter, the Christian band For King & Country was performing at Southwestern Seminary's MacGorman Chapel and Performing Arts Center in 2015. About two-thirds through the concert, they presented the gospel and directed those who wanted to discuss what they had heard to designated prayer rooms where seminary students and faculty were stationed to provide decision counseling.

Brenda and her friend Emily exited the auditorium and found my wife and me. They shared with us that they had traveled several hours from the Houston area to attend the concert of their favorite band. I asked Brenda, "If you came to see For King & Country, then why have you left the concert to come and talk with Hope and me?" She replied, "I want to know more about the Jesus they were talking about and how he can change my life." Hope and I then shared the gospel and asked both of them whether or not they wanted receive God's forgiveness in Jesus. They both enthusiastically said, "Yes!"

Hope prayed with Emily, and I invited Brenda to bow her head and have her first conversation with God. After bowing her head, I instructed her, "Brenda, would you tell God in your own words why you left the concert you came to see to take this time to pray to him right now?" Fighting tears she responded, "God, you know about all the things I am caught up in." She then began to confess a list of all her sins to God and then paused. I said, "Now, Brenda, will you tell God in your own words what can forgive all those sins and make you a new person?" Through her tears she told God, "God, the only thing that can make me right with you is your Son, Jesus, who died, was buried, and raised." I then asked her, based on the scriptural imperative, to confess the lordship of Jesus. She calmly told God, "Jesus is Lord." Finally, I instructed her to thank God in her own words for what he had just done for her and in her. Immediately, her tears of sorrow turned to joy and she began to exclaim, "Dear God, I feel like I can fly. You have taken the burden and guilt of all my sins off of me. Thank you, God!" After she finished thanking God, I closed in a prayer for her to profess her faith through believer's baptism. Using a sinner's prayer prompt enabled me to hear Brenda's comprehension of the gospel in her own words and determine, to the best of my finite knowledge, that she was placing her faith in Christ alone and becoming his disciple. I subsequently directed her to a Baptist church near her home, where one of my students served on its ministry staff. I was confident he would assist her in the next steps of her discipling.

Fear and Evangelism

Personal evangelists also face the spiritual, and sometimes emotional, effects of fear when they share the gospel. No personal evangelist is immune from experiencing some measure of fear. In fact every personal evangelist's scariest witnessing conversation will likely be the first one each day. But after doing it, subsequent evangelism conversations become less frightful and much easier to begin. Although believers face multiple fears in their practice of evangelism, some of the most common ones include fear of the unknown, fear for safety, fear of rejection, fear of failure, fear of repeating past evangelistic experiences that were negative, fear of manipulation, and fear of fanaticism. What causes these evangelistic fears and how can they be overcome?

Fear of the Unknown

Fear of the unknown impedes believers' evangelism because they are reticent to engage in unfamiliar experiences. Some believers do not evangelize because they do not know what to expect if they were to share the gospel with others. Perhaps they are unsure about who is inside the houses they visit. Maybe they are uncertain about the reactions they will receive from those sitting nearby at the local coffee shop or from unbelieving friends. Regarding the fear of the unknown, every believer has a choice—either allow the unknown to remain mysterious by not evangelizing or make known the unknown by evangelizing. Believers will never know what will or will not happen in a particular witnessing situation if they do not clearly and completely testify to others about the saving power of Jesus Christ's death, burial, and resurrection and call for a commitment. Of all the possible responses believers who share the glorious gospel of Jesus Christ can get, more than likely, their hearers will either want to hear more or politely decline the conversation.

Fear for Safety

Fear for safety hinders some believers from evangelizing due to their desire for self-preservation. In an environment where reports of persecution of Christians for preaching the gospel around the globe have become more and more normative, some believers naturally fear for their own safety. Such scenarios should come as no surprise to believers who follow a Savior who was despised and rejected by men to the point of death. In fact, when Jesus warned his followers of the dangers they would endure for his name's sake, he did not excuse them from evangelizing for the sake of safety. Rather, he charged them "that the gospel be preached to all nations" despite the threats of arrest, betrayal, and persecution (cf. Mark 13:9–13).

Although danger is not out of the realm of possibility, most believers in America need not fear for their safety while sharing the gospel in their own communities. Of course, all believers should exercise wisdom when witnessing (i.e., not trespassing on property with clearly marked "No Trespassing" signage; not arguing with someone who disagrees with gospel premises, etc.). In fact, those who evangelize on a consistent basis generally experience few, if any, dangerous encounters when evangelizing.

Fear of Rejection

The fear of rejection prevents believers from evangelizing by shifting attention away from Jesus to themselves. Generally speaking, most people want to be accepted by others. Some believers do not evangelize for fear that those with whom they share the gospel will reject them when they call for decisions. Those who battle the fear of rejection should remind themselves of Jesus's words: "But whoever denies me before others, I will also deny him before my Father in heaven" (Matt 10:33). When evangelizing, believers must first convey the message that only Jesus Christ can reconcile men and women to God through his death, burial, and resurrection, and then call their listeners to a commitment of believing in Jesus alone for salvation and repenting of their sins. After the gospel is clearly communicated, any rejection on the part of the evangelized is much more serious than whether or not the personal evangelist has been rejected. Any denial to the clearly communicated message of the gospel is a repudiation of Jesus Christ himself.

Believers must anticipate rejection and resistance to some extent when they evangelize. A gospel presentation that is rejection-proof every time, or even the majority of times, does not exist. When personal evangelists' presentations of the gospel are not accepted, they must resist the temptation to take the rejection personally, even though the love of Christ for unbelievers makes their hearts ache. Rico Tice explains, "The Bible tells us to answer those who attack us. But most books I've read on evangelism don't tell you that. There's always this suggestion that if you do evangelism in a certain way, or if you learn to be charming or funny or interesting as you share the gospel, you can avoid getting hit. I want to be honest: if you tell non-Christians about Jesus, it will be painful."[16]

Throughout the Scriptures unbelievers rejected either God's message or his messengers (e.g., 1 Kgs 19:10, 14; Ps 41:5–8; Jer 2:4–27a; 18:12; 32:28–32, 34–35; Ezek 2:3–7; 3:4–9; Luke 11:47–51, 53–54; John 13:26–27; Acts 13:50–51; 18:6; 20:22–23; 22:22–23). In some instances when unbelievers showed contempt for God, they were characterized either metaphorically or physically as lifting their heels against him (e.g., Ps 41:9; John 13:18) or turning their backs to God (cf. Jer 2:27b; 7:24; 32:33). On other occasions, however, unbelievers' rejection of God or his messengers elicited dramatic forms of public

---

[16] Rico Tice with Carl Laferton, *Honest Evangelism: How to Talk about Jesus Even When It's Tough* (Purcellville, VA: Good Book, 2015), 18.

repudiation.[17] Some included God turning his back on them (Jer 18:17), Jesus instructing his disciples to shake the dust off their feet against them (cf. Matt 10:14; Luke 9:5; 10:10–11), Paul and Barnabas shaking the dust off their feet against them (Acts 13:51), and Paul shaking his garments within the Corinthian synagogue (Acts 18:6b). Believers will never "shake the dust off their feet," in terms of their witness for Christ, if they do not take the gospel to people who sometimes, if not many times, reject it.

Fear of Failure

The fear of failure obstructs believers from sharing the gospel because of a faulty understanding of success. Many believers accept the false premise that evangelism is successful only if someone makes a profession of faith in Jesus Christ for salvation. This misunderstanding, if accepted by believers, can prove devastating to the consistency of their evangelism. Believers will not see someone come to Christ each time they share the gospel, but they will never see anyone come to Christ if they do not ever share the gospel. Only after they present the gospel and call unbelievers to repent and believe can they know with any certainty (1) if, or how, the Holy Spirit might be working in the unbelievers' hearts and minds, and (2) how the unbelievers might actually respond (i.e., receive, reject, delay, etc.) to the gospel's appeal.

While no one will deny that a profession of faith brings great joy, encouragement, and affirmation to a personal evangelist, these results must never be equated with success. If the decisions of those who are evangelized rested solely on the abilities of believers to convince them, then perhaps professions of faith, or the lack thereof, could be categorized

---

[17] For further discussion about these public displays in response to unbelievers' rejection, see Craig S. Keener, *Acts: An Exegetical Commentary: 3:1–14:28*, vol. 2 (Grand Rapids: Baker, 2015), 2105–6.

in terms of success or failure. But the decisions of those who are evangelized rest with them and the work of the Holy Spirit. John Stott stated,
"To 'evangelize' in biblical usage does not mean to win converts (as it
usually does when we use the word) but simply to announce the good
news, irrespective of the results."[18]

Therefore, in terms of evangelism, believers' successes, as well as their
failures, are measured by their obedience or disobedience to the Great
Commission of Jesus Christ. In other words, the only failure in evangelism is a failure to evangelize. Likewise, success in evangelism is measured
in terms of believers' obedience in practicing it, not in terms of someone
else's acceptance of or rejection to their sharing the gospel (cf. Ezek 3:19;
33:9; Acts 18:5–6; 20:25–27). In correcting the Corinthians, who aligned
themselves with those personal evangelists whom they viewed as most
successful, Paul explained, "Neither the one who plants nor the one who
waters is anything, but only God who gives the growth" (1 Cor 3:7).
Therefore, personal evangelists should rejoice that they are part of the
evangelistic process, no matter what role they play in it, while giving all
the glory to God for those whom he saves.

Fear of Past Negative Evangelistic Experiences

*The dread of past negative evangelistic experiences results in a fear that para-
lyzes some believers in their evangelism.* Some believes do not evangelize
because they fear repeating previous negative evangelism experiences.
Whether because of their own mistakes, such as forgetting a Scripture
reference, or because of unwanted reactions by others, these negative experiences can easily sideline formerly eager witnesses. Even the memories of
negative circumstances, such as seeing no one come to the door on church
visitation night, can evoke fear of their next opportunity to evangelize.
Although many believers tend to let these negative experiences push

---

[18] John Stott, "The Biblical Basis of Evangelism," in *Let the Earth Hear His
Voice*, ed. J. D. Douglas (Minneapolis: World Wide, 1975), 69.

them into evangelistic paralysis, they should instead evaluate and learn from them to emerge stronger and more prepared for the next encounter.

Fear of Manipulating

A fear of emulating perceived manipulation in others' evangelism fosters a desire to overcorrect by not evangelizing at all. While some believers let their own negative experiences paralyze them, others focus on the perceived manipulation others have practiced to excuse themselves from evangelizing. They cite examples of manipulative attempts at evangelism and overcorrect by not evangelizing at all. In reality, however, manipulation is a matter of the heart much more than it is a matter of practice. By guarding their own hearts, these believers can minimize their risk of manipulating others, who desperately need to hear the gospel proclaimed to them personally.

Fear of Fanaticism

Fear of perceived fanaticism promotes an aversion to evangelize within believers. Other potential evangelists fail to share the gospel because they do not want their hearers to call them "fanatics." In truth, obedient believers almost always face ridicule for acting on their love for Christ, but they should remember that this ridicule generally stems from misunderstanding, jealousy, or guilt. With their eyes on Christ, they must echo the apostles' determination to obey God rather than man (cf. Acts 4:19–20). Concern about the opinions of others will fade in the light of Christ's approval.

An Absence of the Fear of God

An absence of the fear of God strips believers of a healthy motivation to evangelize the lost. To this point in the discussion, believers have been encouraged to shun fear as an obstacle to evangelism. Yet all believers must embrace the fear of God, especially in terms of their witness for Christ. Randy Newman offers a helpful reminder when it comes to the fear of

God, as opposed to the other fears related to evangelism discussed previously: "I've heard some people offer 'the fear of the Lord' as the solution to 'the fear of man.' But . . . replacing one fear with another still leaves us in fear. It also fails to grasp the significant differences between the two kinds of fear. The fear of man paralyzes. The fear of God transforms."[19] The apostle Paul wrote, "Therefore, since we know the fear of the Lord, we try to persuade people. . . . Therefore, we are ambassadors for Christ, since God is making his appeal through us. We plead on Christ's behalf, 'Be reconciled to God'" (2 Cor 5:11, 20). David Garland explains this context's meaning of *fear* refers to "a religious consciousness, a reverential awe of God, that directs the way one lives."[20] Believers consistently living devoid of the fear of God, at best, will end in forfeiture of heavenly rewards and, at worst, will generate apathy toward the lost.

Aware of the day he would appear before the *bēma* (judgment) seat of Christ (2 Cor 5:10), Paul sought to persuade, implore, and plead with others to be reconciled to God by proclaiming the gospel of Jesus Christ. Believers must fear God because they, like Paul, will one day stand before the *bēma* seat of our Lord and give account for what they have and have not done during their lives, which includes the extent of their faithfulness in evangelism. Christ's judgment at the *bēma* seat will result either in receiving or in forfeiting heavenly, eternal rewards.

Much more urgent than what heavenly rewards believers will or will not receive is God's impending wrath and judgment upon unbelievers. While believers will appear before the *bēma* seat of Christ, unbelievers will appear before the great white throne to be judged and condemned (Rev 20:11–15). Those who appear at this judgment will be punished eternally in hell because they have neglected to respond in faith and repentance to Jesus Christ. Believers must embrace the fear of God and

---

[19] Randy Newman, *Unlikely Converts: Improbable Stories of Faith and What They Teach Us about Evangelism* (Grand Rapids: Kregel, 2019), 130–31.

[20] David Garland, *2 Corinthians*, New American Commentary, vol. 29 (Nashville: B&H, 2014), 269–70.

evangelize to avoid an uncompassionate apathy for the final state of the lost. If they would become more familiar with the fear of the Lord than their fear of people, they would proclaim the gospel to men, women, boys, and girls in such a way as to persuade them to repent and believe.

The Holy Spirit and Overcoming Evangelistic Fears

All believers at some time or another face one or more of these fear-related obstacles to evangelism. The two primary and greatest catalysts for overcoming them in one's personal practice of evangelism include the empowering filling of the Holy Spirit and the convincing power of God's Word. Two examples of these fear-expelling catalysts were demonstrated when the Holy Spirit filled Peter and John before the Sanhedrin (Acts 4:1–22), and when the convicting power of Christ's words enabled Paul to overcome his fear to evangelize in Corinth (Acts 18:1–11).

Evangelistic Confidence through the Filling of the Holy Spirit (Acts 4:1-22)

Instead of seeking after the lost, many believers spend time searching for the confidence to evangelize. They tell themselves, "If only I had more confidence, I would share the gospel with my friends and acquaintances that I know need Christ." Imagine how much confidence they believe they would need to share Christ with someone who is hostile to the gospel.

Have you ever been in need of evangelistic confidence? Every believer, at some time or another, has needed courage to share their faith. One way they have been emboldened has been to enroll in evangelism training. This can provide willing personal evangelists confidence by teaching them a gospel script they can memorize, giving them the words to say when they share the good news of salvation.

While evangelism training provides believers with confidence to know what to say when they witness, it does not necessarily give them the courage to begin evangelistic conversations. How then do they find confidence to share the gospel with those who are open to hear it as well those who are hostile against it? Consider the boldness of Peter and John as recorded in Acts 4:13–20.

Having healed a lame man in the name of Jesus (Acts 3:1–10), Peter and John were preaching the resurrection from the dead through Jesus in Jerusalem (3:11–26; 4:1–2). The priests, the captain of the temple guard, and the Sadducees took offense and arrested them (4:1–3). Nevertheless, five thousand of those who heard their message believed in Jesus (4:4).

The next day, the apostles were put on trial (4:5–7) and asked by their accusers, "By what power or in what name have you done this" (4:7)? With complete confidence and filled with the Holy Spirit, Peter responded that they had done this in the name of Jesus Christ the Nazarene (4:8–12). Then, in Acts 4:13–20, Luke recorded:

> When they observed the boldness of Peter and John and realized that they were uneducated and untrained men, they were amazed and recognized that they had been with Jesus. And since they saw the man who had been healed standing with them, they had nothing to say in opposition. After they ordered them to leave the Sanhedrin, they conferred among themselves, saying, "What should we do with these men? For an obvious sign has been done through them, clear to everyone living in Jerusalem, and we cannot deny it. But so that this does not spread any further among the people, let's threaten them against speaking to anyone in this name again." So they called for them and ordered them not to speak or teach at all in the name of Jesus. Peter and John answered them, "Whether it's right in the sight of God for us to listen to you rather than to God, you decide; for we are unable to stop speaking about what we have seen and heard."

Notice that the members of the Sanhedrin were amazed as they observed Peter's and John's confidence despite being both uneducated and untrained men. They attributed the apostles' boldness to the fact that they had been with Jesus. The courage they exhibited undoubtedly resulted from the time they had spent with Jesus during his earthly ministry. In describing them, Trueblood wrote, "Once they had been broken and defeated men, but soon afterward they exhibited a courage and confidence which lasted, not merely for the moment, but for the remainder of their lives. They were immovable in spite of persecution and every external discouragement."[21] In addition to the years they spent with Jesus, their confidence was also attributed to his Holy Spirit filling them (Acts 4:8).

Evangelistic confidence is not attained merely by what believers know (such as a memorized, evangelistic script); it is attained by whom they know (Jesus Christ). Many believers today have received more evangelism training than those in the early church did. How then did early believers know what to say when they evangelized? What was the secret of their evangelistic confidence? They were with Jesus (4:13). They remembered what they had seen (4:20). They recalled what they had heard (4:20). Those seeking evangelistic confidence will find it whenever they spend time with Jesus. Those who do this cannot help but tell others about Jesus. In addition, those with whom believers share Jesus can tell whether they have spent time with Jesus (4:13).

Evangelistic Confidence through the Convincing Power of God's Word (Acts 18:1-11)

Doubtless, all believers at some time or another face some fear evangelizing others. Before his arrival to Corinth, Paul's preaching of the gospel was met with persecution and expulsion from Pisidian Antioch (Acts 13:50), mistreatment and the threat of stoning in Iconium (Acts 14:5), stoning almost to the point of death in Lystra (Acts 14:19), flogging and imprisonment in Philippi (Acts 16:22–23), and ridicule in Athens (Acts 17:32). No wonder Paul's first written correspondence to the Corinthians states that he came to them "in weakness, in fear, and in much trembling"

---

[21] Elton Trueblood, *The Validity of the Christian Mission* (New York: Harper & Row, 1972), 64.

(1 Cor 2:3). To a greater extent than any of us, the apostle experienced his own fears in evangelism. Paul encountered the first of two specific evangelistic fears upon arriving at Corinth—*isolation*. Paul came to Corinth alone (Acts 18:1). While in Macedonia, Thessalonican Jews who opposed the gospel began a riot in Berea, forcing Paul to leave immediately by sea for Athens. His abrupt departure temporarily separated him from his close companions, Silas and Timothy (Acts 17:13–14), until he was able to send word for them to come to him as soon as possible (Acts 17:15). Though fearfully alone and isolated in Corinth, Paul nevertheless testified about Christ every Sabbath in the synagogue (Acts 18:4). After Silas and Timothy arrived from Macedonia to Corinth (Acts 18:5a) with a gift from the Philippian church (2 Cor 11:8–9; Phil 4:15–16), Paul devoted himself to preaching the word daily (Acts 18:5).

Paul also experienced the fear of *rejection*. The Corinthian Jews opposed, reviled, and resisted Paul's preaching that Jesus was the Messiah (18:5–6). Rejected once again by his own people, Paul turned to preach the gospel to the Gentile Corinthians (18:6–8).

Despite the belief and baptism of numerous Corinthians, as well as the leader of the synagogue and his family (18:8), Paul feared preaching the gospel any further. He seriously considered the possibility of becoming a muted evangelist. In fact, his fear became so overwhelming that the Lord himself appeared to him in a night vision. The Lord commanded him, "Don't be afraid, but keep on speaking and don't be silent" (18:9). On what basis was Paul to continue preaching? He was to keep preaching because Jesus was with him! Jesus assured him, "I am with you, and no one will lay a hand on you to hurt you, because I have many people in this city" (18:10).

When Christians feel alone either because no one evangelizes with them or when unbelievers reject their attempts to persuade them, they should remember the comforting words of the Lord to Paul, "I am with you" (18:10). The presence of Jesus will help believers to overcome their fear of evangelizing. Because he is always with them, they should not "be afraid, but keep on speaking and [not] be silent" (18:9).

DISCUSSION AND REFLECTION QUESTIONS

1. Complete this exercise to identify someone for whom you can begin praying about salvation and with whom you can intentionally share the gospel.

   a. Identify five of your closest relationships for each category.

MY FAMILY

○ _____

○ _____

○ _____

○ _____

○ _____

PEOPLE WHO LIVE IN MY COMMUNITY/
NEIGHBORHOOD

○ _____

○ _____

○ _____

○ _____

○ _____

PEOPLE WITH WHOM I WORK OR GO TO SCHOOL

◯ _____

◯ _____

◯ _____

◯ _____

◯ _____

MY EXTENDED FRIENDS/ACQUAINTANCES

◯ _____

◯ _____

◯ _____

◯ _____

◯ _____

b. In the circle preceding each name, place the symbol that best describes how you would classify their relationship to Christ.

  ?

BELIEVER   UNBELIEVER   UNSURE

    c. Circle one of the people you marked as **X** or **?** and pray that the Holy Spirit prepares this person to hear the gospel and receive it. Also pray that he prepares you to share the gospel intentionally.

2. Who are three believers for whom you can specifically pray that God will lead them to begin sharing the gospel consistently? In what ways can you encourage them to begin evangelizing without embarrassing or pressuring them?

3. What do you see as the strengths and the weaknesses of using a sinner's prayer to lead people to call upon the name of the Lord for their salvation, in keeping with repentance and belief? Do you intend to use a sinner's prayer in some form when you make new disciples? If so, how do you plan to avoid the problems mentioned in this chapter? If not, how will you lead people to call upon the name of the Lord for their salvation?

4. As you read the Bible for conviction and pray for the Spirit's empowerment to evangelize, identify which of the fear-related obstacles threaten your evangelistic faithfulness and applying the suggestions to address them.

6

Philosophical and Practical Issues in Evangelism

A lady once criticized the evangelism methods nineteenth-century pastor Dwight L. Moody used to win people to saving faith in the Lord Jesus Christ. Moody replied, "I agree with you. I don't like the way I do it either. Tell me, how do you do it?" Moody's critic answered, "I do not do it." Moody quipped, "Then I like my way of doing it better than your way of not doing it."[1] Like Moody, I would rather be a criticized personal evangelist than a non-evangelistic critic. Sometimes another's critique of our evangelism is biblically warranted. At other times critical comments about our evangelism discourage us because constant criticism begets cankerous complacency. Perhaps the evangelistic enterprise would be served best if, before believers critique and question the evangelistic practices of someone else, we sternly look ourselves in the mirror and say, "I question your evangelism!"

---

[1] Nancy Corbett Cole, *Tapestry of Life: Devotions for the Unique Woman* (Tulsa: Honor Books, 1992), 30.

What questions can believers ask themselves to assess their evangelistic practices? This chapter will include some questions that personal
evangelists can use to evaluate their evangelism methods biblically, theologically, and practically. Honest responses to these will help them discern whether others' critiques of their evangelism are warranted and what
aspects of their evangelism fail to meet the biblical ideal and are in need
of recalibration.

(1) Do the Scriptures teach the gospel you communicate?

The gospel originates within the Scriptures. Personal evangelists should
assess their evangelistic practices by ensuring that the gospel they advance
conforms to the specific content and soteriological nature of the gospel
taught and observed in the Bible. In relation to biblical and theological convictions regarding salvation, the gospel, and evangelism, David
M. Gustafson suggested, "[In considering] gospel proclamation and
seek[ing] to formulate its practice, we [should] develop means and methods that are informed by the Scriptures and theological understanding,
and shaped by various forms of disciplines of human inquiry that lead to
sound evangelistic practices."[2]

Mark McCloskey encouraged personal evangelists to ask themselves,
"Is my approach to evangelism grounded in theological convictions
regarding salvation, the gospel, and evangelism? Is it grounded in the cer-
tainties of God's plan to redeem a lost creation, the lostness of man, and
responsibilities of our ambassadorship?"[3] Personal evangelists' theological
convictions concerning salvation inevitably contribute to the gospel content they present to unbelievers. Therefore, personal evangelists' biblical

---

[2] David M. Gustafson, *Gospel Witness: Evangelism in Word & Deed* (Grand
Rapids: Eerdmans, 2019), 11.

[3] Mark McCloskey, *Tell It Often—Tell It Well: Making the Most of Witnessing
Opportunities* (San Bernardino: Here's Life, 1986; repr., Nashville: Thomas
Nelson, 1995), 185.

and theological convictions, as well as the message they proclaim, must be tested continually by biblical doctrine, instruction, and principles.

Chapter 4 surveyed several misconceptions about the gospel and its message. These included the *social gospel*, the *liberation gospel*, the *full gospel*, the *prosperity gospel*, and the *moralistic therapeutic gospel*. Erroneous soteriological conclusions about the gospel also exist. For example, chapter 1 discussed exclusivism, inclusivism, and pluralism—beliefs about the gospel that address whether the salvation claims that Jesus made (e.g., John 14:6) and those made about Jesus (e.g., Acts 4:12) in the New Testament are restrictive or not. Yet even within these seemingly distinct soteriological categories, some people who claim to affirm *exclusivism*—the view that "Christianity offers the only valid means for salvation"—reject *restrictivism*—the view that "access to salvation is not universal but is restricted to those who hear the gospel from a human agent before death."[4] For example, John Sanders explained, "Both Karl Barth and Carl F. H. Henry are exclusivists regarding the relationship between Christianity and other religions, but they disagree strongly when it comes to the destiny of the unevangelised. Henry is a restrictivist, while Barth hoped for universal salvation."[5]

As in the case of Barth and Henry, the soteriological "labels" people wear do not always match the theological assumptions they make about the gospel, so personal evangelists should study the gospel presentations in the New Testament. John the Baptist, Jesus, Peter, Stephen, and Paul are good examples of those whose gospel proclamations should be studied. The goal is for personal evangelists to compare the level of consistency between their own message of salvation and the concept of salvation in these biblical presentations. The extent to which their gospel

---

[4] John Sanders distinguishes *exclusivism* from what he calls *restrictivism*. He defines *exclusivism* in *What About Those Who Have Never Heard: Three Views on the Destiny of the Unevangelized* (Downers Grove, IL: IVP, 1995), 12. He defines *restrictivism* in "Evangelical Responses to Salvation Outside the Church," *Christian Scholar's Review* 24 no. 1 (September 1994): 46.

[5] Sanders, 13.

presentations conform to salvation as taught by Jesus, the prophets, the apostles, and deacons in the Bible says more about their biblical and theological convictions regarding salvation than the "labels" they wear or ascribe to others.

(2) Does your practice of evangelism resemble the practices of first-century churches?[6]

Our Lord initially gave the Great Commission to the apostles, who then passed it down to all believers who would follow them (Matt 28:16–20; *Mark 16:15*; Luke 24:46–48; John 20:21; Acts 1:8).[7] The apostles refer to Christ's command to make disciples several times in their defense before magistrates, during their proclamations of the gospel, and within their correspondences with churches and believers (cf. Acts 4:19; 5:29, 32; 10:42; Rom 16:25–27; 1 Cor 9:16–17; Titus 1:3). For this reason, believers interested in assessing their evangelism should consider the philosophy, practice, and pattern of the primitive, apostolic churches. To assist them in this dimension, McCloskey posed some supplemental questions: "Has my philosophy and practice of evangelism been modeled by the first-century church? Have the theological realities that drove the first-century church to proclaim the gospel with boldness and sensitivity caused me to develop similar patterns for communicating my faith?"[8] Because the New Testament serves as the authoritative and foundational source for evangelism, the philosophies, practices, and patterns found within it should inform the reasons for and ways in which believers evangelize.

Believers in first-century churches used an evangelistic philosophy that sought to evangelize as many as possible as quickly as possible as

---

[6] McCloskey, *Tell It Often—Tell It Well*, 185–86.

[7] Emphasis added to indicate that the earliest manuscripts of Mark generally end around verse 8. Verses 9–20, where Mark 16:15 resides, is usually identified as the longer ending of Mark.

[8] McCloskey, *Tell It Often—Tell It Well*, 185–86.

clearly as possible. Though they used other evangelistic methods, Luke recorded numerous times in which the apostles (e.g., Acts 2:12–41; 3:11–26; 4:5–12; 5:19–21), deacons (e.g., Acts 6:8–7:60; 8:4–6, 12, 40), and disciples (e.g., Acts 2:5–11) of the Jerusalem church evangelized the greatest number of people by preaching the gospel publicly. The first Christians knew what is still true today—that the only way that personal evangelists can have absolute certainty that the unbelievers they encounter will ever hear the gospel is if they, themselves, share the gospel with them. For this reason, they and those who follow them are under obligation, without excuse, to share the gospel of Jesus Christ with everyone everywhere.

Additionally, members of the first church also evangelized as quickly as possible. The New Testament indicates at least two reasons for the urgency. First, in order that the gospel of Jesus Christ "not spread any further among the people," the elders, rulers, and scribes charged Peter and John not to speak or teach in the name of Jesus (Acts 4:17–20). Nevertheless, Peter and John claimed that they could not help but speak of what they had seen and heard. Second, upon being brought back before the Jewish Council a second time for evangelizing in the temple, the high priest questioned why Peter and John continued to fill Jerusalem with their teaching (Acts 5:27–29). They responded that they must obey God and not men. Obedience to Christ's commission necessitated the practice of urgent evangelism by the first Christians.

In the contemporary era personal evangelists encounter two philosophies related to the *duration* of their evangelistic witness for Christ: an *incremental* philosophy—evangelism should take place over a period of time, and an *immediate* philosophy—evangelism should be done at specific points in time. McCloskey referred to the first philosophy of evangelistic duration as the *relational-incarnational* model and defined it as the practice of "sharing Christ in the context of interpersonal relationships . . . [that is, a] warm, ongoing personal relationship where the messenger's life, demonstrating the power of the gospel, has been witnessed."[9]

---

[9] McCloskey, 154, 156.

He called the second philosophy the *comprehensive-incarnational* model, which he defined as taking the initiative and using all ethically appropriate methods to evangelize as much of the gospel as soon as possible with as many as possible, while exercising sensitivity both to the hearers and to the Holy Spirit.[10]

Tim Beougher used different verbiage for these philosophies, referring to them as the *lifestyle* and *initiative* approaches. Concerning the *lifestyle approach*, Beougher explained, its "advocates argue that the chances that a nonbeliever will come to a true understanding of the gospel with a person with whom they have an established relationship are higher than when a person shares Christ with a stranger."[11] He described the *initiative approach* as the readiness and willingness to witness to anyone, anywhere, at any time.[12]

The Incremental Evangelism Approach

The *incremental evangelism* approach describes the practice of intentional evangelism in the context of ongoing, interpersonal relations, where Christians share the gospel over a period. In McCloskey's and Beougher's concepts of this approach, they emphasize the role of established relationships and evangelistic demonstration. The roles of relationship and demonstration are integrated in this model of evangelism. Because chapter 7 explores the roles of relationship and demonstration as an evangelistic strategy and method, the issue of duration will be considered.

The New Testament provides a few incidents and indications of incremental evangelism. First, Jesus made disciples incrementally in the Gospels. Throughout the Gospels, Jesus spent substantial time making disciples during his ministry. Over a period of three years, Jesus taught the Twelve, as well as those in the crowds, to become his disciples. Some

---

[10] McCloskey, 154, 160.

[11] Beougher, *Invitation to Evangelism*, 171 (see chap. 1, n. 31).

[12] Beougher, 170.

of them, including the eleven apostles and those counted among the 120 present in the upper room (Acts 1:12–15), endured and received the Spirit at Pentecost. Others, like Judas (Matt 26:14–16; Mark 14:10–11; Luke 22:3; John 6:70–71; 13:27) and some of his Jewish disciples (John 6:66; 8:30–59), betrayed, abandoned, or attempted to stone him. But a shift happened after Jesus sent the Holy Spirit to fill his disciples during Pentecost (Acts 2:1–4); the interval of time it took for the believers to present the gospel and for unbelievers to be made disciples by the gospel shortened.

On at least two occasions Paul practiced incremental evangelism. In Acts 17:16–34 Paul shared Christ and his resurrection with those in the marketplace, among whom were the Epicurean and Stoic philosophers. They brought him to Mars Hill (the Areopagus) to share the gospel with them a second time. After Paul called for their repentance and referred once again to Christ's resurrection, some ridiculed him, some believed and joined him, and others said, "We'd like to hear from you again about this" (Acts 17:32), indicating an incremental approach to evangelism.

Acts 24:1–27 recounts Paul's defense before Felix, in which he referred to the Way and his association with it. Several days after Paul had first appeared before him, Felix summoned Paul to return. During their second meeting, Paul preached faith in Christ Jesus, as well as righteousness, self-control, and the judgment to come, to both Felix and his wife Drusilla. Motivated by fear in what Paul said and hoping that Paul would offer him a bribe, Felix sent him away. Nevertheless, Felix "sent for him quite often and conversed with him" (Acts 24:26b), indicating that Paul preached the gospel to him over a period of two years.

Some of the strengths of this approach include that it provides (1) a relational context for new disciples to be baptized and taught obedience to Christ's commands in the church of their disciple-makers; (2) a consistent demonstration to unbelievers of the gospel's effects upon their disciple-makers; (3) an environment where disciple-makers can learn about unbelievers and use those observations to contextualize the gospel for them; and (4) an alleviation of stress on the part of disciple-makers to press for decisions and for unbelievers to feel pressured to make a decision they may not be ready to make.

Some weaknesses also accompany the incremental evangelism approach, such as: (1) the overwhelming examples of evangelism in the New Testament are immediate rather than incremental; (2) too great an interval of time may pass, and unbelievers may die before ever hearing the entire gospel; (3) disciple-makers may struggle with being intentional over perceived fears that the gospel's demands may threaten harmony within existing relationships; and (4) the tendency for disciple-makers to rely on the elements of building trust, relational capital, etc., over the preemptive and proactive work of the Holy Spirit in unbelievers.

The Immediate Evangelism Approach

The *immediate evangelism* approach describes the practice of intentional evangelism by believers to strangers, acquaintances, family, and friends, where they share as much of the gospel as possible in one particular setting or time. The comprehensive-incarnational and initiative philosophies align with immediate evangelism. A couple of theological presuppositions advance this approach. First, it trusts in the power and persuasion of the gospel message itself (cf. Rom 1:16; 1 Cor 1:18). As McCloskey explains, "[the gospel itself] has the inherent ability to win its own hearing, create its own platform of relevance and engage the hearts of the lost toward the end that sinners, convinced of its truth, can be saved."[13] Second, it recognizes that the Holy Spirit precedes presentations of the gospel to prepare unbelievers to hear them (Acts 10:19). Together these theological presuppositions form the following philosophy of immediate evangelism: "Since the gospel message, in conjunction with the convicting work of the Spirit, is sufficient to produce authentic conversions, legitimate and effective communication of the gospel can and often does

---

[13] McCloskey, *Tell It Often—Tell It Well*, 158.

take place in a context lacking demonstration, deed, presence, and generally, the relational element."[14]

Those who shared the gospel in the New Testament did not evangelize unbelievers by building friendships and sharing a little of the gospel over a period of time. Rather, they shared complete presentations of the gospel at specific points in time. In fact, the overwhelming majority of evangelism encounters in the New Testament occur at a particular point in time rather than over a prolonged period of time. Consider the evangelistic encounters of Jesus (in John 3:1–12; 4:1–30), Peter (in Acts 2:14–41; 3:11–26; 10:1–48), Philip (in Acts 8:26–38), and Paul (in Acts 16:6–15, 25–34). Note the prior relationship, if any, believers had with those with whom they shared the gospel, and how much time elapsed between when they met and when they presented the gospel.

In John 3:1–12 Jesus did not wait until he had met with Nicodemus several times before he shared the new birth from above with him. When Jesus encountered the woman at the well in Samaria, as recorded in John 4:1–30, he initiated their introduction to one another by telling her to give him a drink. By doing so, he directed their conversation in such a way that he told her about the living water and worshiping God in Spirit and in truth within the first few minutes of their meeting.

Peter neither took the time nor considered it necessary to meet and intimately know the thousands of people at the temple in Acts 2:14–41 and 3:11–26 before he preached the gospel to them. In Acts 10:1–48 Cornelius wasted no time sending two household servants and a devout soldier to request that Peter—a complete stranger to him—come share the gospel with him after receiving a vision from God to do so (Acts 10:30–33). Having received his own vision from the Lord, Peter obliged. Upon arriving in Caesarea, he immediately presented the gospel to Cornelius, his relatives, and his close friends, who believed and were baptized. Like Peter, God assigned Philip a divine appointment to meet with the Ethiopian official whom he had led to be reading Isaiah (Acts

---

[14] McCloskey, 159.

8:26–38). The Holy Spirit had already prepared the official to be willing to hear and respond to the gospel. As a result, he was waiting on God to send him one of his messengers to guide him in the gospel.

Paul also practiced immediate evangelism. Acts 16 describes two occasions when he practiced it. Verses 6–15 describe how he and his companions evangelized Lydia and her household immediately when they met them by the river. In verses 25–34 the suicidal Philippian jailer wasted no time in asking Paul and Silas what he needed to do to be saved; and Paul and Silas wasted even less time telling him, "Believe in the Lord Jesus, and you will be saved—you and your household" (Acts 16:31).

Immediate evangelism has a number of strengths to merit its practice. First, due to its presuppositions concerning the gospel and the Holy Spirit, biblical and theological conclusions serve as both motivation for and encouragement in this evangelistic practice. Second, immediate evangelism closely follows the duration model of how evangelism was overwhelmingly practiced in the New Testament. Third, this approach promotes an intentional and proactive, rather than a passive and reactive, practice of evangelism. It leads believers to adopt a philosophy that they make the gospel part of all their conversations, even the first ones. Last, due to its urgent nature of sharing the gospel in light of the uncertainty in the timing of unbelievers' deaths, the approach of immediate evangelism exposes more people to the gospel than incremental evangelism does.

Nevertheless, it also has some weaknesses. It can lead practitioners to adopt a legalistic view of evangelism and to incur self-imposed guilt for missing opportunities to share the gospel. Second, immediate evangelism can cause personal evangelists to find difficulty extending the disciple-making process beyond their evangelism to ensure new believers are baptized and taught obedience to Christ's commands. Last, it can promote a "one and done" mentality that leads personal evangelists to stop evangelizing those who, upon first hearing the gospel, do not believe.

The Dual Practice of Incremental and Immediate Evangelism

While most, if not all, personal evangelists will gravitate toward practicing either incremental or immediate evangelism, they should not practice their preferred approach to the exclusion of ever practicing the other. They should practice both incremental and immediate evangelism because the New Testament includes (1) occurrences of either incremental or immediate evangelism; (2) occasions of simultaneous incremental and immediate evangelism; and (3) a commendation for both forms of evangelism.

Refer to the previous descriptions for evidence of the New Testament's inclusion of one or the other. Acts 13:14b, 42, 44; 18:4, 7–8; and 19:8–10 exemplify the simultaneous practice of incremental and immediate evangelism. Each of these instances occurs in places of assembly, particularly synagogues and the hall of Tyrannus. Upon arriving to Pisidian Antioch, Paul preached the entire gospel at a particular point in time within the synagogue (Acts 13:14b). The people urged him to return there the following Sabbath and preach it (Acts 13:42, 44). He obliged, and in doing so, also preached the gospel over a period of time. In like manner, while he was in Corinth, he visited its synagogue every Sabbath (incrementally), each time (immediately), attempting to persuade Jews and Greeks to believe in Jesus the Messiah (Acts 18:4). In fact, when the Jews resisted him to the point that they blasphemed, he left the synagogue, pledging to turn his attention to the Gentiles. Nevertheless, he continued to preach the gospel at Titius Justus's house, within earshot of the Jews in their synagogue, with the result that Crispus, the synagogue leader, and his family believed in the Lord (Acts 18:7–8). One other example of this dual practice includes Paul boldly preaching the gospel for three months (incrementally) in the Ephesian synagogue (Acts 19:8) until he withdrew from it and discussed the gospel daily (immediately) in the lecture hall of Tyrannus (Acts 19:9–10).

Paul also referenced the practice of incremental and immediate forms of evangelism in an evangelistic dialogue at his defense before Agrippa.

Luke recounted, "Agrippa said to Paul, 'In a short time are you persuading me to become a Christian?' And Paul replied, 'I pray to God, whether in a short time or in a long time, not only you but also all those who are listening to me today may become such people as I also am, except for these bonds!'" (Acts 26:28–29 LEB). Bible translations vary on the meaning of *en oligō* (Acts 26:28) and *en oligō kai en megalō* (Acts 26:29). Most formal equivalent translators render verse 28 as "in a short time" (LEB, NASB, ESV) or "so quickly" (NRSV), and verse 29 as "in a short [time] or in a long [time]" (LEB, NASB) or "whether quickly or not" (NRSV). The KJV and NKJV, as well as the optimal equivalent CSB, translate these phrases to mean ease of ability, rather than an interval of time, as in the formal equivalent translations. Craig Keener discusses the reasons undergirding these translation decisions but is himself aligned with those scholars and translators who understand the phrases to convey sudden (Acts 26:28) and gradual (Acts 26:29) intervals of time.[15] Therefore, Paul demonstrated an openness to evangelism over short and long times.

Believers in the first century evangelized as clearly as possible. This involves two dimensions to ensure the clear and consistent communication of the gospel—sharing the message of the gospel as precisely and understandably as possible and exhibiting a lifestyle as consistent with the message of the gospel as possible. When evangelizing, believers should share the gospel in as clear and precise a way as they can so that their hearers can comprehend it, its offer, and its demands. They should use vocabulary their hearers can understand, or at least define unfamiliar terms.

Also, personal evangelists must exhibit lifestyles that are as consistent as possible with the gospel. They will face temptations to adopt worldly, even sinful, standards in order to gain a hearing and become relevant.[16]

---

[15] See Craig S. Keener, *Acts: An Exegetical Commentary: 24:1–28:31*, vol. 4 (Grand Rapids: Baker, 2015), 3545–49.

[16] Though not commenting on this particular temptation, Edward Rommen articulates the danger of yielding to such a temptation when he writes: "We are

Nevertheless, they must be convinced that evangelistic lifestyles incorporate a pattern, or lifestyle, of biblical holiness. As Vance Havner has been attributed with saying, "It is not our business to make the [gospel] message acceptable, but to make it available. We are not to see that they like it, but that they get it." While not every evangelistic approach practiced today can be found in Scripture (for example, internet evangelism), an evangelistic practice consistent with Scripture conforms to its standards of holiness, as those within the first-century church practiced it.

(3) Do your philosophy and practice of evangelism ground themselves in the authoritative command of Jesus found in the Great Commission?

McCloskey suggests believers should not ask themselves "why men are not coming to us, but why we are not going to men."[17] Though many symptoms prevent believers from going to people with the gospel, they all result from disobedience to Jesus's authoritative command in the Great Commission.

William Carey confronted such disobedience in the eighteenth century when he published *An Enquiry into the Obligations of Christians to Use Means for the Conversion of the Heathens*. He described the Great Commission disobedience of believers in his day thus:

> The work has not been taken up, or prosecuted of late years (except by a few individuals) with the zeal and perseverance with which the primitive Christians went about it. It seems as if many thought the commission was sufficiently put in execution by what

---

under great pressure to adapt the [g]ospel to its cultural surroundings. While there is a legitimate concern for contextualization, what most often happens in these cases is an outright capitulation of the [g]ospel to the principles of that culture." *Get Real: On Evangelism in the Late Modern World* (Pasadena: William Carey Library, 2010), 371.

[17] McCloskey, *Tell It Often—Tell It Well*, 191.

the apostles and others have done; that we have enough to do to attend to the salvation of our own countrymen; and that, if God intends the salvation of the heathen, he will some way or the other bring them to the gospel, or the gospel to them. It is thus that multitudes sit at ease, and give themselves no concern about the far greater part of their fellow-sinners, who to this day, are lost in ignorance and idolatry. There seems also to be an opinion existing in the minds of some, that because the apostles were extraordinary officers and have no proper successors, and because many things which were right for them to do would be utterly unwarrantable for us, therefore it may not be immediately binding on us to execute the commission, though it was so upon them.[18]

Nevertheless, he contended that all believers have a duty to obey the Great Commission of our Lord. Otherwise, he argued, why do we continue to baptize in obedience to his command? Why do we honor the obedience of others who have evangelized throughout history? Why, then, do we believe we have available to us the divine promise of his presence?[19]

Personal evangelists should imitate the way in which the apostles and first Christians made disciples through evangelism. Making disciples requires evangelism. The disciple-making process will not ensue apart from believers initiating it by evangelism. Nevertheless, disciple-making does not equal evangelism only—it also requires the subsequent dimension of discipleship.

For years within evangelicalism, the erroneous idea that evangelism aims merely to encourage unbelievers to repeat a scripted prayer has somehow emerged and persisted. Of course, unbelievers who become new disciples of Jesus must call on the Lord and confess Jesus as Lord. Personal evangelists should not view an unbeliever's prayer as a culmination of a

---

[18] Carey, *An Enquiry into the Obligations of Christians to Use Means for the Conversion of the Heathens*, 8 (see chap. 1, n. 5).

[19] Consider the reasons Carey offered in *An Enquiry into the Obligations of Christians*, 8–9.

new disciple's relationship with Christ; but rather as a commencement of it. In other words, the evangelistic philosophy and practice of personal evangelists regarding biblical salvation should not be focused only on unbelievers' regeneration and justification at the expense of their sanctification and future glorification.

A philosophy of evangelism that achieves the biblical standard of Great Commission disciple-making prioritizes the profession of faith through believer's baptism and obedience to Christ's commands just as much as it encourages unbelievers to repent and believe. Chapter 10 discusses evangelism as disciple-making in greater detail and offers a practical way that personal evangelists can share the gospel in a manner that forms the kind of Christian disciples they intend to make. In addition, believers should study the ways that first-century believers moved from evangelism to baptism by studying the passages in Acts that describe this scenario (cf. Acts 2:37–47; 8:4–25; 8:26–40; 9:1–20; 10:1–48; 11:1–18; 16:11–15; 16:25–34; 18:1–11; 22:6–16).

(4) Do your philosophy and practice of evangelism demonstrate urgency, out of a genuine concern for lost souls, considering the reality of heaven and hell?

Concerning the reality of heaven and hell, believers' attitudes toward evangelism can be described in terms of two opposite extremes—either lethargic or urgent. Though most evangelicals identify themselves as believing exclusivists, those who exercise a less-than-urgent kind of evangelism appear as practicing universalists.[20] The author of Hebrews asked, "How will we escape if we neglect such a great salvation?" (Heb 2:3). But how

---

[20] John Mark Terry says, "Professor Roy Fish of Southwestern Baptist Seminary has stated that most Christians are functional universalists. A universalist believes that all people will ultimately be saved. Most believers reject that concept, but they live as if they believe it because they never witness to others." *Church Evangelism: Basic Principles, Diverse Models* (Nashville: B&H, 1997), 11.

can the lost endure if Christians neglect to tell them of such a great salvation? If heaven and hell really exist and one's eternal destiny hangs in the balance, a holy evangelistic urgency must compel every Christ-follower.

Some well-meaning commentators have critiqued urgent evangelism driven by the reality of heaven and hell. Their critiques do not dispute the reality of hell; rather, they argue that urgent evangelism motivated by final states (1) attempts to influence hearers to profess Christ solely out of a fear of hell, or that it (2) minimizes the importance of discipleship. Concerning the first critique, many evangelistic discussions about hell will illicit fear in those who listen—and it should. But as long as personal evangelists are motivated by a sincere concern to convey the entire counsel of God, rather than being manipulative, such a fear in their hearers' hearts is a healthy one. Although the practices of a few modern-day personal evangelists may validate these concerns on occasion, urgent evangelism in light of death, the coming day of the Lord, and God's judgment, as was practiced in the New Testament, neither precludes discipleship nor necessitates the use of fear tactics (e.g., Matt 3:1–12; 7:13–14; 7:21–23; 12:38–42; 13:24–30, 36–44; 21:33–46; 22:1–14; Mark 12:1–12; Luke 3:1–18; 11:29–32; 13:1–5, 22–30; 16:19–31; Acts 2:14–21; 17:22–31; 24:25). As long as personal evangelists ground their evangelism in the authoritative command of Jesus in the Great Commission, they will evangelize in such a way that anticipates the disciples they make will profess their faith through believer's baptism and be taught obedience to all the commands of Christ (Matt 28:19–20).

To the other critique about diminishing the importance of discipleship, Dean Inserra exclaimed at the 2021 National Conference on Preaching, "People have no trouble choosing heaven over hell, but they have a hard time choosing heaven over earth."[21] While accenting the choice between heaven and hell, personal evangelists and churches must expand their practice of evangelism so unbelievers also understand

---

[21] Dean Inserra quoted by Charlie Dates, Twitter post, June 17, 2021, 8:05 p.m., https://twitter.com/CharlieDates/status/1405693140254789634.

the choice between receiving the righteousness from above and retaining the unrighteousness here below. Doing so necessitates that believers and churches evangelize in such a way that their hearers anticipate the demands of discipleship without preaching a "works salvation." Chapter 10 instructs further about how to evangelize with discipleship in view; however, the element of Christ's lordship embedded within the gospel provides an intuitive way for believers to portend discipleship while avoiding a works-based gospel.

Question two of this chapter explored the theme of the duration of time in relation to evangelism. Because this particular question deals with the subject of urgency, we now turn to a discussion about the theme of frequency. Generally, believers' evangelism can be categorized in three different frequencies: sporadic, casual, or intentional.

Sporadic Evangelism

Sporadic evangelism describes the kind of evangelistic frequency in which believers share the gospel intermittently and infrequently. No examples of sporadic evangelism appear in the New Testament. Those believers whose evangelism classifies as sporadic should endeavor, as the New Testament portrays personal evangelists, to become more consistent and more urgent in their practice of evangelism. Usually, sporadic evangelism results from believers either (1) having feelings of indifference toward unbelievers' hopelessness apart from Christ, or (2) routinely finding themselves in environments where they are almost exclusively surrounded by other believers.

L. R. Scarborough warns about the trajectory upon which believers indifferent about the lost would find themselves: "When the soul ceases to yearn for the salvation of men, it cares less and less for the authority of God and the truth revealed in His book."[22] Believers express indifference

---

[22] Lee Scarborough, "The Supreme Passion of the Gospel," in J. C. Massee, *Baptist Doctrines: Addresses Delivered at the North American Pre-Convention Conference* (Des Moines: Union Gospel Printing, 1921), 145.

toward the salvation of the lost for a multitude of reasons. While this indifference generally stems from their lack of a consistent, intimate relationship with Christ, it likely manifests itself in the time they spend indulging in other interests or forms of entertainment. One way that sporadic personal evangelists can gain a greater sensitivity about the frequency of their evangelism is by asking themselves, "What if the person who led me to Christ had evangelized then with the same urgency and frequency with which I witness now?" After pondering the consequences of such a scenario and hopefully being inspired to evangelize more frequently as a result, they can begin to deliberate the ways they can imitate the evangelistic frequency of the person who evangelized them.

Believers who always find themselves with little to no access to unbelievers must realize that this is due to not having an intentional plan to engage the lost. This plan could include scheduling time to engage with them, finding a venue in which to interact, and then evangelizing them. Some believers have found access to unbelievers by using a *third space*, a modification of sociologist Ray Oldenburg's *third place*, for evangelistic purposes. Oldenburg suggested concerning *first, second,* and *third places*: "[A first place] is domestic, a second [place] is gainful or productive, and the third [place] is inclusively sociable, offering both the basis of community and the celebration of it."[23] Translated from his sociological observations for evangelistic purposes, believers' *first space* is their homes, their *second space* is their workplace or school, and their *third space* refers to environments like gyms, coffee shops, barbershops or hair salons, or parks. Locations such as these third spaces become places where they can meet and discuss issues and the gospel with secular unbelievers, along

---

[23] Ray Oldenburg, *The Great Good Place: Cafés, Coffee Shops, Bookstores, Bars, Hair Salons, and Other Hangouts at the Heart of a Community* (Philadelphia: Da Capo, 1999), 14. Despite Oldenburg's inclusion of "Bars" in his book's title, my reference to this book should not be mistaken as an endorsement for using alcoholic beverages to evangelize.

with any unbelievers in their first and second spaces with whom they are more familiar.

Casual Evangelism

Casual evangelism refers to an evangelistic frequency in which believers' urgency to share the gospel is relaxed and nonchalant. Intending to work steadily toward communicating the entire gospel and call for a response, casual personal evangelists gradually share small amounts of the gospel progressively over time. Although they will discuss the gospel more frequently than those who practice sporadic evangelism, they likely do so either (1) because the need to cultivate trust and relational capital exceeds the uncertainty about whether unbelievers will get another chance to hear the gospel before their death, incapacitation, or in the absence of the Holy Spirit's conviction; or (2) because they know they are obligated to evangelize, but they yield to fear or lack the passion to obey. When believers feel comfortable talking about spiritual things or inviting neighbors and friends to church, but do not give a complete or faithful gospel presentation of the gospel, it is not evangelism—it is only conversation. Those who are inclined toward a more casual approach to evangelism must be careful not to substitute evangelistic witness with casual, spiritual conversation.

Casual evangelists should be commended for their consistent work in evangelism, but they should also be cautioned not to lose biblical urgency. They should evaluate the extent of the time they have taken to present the complete gospel, if at all, to those they evangelize. Then they should determine whether or not the frequency they take to share the gospel meets biblical expectations. If so, then they should persistently continue toward making disciples evangelistically. If not, they should devise a more deliberate and direct plan to discuss the gospel in the conversations they have with unbelievers.

Intentional Evangelism

Intentional evangelism describes the evangelistic frequency with which believers consistently and urgently share the gospel with unbelieving family members, friends, acquaintances, and strangers. This frequency does not happen by mere coincidence. Evangelism seldom occurs when believers relegate it to a pastime. Those who fail to plan time to practice obedient evangelism will fail to find time to be obedient in evangelism. Nevertheless, evangelism ensues when believers in Jesus Christ submit themselves to the authoritative command of Jesus and discipline themselves to make disciples. As C. H. Spurgeon says, "A burning heart will soon find for itself a flaming tongue."[24]

This evangelistic frequency has been practiced both in the New Testament and throughout Christian history. Intentional evangelism results from a principle suggested by Scarborough: "Put Christ's value on men and we will long to see them right with God."[25] Intentional personal evangelists should guard against (1) being motivated to evangelize out of love for self over love for unbelieving others, and (2) practicing rushed methods of evangelism.

Intentional evangelism can sometimes motivate personal evangelists to attempt to retain a reputation for the frequency of their evangelism. A thin but discernable line separates this motivation from evangelistic accountability. To identify it, personal evangelists should evaluate the reasons they want others to know about their evangelism and determine whether they are selfish or spiritual. They can also assess whether (1) they use their evangelism as a way to manipulate people into doing things that gives them credit, and (2) they incessantly brag in conversation or on social media about their evangelistic efforts and results.

Practicing intentional evangelism can also lead personal evangelists to rush through their gospel presentations. Whereas casual evangelism

---

[24] C. H. Spurgeon, *Second Series of Lectures to My Students* (London: Passmore and Alabaster, 1877), 148.

[25] Scarborough, *With Christ after the Lost*, 42 (see chap. 2, n. 9).

can sometimes demonstrate a lack of urgency, intentional evangelism can cultivate a type of urgency that shares the gospel so quickly and shallowly that the content and demands of the gospel are lost upon unbelievers. To correct this excessive form of evangelistic frequency, intentional personal evangelists should seek to balance the quantity of their gospel presentations with the quality of their content.

(5) Do your philosophy and practice of evangelism consider the role and work of God, specifically the Holy Spirit?

According to the Bible, personal evangelists and God cooperatively partner with one another. Evangelism that fails to depend upon the Spirit of God has a tendency to become manipulative. On the other hand, the Holy Spirit does not evangelize on his own apart from the evangelistic witness of believers. Rather, he assists believers in their proclamation of the gospel to unbelievers.

The New Testament teaches that God aids believers in their evangelism in at least four ways. First, God is working before the evangelistic witness (e.g., Acts 8:27–28, 30–34; 9:1–9; 10:1–8, 24, 30–33; 11:13–14; 22:6–10; 26:12–18). The concept of pre-evangelism has been commonly taught and advocated as an essential step within the evangelistic process. *Pre-evangelism* generally refers to a human-influenced process where believers earn sufficient levels of trust, relational capital, and goodwill to incline unbelievers to listen to the gospel, leading to repentance and belief. But pre-evangelism, as observed in the New Testament verses provided, refers to the way in which the Holy Spirit preceded believers' witness of the gospel so that unbelievers might repent and believe. Personal evangelists must resist the temptation to convince themselves that they have the ability and responsibility to do what only the Holy Spirit can do to prepare someone with a readiness to hear, understand, and be interested in the gospel. Therefore, they must convince themselves to evangelize rather than pre-evangelize. I have found that my evangelism is much more effective when the Holy Spirit does the pre-evangelizing than when I attempt to do it.

Second, he prompts and directs the evangelistic witness (e.g., Acts 8:27, 29; 9:10–16; 10:9–22, 28–29; 11:4–12; 13:1–4; 16:6–10; 18:9–10). Believers commonly refer to *divine appointments* as occasions where the preeminent Holy Spirit preempts believers' intentional conversations with others about the gospel's claims and its appeal. When they occur, God uses events and circumstances to prompt believers to witness, while preparing unbelievers beforehand to hear and respond to the gospel. Many times when personal evangelists sense they should evangelize someone, they likely question whether God is prompting them or if they have surmised it on their own. When this happens, they should reassure themselves that neither their own flesh nor the devil would ever prompt them to do such a thing; instead, any prompting to share the gospel always comes from God. Yet Christians should not wait until they encounter a divine appointment before they evangelize. God issued the Great Commission to prompt believers to evangelize at all times, even in the absence of what some have traditionally considered a divine appointment.

Third, the Spirit fills and emboldens the personal evangelist (e.g., Acts 2:1–4, 14–18; 4:8–13, 29–31; 7:55; 13:9–12). When the Holy Spirit fills believers, they naturally and consistently share Christ with unbelievers. D. L. Moody explains, "You can tell a man who is filled by the Holy Ghost: he is all the time talking about Christ; he has nothing to say of himself, but is constantly holding Jesus Christ up as an all-sufficient Saviour."[26] Being Spirit-filled witnesses for Jesus Christ is not synonymous with being "super-Christians." Instead, it entails believers walking in the Spirit, being led by the Spirit, exhibiting the fruit of the Spirit, living in the Spirit, and keeping in step with the Spirit (cf. Gal 5:16–18, 22–25). As a result, Spirit-filled witnesses experience nothing more joyous than when they practice Spirit-dependent evangelism.

---

[26] D. L. Moody, *"To All People": Comprising Sermons, Bible Readings, Temperance Addresses, and Prayer-Meeting Talks* (Boston: Globe, 1877), 61.

Fourth, he enables and empowers the evangelistic witness (e.g., Matt 10:17–20; Mark 13:9–11; Luke 12:1–12; 21:12–15; Acts 23:11; 2 Cor 5:20). Often, believers try to muster up their own courage or rehearse the ways they will respond to each objection. Perhaps the reason Christians intend to evangelize but never follow through is because they spend more time attempting to evangelize in their own power, rather than the power of the Spirit. But, by relying on the enablement and empowerment of the Holy Spirit, believers will learn they do not need to muster enough courage to act, premeditate their exact words, or anticipate every question unbelievers may ask in order to evangelize. Instead, he will give them the boldness (cf. Acts 4:8–13, 29–31; 28:30–31) and the words and answers (cf. Matt 10:17–20; Mark 13:9–11; Luke 12:11–12; 21:12–15) they require to share the gospel with unbelievers.

The New Testament also includes eight ways the Holy Spirit operates in unbelievers in the evangelistic process. First, he prepares the minds and hearts of those who will hear the gospel (e.g., Acts 9:1–9; 10:1–8, 24, 30–33; 11:13–14; 16:14; 22:6–11; 26:12–19). Christians must avoid thinking that unless they observe God working in some supernaturally explicit way in the life of an unbeliever that God is not at work. Kenneth L. Chafin says:

> For too long God's people have failed to realize that he is already at work in the lives of the people to whom he sends us. We are not being sent out to a hostile world into which God has not gone. We are invited to *follow* him into his world and bear witness. This means we will never encounter a person whom God does not love. We will find out some we do not love, or that others do not love, or even people who do not love themselves. But we will never meet a person God does not love. This means we will not meet a person who would not be better off if they followed Christ.[27]

---

[27] Kenneth L. Chafin, *The Reluctant Witness* (Nashville: B&H, 1974), 19.

No personal evangelist can know how someone else will respond to the gospel until that person hears it. Sometimes the Spirit works to prepare unbelievers to comprehend the gospel at the same time believers share it with them. In other cases, he will have already worked before unbelievers hear the gospel. In these preemptive cases the unbeliever may be the only one aware of his activity (and in some cases that person doesn't even realize it). At other times believers can recognize his working by the questions the unbelievers are asking, their longings for inner peace, or their cries for help.

Second, the Spirit convicts those who hear the gospel (e.g., John 16:8–11; Acts 2:37; 2 Cor 7:10). He convicts unbelievers in a myriad of ways, including but not limited to, their sin, Christ's righteousness, the coming judgment, and the truth of the gospel. While the Spirit's conviction sometimes manifests as "piercing unbelievers' hearts," it always aims to produce a godly sorrow that leads to repentance.

Third, he regenerates those who repent and believe the gospel (e.g., John 3:1–8; 6:63; 2 Cor 5:17–18; Titus 3:5; 1 Pet 1:22–23). Despite their resolutions, desires, turned-over leaves, and commitments to change, humans do not possess the ability to nullify the nature and effects of their personal sin. Only God can regenerate human beings so that they become new creations in his Son. Regeneration occurs as people repent of their sins, believe in Jesus Christ, and receive him by confessing him as Lord and Savior. At that moment, they experience justification—that is they are both declared and made righteous in God's sight—because Christ's righteousness is imputed to them (e.g., Rom 3:21–22; 5:1–21; 2 Cor 5:21; Gal 2:15–16; 3:10–14; Titus 3:7).

Fourth, the Holy Spirit fills and indwells those who have repented and believed (e.g., Matt 3:11; Mark 1:8; Luke 3:16; John 1:33; Acts 8:17; 10:44–47; 11:15–17; 19:6; Titus 3:6). Along with being regenerated by the Spirit, those who have repented and believed the gospel are also filled by the Holy Spirit and permanently indwelled by him. This initial filling of the Holy Spirit is referred to in the Scriptures as the "baptism of the Holy Spirit" and is synonymous with regeneration (Matt 3:11; Mark 1:8;

Luke 3:16; John 1:33; Acts 1:5; 2:38; 11:16; 19:1–6; 1 Cor 12:13). Yet the Spirit continually fills believers, and Paul commanded in Eph 5:18 that believers be filled with the Spirit. This continual filling enables believers to be submissive to God in the Christian life and to be empowered for service to him.

Fifth, God's Spirit seals those who have repented and believed (e.g., Rom 8:16; 2 Cor 1:21–22; 5:5; Eph 1:13–14; 4:30). Related to his permanent indwelling of believers, the Holy Spirit seals them for salvation and the day of redemption. For this reason, regenerated believers can never lose their salvation. The Spirit's seal also serves as an authentication of a believer's relationship with God to themselves and others.

Sixth, he sanctifies those who have repented and believed the gospel (e.g., Rom 8:13; 15:16; 1 Cor 6:11; 2 Cor 3:18; Gal 5:16–26; 2 Thess 2:13; 1 Pet 1:2). By virtue of sealing believers for the day of redemption, the Holy Spirit continually convicts believers of sins they commit, assists them in overcoming their struggles with sin, and conforms them into the image of Christ. He leads, guides, empowers, convicts, enables, and transforms believers throughout their lifetimes, that they might please God.

Seventh, he gifts those who have repented and believed (e.g., Rom 12:3–8; 1 Cor 12:1–31; Eph 4:7–16; 1 Pet 4:10–11). Every believer receives at least one spiritual gift; however, the Spirit may give them more than one. The gifts he endows upon believers are not to meet their own needs or bring attention to themselves; rather, they are for the common good of the body of Christ. As such, God intends that the interdependent nature of the gifts unifies the body without creating division.

Last, the Holy Spirit will glorify those who have repented and believed the gospel (e.g., 1 Cor 15:50–57; Phil 3:20–21; 1 Thess 4:13–18; 1 John 3:2). At Christ's return, both the dead in Christ and those who are alive will ascend to meet him in the clouds. Instantaneously, the Spirit will transform their mortal bodies into glorified bodies that will live forever. Believers' glorification will consummate their sanctification, whereby their sins will be put to death and they will live holy and pure lives throughout eternity.

(6) Do your philosophy and practice of evangelism incorporate the Scriptures?

This question expands on the first question in the chapter: "Do the Scriptures teach the gospel you communicate?" This first question was concerned with the doctrinal consistency between believers' concept of salvation in the gospel and the Bible's teaching about salvation in the gospel. This new question; however, builds upon it to help believers incorporate the Scriptures in their verbal presentations of the gospel.

The New Testament presents three obvious reasons for incorporating the Scriptures in gospel presentations. First, hearing the Word of Christ is a prerequisite for biblical faith (Rom 10:17). Second, the Scriptures provide verification of the gospel to those who hear it (Acts 17:11). Last, evangelistic proclamations in the New Testament overwhelmingly incorporate the Scriptures (e.g., Luke 24:14–32; Acts 2:14–41; 3:11–26; 4:1–12; 7; 8:4, 35; 13:13–49; 16:25–32; 17:10–13; 18:5, 28; 20:27; 26:22–23; 28:23–27).

Unfortunately, several of today's would-be personal evangelists use general revelation (i.e., creation) more than they do special revelation (i.e., the Bible) in their evangelism. Other personal evangelists often summarize the gospel in their own words or in the words of someone else (if they use a witness training model). Whether they use their own words or the words of others, personal evangelists should ensure that their evangelistic proclamations both incorporate and are structured around the Word of God. They must incorporate Scripture in their gospel presentation, proving consistent with both the text's immediate context and intended meaning. Only through hearing the Scriptures can those whom the Spirit convicts heed them, as a lamp shining in a dark place, until the day dawns and the morning star rises in their hearts (2 Pet 1:19).

Personal evangelists should compose, in written form, the gospel that they present when they evangelize alongside the specific Bible references that teach it. Consider the following example as a template:

1. All humans sin by disobeying and rebelling against God (Rom 3:10, 23).
2. To demonstrate his love for humanity, God sent his Son, Jesus Christ, who was fully God and fully man, to die for their sins, be buried, and be raised from death on the third day (John 3:16; Rom 5:8; 1 Cor 15:3–4).
3. To receive forgiveness for sins and be made right with God, humans must repent of their sins and place their faith in Jesus Christ alone, confessing him as Lord (Acts 3:19; 16:31; Rom 10:9–10).

After identifying verses that teach the gospel propositions they generally share, personal evangelists should either commit one or more of the Scriptures to memory or use a marked New Testament. Two ways they can use a marked New Testament include: (1) marking the verses in their Bible—either by highlighting, underlining, or bracketing—and composing a table of contents in the front with the passages and corresponding page numbers; or (2) typing the verses into a digital note program on their phone to consult when they evangelize. By using Scripture, personal evangelists convey the gospel according to the Bible instead of one of their own making, and they follow the example of Jesus and the apostles, who incorporated Scripture in their gospel presentations.

(7) Do your philosophy and practice of evangelism call for a decision and instruct unbelievers to repent and believe?

Personal evangelists do not evangelize merely to communicate information about Jesus but rather, to call people to faith in Jesus. Edward Rommen states, "Given the personal nature of the [g]ospel, evangelism is essentially the issuing of an invitation to participate in the restoration offered by Christ."[28] He continues, "Talking about conversation instead

---

[28] Rommen, *Get Real*, 183.

of conversion misses the point, since the end result of evangelism is an acceptance of the invitation and a radical transformation of the recipient's life."[29] John Stott also aptly admonishes:

> We must not be afraid to ask for an immediate decision. We shall not press those who are not ready, but neither shall we encourage those who are willfully seeking to escape Christ's challenge. There are just as many dangers in going too slow as there are in going too fast. Procrastination is as subtle an enemy as precipitation. Indeed, I find that there are more warnings in Scripture against the folly of delay than against the dangers of decision.[30]

An evangelistic presentation must include a call for decision for at least two reasons. First, evangelistic presentations recorded in the New Testament include a call for unbelievers to repent of their sins and to believe in Jesus Christ for salvation (e.g., Matt 3:2; 4:17; Mark 1:14–15; Acts 2:38; 3:19; 14:15; 26:20). Unbelievers must have been convicted by the Spirit of God and heard the complete gospel message before they can repent. Repentance refers to the changing of one's mind about God and his one way of salvation through his Son Jesus Christ. It is not as much about changes new believers must make in themselves, but what their surrender will allow the Holy Spirit to change within them. Repentance must not be presented or understood as an exchange for God's forgiveness—a quid pro quo, if you will. David Allen explains spiritual forms of quid pro quo this way: "If you give to get, you're not giving, you're trading."[31] In other words, repentance is not something that God needs from sinners so he can save them—that is Christ's death, burial, and resurrection for our sins; it is something he demands of them in order that they can be saved.

---

[29] Rommen, 183.

[30] John Stott, *Fundamentalism and Evangelism* (London: Crusade, 1958), 39.

[31] David Allen, Twitter post, May 10, 2014, 4:00 p.m., https://twitter.com/DrDavidLAllen/status/465234909620346881.

Whenever repentance and faith are paired together within the New Testament, and in the context of responding to the gospel, repentance always precedes faith. Therefore, no one can believe in the heart without having first repented in the mind. Whereas repentance deals with the mind, faith operates within the heart. Faith is a complete trust that unbelievers' sins can be forgiven, no matter how heinous or how many, only by Jesus's death for sin. By exercising faith in Jesus Christ for salvation, unbelievers not only place it in Christ, but also receive salvation from him.

Second, unbelievers do not know how to respond to the gospel apart from receiving instruction through an evangelistic invitation, even when they are convicted of their sins. At least three times the New Testament included accounts of unbelievers who both heard the gospel presented and were convicted of their sins by the Holy Spirit; however, they did not know how to respond (e.g., Luke 3:7–14; Acts 2:37–39; 16:30–33). In each of these cases, a personal evangelist explained to them how they were to respond to the gospel and the Spirit's conviction.

In the first account, Luke 3:7–14 records John the Baptist imploring the crowds to "produce fruit consistent with repentance" (v. 8). In response to his plea and to the Spirit's conviction by implication, the crowds, tax collectors, and some soldiers indicated their desire to repent, as well as their need to know how to. Luke wrote concerning these groups' responses and John's reply to them:

> "What then should we do?" the crowds were asking him. He replied to them, "The one who has two shirts must share with someone who has none, and the one who has food must do the same."
>
> Tax collectors also came to be baptized, and they asked him, "Teacher, what should we do?" He told them, "Don't collect any more than what you have been authorized."
>
> Some soldiers also questioned him, "What should we do?" He said to them, "Don't take money from anyone by force or false accusation, and be satisfied with your wages." (Luke 3:10–14)

When John told the crowds of people to share, the tax collectors to collect only what was required, and the soldiers to be satisfied with their wages and not steal, he was not preaching works salvation. Rather, he was explaining to them specific kinds of fruit they would produce were they to repent.

On the second occasion, Luke recounted in Acts 2:37–39 how the crowds responded to Peter preaching the gospel during Pentecost. Upon hearing him preach Christ, Luke described that they were "pierced to the heart" (v. 37), indicating that the Holy Spirit was convicting them. Convinced by the Spirit that they needed to respond, yet not knowing exactly how to respond, they asked Peter and the apostles, "Brothers, what should we do?" Peter instructed them to repent and be baptized.

In the third occurrence, Acts 16:30–33 described Paul and Silas's imprisonment in Philippi. A violent earthquake shook the doors open and the chains off of all the prisoners. Believing his captives had escaped and would be punished by death, the jailer decided to kill himself, but Paul stopped him. Apparently under conviction by the Holy Spirit after having heard Paul and Silas's prayers and songs, the jailer asked, "Sirs, what must I do to be saved" (v. 30)? They instructed him to believe in the Lord Jesus.

Unbelievers are called to salvation through both the Spirit's conviction and believers' invitation (i.e., Isa 53:1; Rev 22:17). By answering this call, they must repent of their sins and believe in Christ's death, burial, and resurrection. In doing so, they receive forgiveness for their sins, the imputation of Christ's righteousness, and the indwelling of the Holy Spirit. As these three accounts have demonstrated, personal evangelists should not assume unbelievers understand and comprehend the gospel's and Spirit's appeal when evangelizing. Unbelievers will likely also need their assistance to know how to repent and believe in a tangible way.

The inherent nature of the gospel prompts those who share it to offer an opportunity for their hearers to respond, and it also requires a response from those who hear it. For these reasons, personal evangelists should ask themselves at least three questions. First, "Does my evangelistic proclamation incorporate an invitation to receive Christ, as recorded in the New Testament?" Second, "After I present the gospel to unbelievers, do they understand how they can receive Christ?" Last, "Do I present the gospel in such a way that my hearers realize they have a decision to make? Or do they leave the conversation indifferent and unaware of their responsibility to receive the forgiveness of sins, reconciliation with the Father, eternal life, and the indwelling of the Holy Spirit by repenting of their sins and believing in Christ for salvation?" In the New Testament, those who hear the gospel make a decision, whether positive or negative, regarding what they have heard (e.g., Acts 17:32–33).

Reconciling Divine and Human Agency in Salvation with Evangelism

Gospel invitations in evangelism instinctively correlate with beliefs about soteriology. The doctrines personal evangelists believe concerning the nature and means of salvation have implications on how, or whether, they call unbelievers to salvation. A longstanding soteriological debate concerning evangelistic invitations revolves around God's role in salvation—specifically whom he saves and how he orders the process by which salvation occurs—as well as the extent to which and how unbelievers respond to the call of the gospel.

The most well-known and widely accepted treatise on this debate—*Evangelism and the Sovereignty of God*—was written by J. I. Packer. Due to the complex and seemingly contradictory issues related to the divine and human agencies involved in soteriology and evangelism, most Christians consider them a paradox. Unconvinced they qualify as a paradox; however, Packer convincingly identifies them as a theological *antinomy*—that is, an apparent contradiction of facts that appear to be equally true, necessary, and logical. Although believers may neither like nor comprehend the seemingly theological contradictions surrounding these discussions, he advises, "Accept [this theological antinomy] for what it is, and learn to live with it. Refuse to regard the apparent inconsistency as real; put down the semblance of contradiction to the deficiency of your own understanding; think of the two principles as not rival alternatives but, in some way that at present you do not grasp, complementary to each other."[32] In doing so, Packer concludes:

> It is necessary, therefore, to take the thought of human responsibility, as it affects both the preacher and the hearer of the gospel, very seriously indeed. But we must not let it drive the thought of divine sovereignty out of our minds. While we must always remember that it is our responsibility to proclaim salvation, we must never forget that it is God who saves. It is God who brings men and women under the sound of the gospel, and it is God who brings them to faith in Christ. Our evangelistic work is the instrument that He uses for this purpose, but the power that saves is not in the instrument. We must not at any stage forget that.[33]

A century earlier, C. H. Spurgeon articulated a similar position. In a sermon entitled, "Sovereign Grace and Man's Responsibility," he explained:

> The system of truth is not one straight line, but two. No man will ever get a right view of the gospel until he knows how to look at the two lines at once. I am taught in one book to believe that what I sow I shall reap: I am taught in another place, that "it is not of him that willeth nor of him that runneth, but of God that showeth mercy." I see in one place, God presiding over all in providence; and yet I see, and I cannot help seeing, that man acts as he pleases, and that God has left his actions to his own will, in a great measure. . . . That God predestines, and that man is responsible, are two things that few can see. They are believed to

---

[32] Packer, *Evangelism and the Sovereignty of God*, 21 (see chap. 1, n. 32).
[33] Packer, 27.

be inconsistent and contradictory; but they are not. It is just the fault of our weak judgment. Two truths cannot be contradictory to each other. If, then, I find taught in one place that everything is fore-ordained, that is true; and if I find in another place that man is responsible for all his actions, that is true; and it is my folly that leads me to imagine that two truths can ever contradict each other. These two truths, I do not believe, can ever be welded into one upon any human anvil, but one they shall be in eternity: they are two lines that are so nearly parallel, that the mind that shall pursue them farthest, will never discover that they converge; but they do converge, and they will meet somewhere in eternity, close to the throne of God, whence all truth doth spring. . . . You ask me to reconcile the two. I answer, they do not want any reconcilement; I never tried to reconcile them to myself, because I could never see a discrepancy. . . . Both are true; no two truths can be inconsistent with each other; and what you have to do is to believe them both.[34]

Packer's and Spurgeon's attempts to reconcile the divine and human elements in salvation notwithstanding, what implications do soteriological beliefs—particularly hyper-Calvinism, high Calvinism, and those of moderate Calvinists and non-Calvinists—have on the way in which believers deal with the gospel invitation in evangelism? As the following sections will explain, hyper-Calvinists reject the necessity of invitations, preferring to focus on God's determinative imposition in salvation. High Calvinists affirm the necessity of offering gospel invitations in evangelism and issue them nonspecifically to unbelievers in light of the regenerating work of the Holy Spirit that precedes a human response to the gospel. Those who identify as moderate or non-Calvinists insist on issuing impartial gospel invitations to all unbelievers.

---

[34] C. H. Spurgeon, "Sovereign Grace and Man's Responsibility," *New Park Street Pulpit*, vol. 4, August 1, 1858, https://www.spurgeon.org/resource-library /sermons/sovereign-grace-and-mans-responsibility/#flipbook.

The Determinative, Evangelistic Imposition

Hyper-Calvinistic soteriology both theologically and logically conceives of a *determinative, evangelistic imposition* on the part of God to save those he elects, rendering the need for human agents to issue a gospel invitation as unnecessary. Peter Toon defined *hyper-Calvinism* as

> a system of theology, or a system of the doctrines of God, man and grace, which was framed to exalt the honour and glory of God and did so at the expense of minimising the moral and spiritual responsibility of sinners to God. It placed excessive emphasis on the immanent acts of God—eternal justification, eternal adoption and the eternal covenant of grace. In practice, this meant that "Christ and Him crucified," the central message of the apostles, was obscured. It also often made no distinction between the secret and the revealed will of God, and tried to deduce the duty of men from what it taught concerning the secret, eternal decrees of God. Excessive emphasis was also placed on the doctrine of irresistible grace with the tendency to state that an elect man is not only passive in regeneration but also in conversion as well. The absorbing interest in the eternal, immanent acts of God and in irresistible grace led to the notion that grace must only be offered to those for whom it was intended. . . . So Hyper-Calvinism led its adherents to hold that evangelism was not necessary.[35]

Hyper-Calvinism teaches that in eternity past, before the world was created, God chose some humans as elect recipients of his grace, while also declaring all other humans as vessels of his damnation. This doctrine is known as *double predestination*. It also teaches that at the moment God declared who would be his elect, before space and time, God's grace was irresistibly bestowed upon them through the particular, or limited,

---

[35] Peter Toon, *The Emergence of Hyper-Calvinism in English Nonconformity 1689–1765* (London: Olive Tree, 1967), 144–45.

atonement of Jesus's death. These conclusions, drawn from hyper-Calvinism's understanding of unconditional election, particular atonement, and irresistible grace, reject any need for Christians to offer a gospel invitation when they preach the gospel.

Hyper-Calvinism rose to prominence in the eighteenth century, but it has waned ever since. Although some hyper-Calvinists can be found within evangelicalism today, very few still exist. Regrettably, some evangelicals pejoratively refer to high Calvinists, or five-point Calvinists, as hyper-Calvinists, and claim their form of Calvinism necessitates they do not offer gospel invitations due to God's determinative, evangelistic imposition. But this unfortunate mischaracterization results from an incorrect conflation between two different brands of Calvinism and the false assumption that high Calvinists must affirm double predestination. Instead, high Calvinists issue nonspecific, evangelistic invitations.

The Nonspecific, Evangelistic Invitation

High Calvinism soteriology, both theologically and logically, requires believers to share the gospel and offer a *nonspecific, evangelistic invitation* to sinners. Adherents to this system affirm the five points of Dortian Calvinism, also referred to as the "doctrines of grace"—total depravity, unconditional election, limited (particular) atonement, irresistible grace (effectual calling), and perseverance of the saints. Like hyper-Calvinists, they believe that every person inherits Adam's sin nature and guilt, thereby rendering them with the moral inability to please God, choose righteousness, or save themselves. In eternity past, they also affirm that God chose certain individuals, in his perfect love and wisdom, as his elect who would be saved from his just wrath. They conclude that because God is the sole actor in salvation, he preserves those whom he has predestined and endowed with his grace.

While high Calvinists also affirm unconditional election, limited atonement, and irresistible grace, they differ from hyper-Calvinists' understanding of them. In regards to the doctrine of election, they do not follow the hyper-Calvinistic logic of double predestination. Instead, they argue that prior to election, everyone was already under God's just wrath because of Adam's sin; therefore, they bear the responsibility for their hopeless state. The fact that he would elect anyone demonstrates magnanimous compassion on God's part, as he is not obligated to save anyone.

Concerning their concept of *limited atonement*, also known as particular atonement, Millard Erickson explains it as the belief "that the purpose of Christ's coming [and death] was not to make possible the salvation of all humans, but to render certain the salvation of the elect."[36] Although a few of them believe in the justification of the elect at the time of Jesus's death upon the cross, high Calvinists reject that limited atonement and God's effectual call were applied to the elect in eternity past. Instead, most of them believe that God will apply Christ's atonement at the moment the Spirit effectually calls elect individuals, at which time God will also grant them the faith to repent.

A criticism leveled against high Calvinists concerns the necessity for believers to evangelize due to (1) the certain salvation of the elect because of particular atonement and (2) the effectual call of the Spirit that grants faith to the elect so they will repent. But in multiple places, the Canons of Dort affirmed that believers must proclaim the gospel. Article III of its "First Head of Doctrine" taught, "That men may be brought to believe, God mercifully sends the messengers of these most joyful tidings, to whom he will, and at what time he pleaseth, by whose ministry men are called to repentance and faith in Christ crucified. Rom. x. 14, 15."[37] In fact, the following comprised the "Second Head of Doctrine," which advanced the doctrine of limited atonement: "Moreover the promise of the gospel is, that whosoever believeth in Christ crucified, shall not perish,

---

[36] Erickson, *Christian Theology,* 826 (see chap. 4, n. 34).

[37] Sally Burdick and Jonathan Seymour, *Canons, Ratified in the National Synod of the Reformed Church, Held at Dordrecht in the Years 1618 & 1619* [Electronic Resource] (Reprint, Second Series No. 25289, New York: Whiting & Watson, 1812), 1.

but have everlasting life. This promise, together with the command to repent and believe, ought to be declared and published to all nations, and to all persons promiscuously and without distinction, to whom God out of his good pleasure sends the Gospel."[38]

High Calvinists in the twentieth and twenty-first centuries have also affirmed the necessity for believers to evangelize, while also holding to limited atonement and irresistible grace. R. B. Kuiper writes:

> Are the unsaved to be told that faith is a gift of God? Most assuredly! Wholly, of course, the truth of the matter must be told them. To hide his truth from them would be irresponsible. To permit them to entertain the thought that they can believe of their own volition apart from the regenerating grace of the Holy Spirit is worse than irresponsible. It amounts to encouraging them in the belief that they are masters of their own fate, captains of their own fate, captains of their own souls. However, that faith is a gift of God is not the only truth to be impressed upon the lost. This truth must be coupled with another. As so often in Christian theology, so here also there are complementary truths both of which deserve the strongest stress. The sinner needs to be told emphatically that he *must* believe and that, in case he does not believe, the wrath of God will abide on him.[39]

Wayne Grudem also asserts:

> In answer to the objection that [Calvinists' view on the extent of the atonement] compromises the free offer of the gospel to every person, Reformed people answer that we do not know who they are who will come to trust in Christ, for only God knows that. As far as we are concerned, the free offer of the gospel is to be made to everybody without exception. We also know that everyone who

---

[38] Burdick and Seymour, 7.

[39] R. B. Kuiper, *God-Centered Evangelism: A Presentation of the Scriptural Theology of Evangelism* (1966; repr., Carlisle, PA: Banner of Truth, 2002), 160.

repents and believes in Christ will be saved, so all are called to repentance (cf. Acts 17:30). The fact that God foreknew who would be saved, and that he accepted Christ's death as payment for their sins only, does not inhibit the free offer of the gospel, for who will respond to it is hidden in the secret counsels of God. That we do not know who will respond no more constitutes a reason for not offering the gospel to all than not knowing the extent of the harvest prevents the farmer from sowing seed in his fields.[40]

To be consistent with their theology and logic, high Calvinists must offer nonspecific, evangelistic invitations when they evangelize. In doing so, they will offer a general invitation of repentance to everyone, with the knowledge that only those whom the Spirit has regenerated and given faith will have the ability to do so. Because high Calvinists believe that Christ only died for the elect and they cannot know who is elect because that knowledge lies in God's secret will, such a nonspecific, evangelistic invitation prevents them from looking anyone in the eye and saying, "Jesus died for you and will forgive you of your sins." Instead, they can say to any particular person something like: "Jesus died for sinners, and if you understand the gospel I told you and sense an overwhelming urge to respond to God's love for you in the gospel, you can turn away from your sins." This type of invitation corresponds with the belief that Christ died for some, not all, sinners, and that anyone whom the Spirit has regenerated with faith will supernaturally respond by repentance.

The Impartial, Evangelistic Invitation

Those whose soteriology leads them to espouse an *impartial, evangelistic invitation* include a wide range of theological systems, including but

---

[40] Wayne Grudem, *Systematic Theology: An Introduction to Biblical Doctrine* (Grand Rapids: Zondervan, 1994), 595. Grudem expanded further on this note by defending evangelists (despite their soteriology) who tell unbelievers, "Christ died for your sins," 602.

not limited to moderate Calvinists, Amyraldians, Arminians, Molinists, Provisionalists, as well as evangelicals who appeal to the mystery of God's sovereignty and man's responsibility over the historic, systematized soteriologies.[41] This diverse group differ on numerous points of their theology, and soteriology by extension (such as the *ordo salutis* and varying points of acceptance concerning the doctrines of grace). Nevertheless, they find consensus around the belief that "Christ's atoning work on the cross is intended for everyone without exception, while its application is limited only to those who believe by the power of the Spirit," prompting their critics to call them "hypothetical universalists."[42] Practitioners of

---

[41] A brief description of each of these soteriological systems follows: (1) *Moderate Calvinists* are those who vary on the number of points of Dortian Calvinism to which they ascribe, but usually affirm at a minimum the doctrines of *total depravity* and *perseverance of the saints* (i.e., generally this group consists of individuals who consider themselves either a two-, three-, or four-point Calvinists); (2) *Amyradlians* are four-point moderate Calvinists, who ascribe to the views of Moses Amyraut and thereby reject the Doritan Calvinistic doctrine of *limited atonement*; (3) *Arminians* are those who ascribe to the views of Jacobus Arminius and generally affirm the "Five Articles of Remonstrance"— that is *conditional election, unlimited atonement, total depravity, prevenient grace,* and *conditional preservation of the saints*; (4) *Molinists* are those who ascribe to the views of Luis de Molina and attempt to reconcile the tension between divine sovereignty and human liberty in salvation through middle, or counterfactual, knowledge. They generally affirm the five points that Timothy George proposed as a summary of Molinism: *radical depravity, overcoming grace, sovereign election, eternal life,* and *singular redemption*; and (5) *Provisionalists* are those who align with Leighton Flowers's seven point soteriological acrostic—P-R-O-V-I-D-E: *People Sin,* which separates all from fellowship with God; *Responsible* (people are able to respond) to God's appeals for reconciliation; *Open Door* for anyone to enter by faith; *Vicarious Atonement* provides a way for anyone to be saved by Christ's blood; *Illuminating Grace* provides clearly revealed truth so that all can know and respond in faith; *Destroyed* for unbelief and resisting the Holy Spirit; and *Eternal Security* for all true believers.

[42] David Gibson and Jonathan Gibson, "Sacred Theology and the Reading of the Divine Word," in *From Heaven He Came and Sought Her: Definite Atonement in Historical, Biblical, Theological, and Pastoral Perspective* (Wheaton, IL: Crossway, 2013), 48–49.

the impartial, evangelistic invitation agree with David Allen's reasoning: "The universal call of the gospel and the universal command to believe the gospel indicate a universal provision of the gospel in [the] atonement."[43] He continued, "The gospel is actual in its availability—Christ died for all. The gospel is potential in its application—no one is saved apart from faith."[44]

Proponents of impartial, evangelistic invitations appeal to the impartiality shown in biblical evangelistic invitations to both those who hear the gospel and those who have not yet heard the gospel. Some examples of these calls include, but are not limited to, Peter's offer of forgiveness and the gift of the Holy Spirit to those under his hearing and those beyond his hearing, such as their "children, and for all who are far off, as many as the Lord our God will call" (Acts 2:39), as well as Paul and Silas's admonition that in addition to the Philippian jailer, himself, his own household could be saved (Acts 16:31).

The desire of the Lord, found in 1 Tim 2:4 and 2 Pet 3:9, also informs their philosophy and practice of issuing invitations. In 1 Tim 2:1–7, they apply to their appeals the textual logic that (1) Paul requires that expressions of prayer be made impartially for all people, because (2) these intentional and inclusive prayers please God, due to (3) God's sincere desire that all be saved and come to the knowledge of the truth, as expressed in the fact that (4) Christ Jesus gave himself as a ransom for all; therefore, like (5) Paul they will give testimony of this truth to everyone for whom they also pray. Second Peter 3 specifically addresses questions and

---

[43] David Allen, Facebook post, August 5, 2016, 1:04 p.m., https://www .facebook.com/david.l.allen1/posts/10210146542317816. Allen thoroughly provides his reasons, from biblical, theological, historical, and practical perspectives, for such a conclusion in *The Extent of the Atonement: A Historical and Critical Review* (Nashville: B&H Academic, 2016) and *The Atonement: A Biblical, Theological, and Historical Study of the Cross of Christ* (Nashville: B&H Academic, 2019).

[44] David Allen, Facebook post, December 29, 2016, 10:59 a.m., https:// www.facebook.com/david.l.allen1/posts/10211589483870453.

criticisms concerning the delay of Christ's return. Peter answers these questions by rejecting the logic used by the scoffers of his day and appealing to God's longsuffering patience due to his desire that none perish but all come to repentance (v. 9). In the time they have been given until his return, practitioners of this invitation deduce they should spend it urging every person's repentance so they do not perish at his return.

Unlike those who issue nonspecific invitations, believers who extend impartial, evangelistic invitations have no difficulty looking everyone in the eye and telling them that Jesus died for them. Like high Calvinists, they affirm the necessity of God enabling unbelievers in some way before they are able to repent and believe. For example, moderate Calvinists and Amyraldians maintain the doctrine of irresistible grace; Arminians acknowledge the enablement of God's prevenient grace; while Molinists, Provisionalists, and other evangelicals insist on the preemptive work of the Holy Spirit to convince and convict the minds and hearts of unbelievers. When issuing an impartial, evangelistic invitation, believers will share the gospel with anyone and everyone, calling on their hearers to repent of their sins and believe in Jesus's death, burial, and resurrection to be saved.

(8) Is your doctrinal philosophy of evangelism consistent with your dutiful practice of evangelism?

While believers should evangelize with all excellence and purge ineffective practices, McCloskey had something else in mind when he posed his evaluative question in *Tell It Often—Tell It Well*: "Does [your evangelism] work?"[45] He frames the intended meaning of this assessment question by offering another: "Does my philosophy and practice of evangelism make me effective in getting the gospel out to as many as possible, as soon as possible and as clearly as possible?"[46] Just because Christians merely

---

[45] McCloskey, *Tell It Often—Tell It Well*, 186.
[46] McCloskey, 186.

believe in the necessity and importance of evangelism does not guarantee that they will evangelize.

Numerous helpful campaigns, apparel, and apps exist to assist a personal evangelist in evangelizing consistently. Words such as *gospel*, *Great Commission*, *evangelism*, and *mission* are rising in popularity. Influential blogs, books, and conferences alike use these terms and their cognates (e.g., gospel-centered, missional, etc.) in their titles and themes. As much excitement and encouragement as this trend brings, believers must guard against the temptation of talking about the gospel to those who know it best without taking the gospel to those who need to hear it most.

James F. Love first said, "The gospel was given not to be hoarded but to be heralded,"[47] although it has been popularly attributed to E. D. Head or Vance Havner. Whatever meaning believers ascribe to being "gospel-centered" should incorporate an understanding that in order to be so, their conversations with unbelievers should, like the first Christians, center around the gospel as much as, if not more than, their conversations with believers. For this reason, believers should employ a standard measure by which they test themselves—a *gospel Shibboleth*, so to speak.

In its modern usage *Shibboleth* possesses a range of meanings, including a test to determine the extent to which someone or something is in accordance with established rules, principles, or standards. The concept of a *Shibboleth* is derived from Judg 12:1–6, which recounts how men from the tribe of Ephraim confronted Jephthah about his defeat of the Ammonites. A fight ensued between the men of Ephraim and the Gileadites, who were led by Jephthah. Jephthah and his army prevailed, positioning themselves at the fords of the Jordan River that led to Ephraim. Fugitives of Ephraim came to the fords in order to return

---

[47] James F. Love, *Missionary Messages* (New York: George H. Doran, 1922), 22–23. The quote's context is as follows: "The heart which the gospel regenerates is the only safe keeping place for the gospel. Those who know its power to save, believe it too precious to be lost. You cannot keep the truth pure apart from the missionary use of it. . . . [The gospel] was given not to be hoarded but to be heralded."

home. The Gileadites asked, "Are you an Ephraimite?" If they replied, "No," the Gileadites instructed them to say, "Shibboleth," testing whether or not they were fugitives. Any men from Ephraim said, "Sibboleth," because they could not pronounce the word correctly. So they failed the test and were subsequently executed.

The intentional and consistent practice of personal evangelism serves as the *Shibboleth* by which believers should evaluate their gospel verbiage. The true test of their gospel-centeredness is not that they merely talk about the gospel among sympathetic groups of believers; rather, it encompasses telling the gospel to apathetic, even skeptical, unbelieving audiences. Whereas the men of Ephraim had trouble with pronunciation, personal evangelists' trouble tends to lie with their proclamation (or, rather, the lack thereof). The gospel enterprise is not hindered by their inability to pronounce words like *gospel*, *evangelism*, and *Great Commission* (believers can and do articulate them all too well); however, the work of the gospel will be hindered if they fail to proclaim intentionally and consistently the Word of the cross.

The men of Ephraim were victimized when they failed the Gileadites' test. In contrast, those who fail the test of the gospel *Shibboleth* at one time or another will not become victims, though they will have the blood of those to whom they never preached on their hands. Instead, the victims of this failure to evangelize are the souls of unbelieving men, women, boys, and girls on a trajectory toward hell. For this reason, personal evangelists must evaluate whether they spend most of their time talking about the gospel with believers or telling the gospel to unbelievers. Their frequency in sharing the gospel serves as an accurate measure of their faithfulness to the gospel.

Using evangelism as believers' gospel *Shibboleth* is not a new concept, only a new way of saying it. On August 22, 1903, Henry Crocker published a poem in a Chicago Baptist newspaper. In it he conveyed through the term *watchword* the same idea as a gospel *Shibboleth*. His challenge to his readers in the twentieth century rings true for believers in the twenty-first century:

Give us a watchword for the hour,
A thrilling word, a word of power;
A battle-cry, a flaming breath,
That calls to conquest or to death.

A word to rouse the church from rest,
To heed her Master's high behest;
The call is given: Ye hosts arise,
Our watchword is Evangelize!

The glad evangel now proclaim,
Through all the earth, in Jesus's name;
This word is ringing through the skies,
Evangelize! Evangelize!

To dying men, a fallen race,
Make known the gift of Gospel grace;
The world that now in darkness lies,
Evangelize! Evangelize![48]

All believers should honestly evaluate whether their beliefs related to evangelism encourage or hinder their own practice of it. Adam W. Greenway leverages this principle in terms of Christian integrity when he admonishes Southern Baptists:

> Integrity, however, should demand from us the honest admission that our hearts do not break and our eyes do not weep over the lostness that surrounds us in our own states, much less our subdivisions. Despite our needed public reaffirmations of doctrinal orthodoxy, the overwhelming abandonment of that most central responsibility of our faith—to personally engage individuals who are not yet believers in Jesus Christ, sharing with them that He is

---

[48] Henry Crocker, "Evangelize!" *The Standard* 50, no. 51 (August 22, 1903): 13.

the only Savior and Lord—produces the practical result of contradicting the very faith we claim to embrace.[49]

If Christians discover their beliefs do, in fact, prevent them from adhering to the New Testament's expectation of practicing consistent and intentional evangelism, they must assess and correct this inconsistency between their philosophy of evangelism and their practice of it.

DISCUSSION AND REFLECTION QUESTIONS

1. Is your conceptualization of the gospel supported by the Scriptures? Compose a summary of how you present the gospel when you evangelize. Then, provide biblical support for each doctrinal assertion you make.

2. As a general rule, did Christians in the first century practice evangelism incrementally, immediately, or both incrementally and immediately? Support your claim with pertinent passages and verses. Do the duration patterns of your own evangelism resemble those practiced by believers in the New Testament? If not, what adjustments should you make to bring them into alignment with biblical standards?

3. Select and discuss an example from the New Testament in which someone's evangelistic proclamation resulted in new disciples who were baptized and taught obedience to Christ's commands. In what ways can this example help you connect the people who become disciples with a local church so that they are baptized by immersion and learn to be obedient to Christ?

4. How would you describe the frequency of your evangelistic practice—sporadic, casual, or intentional? What changes, if any,

---

[49] Adam W. Greenway, "Conclusion," in *The Great Commission Resurgence: Fulfilling God's Mandate in Our Time*, ed. Chuck Lawless and Adam W. Greenway (Nashville: B&H Academic, 2010), 403.

do you need to make in the urgency with which you share the gospel, in light of the unpredictable nature of unbelievers' life expectancies, as well as the exact timing of Christ's return?

5. Based on your current presuppositions and practices, in what ways do you either de-emphasize or neglect the role and power of the Holy Spirit in your evangelism? What changes do you need to make before and during your gospel presentations to depend less on yourself or the practice of so-called pre-evangelism, and rely more fully on him and his role in salvation?

6. What are some of the specific Scriptures that you consistently incorporate in your gospel presentations? What principles, if any, guide you in how you select the verses you use?

7. How would you describe (1) your soteriology and (2) the kind of invitation you issue when you evangelize? Are your beliefs about salvation consistent with the way you invite people to repent and believe? If not, is this inconsistency due to a misunderstanding about the doctrine of salvation you hold or a misapplication of the way you call people to be saved?

8. Does what you believe about evangelism encourage or hinder your sense of duty and practice of it? Specifically, what about your evangelistic philosophy encourages you to share the gospel? What hinders you from doing it?

7

Personal Evangelism Methods and Strategies

E vangelism embodies almost as many methods and strategies as those who practice it. Concerning the various number of ways to evangelize, L. R. Scarborough claims, "I have won somebody to Christ every way Jesus did except up a tree and on a cross. And the first chance I get I'm going after them."[1] Many of Roy Fish's students heard him express the same sentiment when he would say, "Jesus wants the most people won to him in every possible way and in every possible place and in the shortest space of time."

What is the best evangelism method for believers to use? John Stott answered, "Fundamentally, there is only one evangelistic method: the proclamation, whether public or private, of the gospel of Jesus Christ.

---

[1] Curtis Hutson, *Great Preaching on Soul-Winning* (Murfreesboro, TN: Sword of the Lord, 1989), 188. Numerous people have quoted Scarborough saying this statement. Apparently, he never wrote it in a book. Hutson is the one source I could find that quotes it directly.

Indeed, this is not a *method* in evangelism; it is the *essence* of evangelism itself."[2] The best evangelism methodology is not the latest, best-selling, or most popular one. It is the one that each believer actually practices; or as Roy Fish often quipped during his "Introduction to Evangelism" lectures, "The only approach with a lost person worse than a bad approach is no approach at all."

Most Christians recognize the importance of evangelism, but they are at a loss when it comes to striking up a conversation with a close friend or a stranger they encounter on a plane, in a grocery line, or at a restaurant. Christians have found different ways to share the gospel based on their personality, level of comfort, and past experiences. In his book *Contagious Faith*, Mark Mittelberg proposed "five *Contagious Faith* styles," or natural approaches to share the gospel, which he identified as "Friendship-Building," "Selfless-Serving," "Story-Sharing," "Reason-Giving," and "Truth-Telling."[3] Priscilla Pope-Levison also offered eight "models of evangelism"—"personal," "small group," "visitation," "liturgical," "church growth," "prophetic," "revival," and "media"—in her book by the same name. Despite the number of approaches or models acknowledged, most personal evangelists demonstrate their preference toward a single method by practicing only it; however, she correctly advises, "a vital promising future for evangelism will happen only as individual models combust to create a model uniquely suited to each particular context."[4]

This chapter identifies and critically analyzes seven common approaches to sharing the gospel. These techniques provide ways for believers to use testimony, storying, questions, conversations, acts of service, relationships, and confrontation to evangelize. Each approach has

---

[2] John R. W. Stott, *Evangelism: Why & How* (Chicago: InterVarsity, 1969), 21–22.

[3] See Mark Mittelberg, *Contagious Faith: Discover Your Natural Style for Sharing Jesus with Others: Study Guide* (Grand Rapids: HarperChristian, 2021), session 1, Kindle.

[4] Priscilla Pope-Levison, *Models of Evangelism* (Grand Rapids: Baker, 2020), 9.

potential strengths and weaknesses, but not all approaches are created equal. All seven have their own advantages and usefulness in particular situations; therefore, effective personal evangelists will learn to use more than one. The leading of the Holy Spirit should dictate which approach, or approaches, should be incorporated in any given evangelistic encounter.

The Witness: Testimonial Evangelism

The *witness* uses his or her testimony to present the gospel. In addressing the witness of the gospel through personal testimony, Trueblood declares:

> It cannot be too strongly emphasized that all witness necessarily involves the use of the first person singular. My testimony bears, I believe, on something independent of me, something objectively real, but I cannot escape the necessity of my personal affirmation. It is never somebody in general who bears witness; it is always an individual with an individual consciousness.[5]

Sharing one's testimony is a strong approach because it is natural and relational.

Nevertheless, evangelism is not just telling your own story. It must include and emphasize his story—the gospel. Mark Mittelberg proposes the following three key words—*discovery, decision,* and *difference*—to recount your salvation testimony. By discovery he recommends you answer the following question: "What [discovery] helped you reach the conclusion that you needed Christ and the salvation he offers?"[6] For decision, he suggested you explain exactly what you decided to do, based on that discovery, to receive God's forgiveness and leadership. Last, he encouraged that you provide evidence of what difference that decision has made in your life.

---

[5] Trueblood, *The Company of the Committed,* 49 (see chap. 1, n. 8).

[6] Mark Mittelberg, *Contagious Faith: Discover Your Natural Style for Sharing Jesus with Others* Grand Rapids: Zondervan, 2021), 90–91.

Those who have both received and experienced salvation in Christ through the gospel bear responsibility to share their own firsthand experiences with unbelievers. They know their story of how they heard the gospel message and believed it better than anyone else does—it is their own story! Their intimate familiarity with the gospel and how it saved them requires no memorization on their part.

Recall the Samaritan woman at Jacob's well in John 4:4–42. After hearing about and receiving the living water, she immediately left Jesus and his disciples to go into town. She took time neither to rehearse her testimony nor to complete evangelism training before she told the people about her personal experience with Jesus. On account of her testimony, that was just as much authentic as it was amateur, many of the Samaritans believed in him.

Some Christians have convinced themselves that discussions about each person's faith is a private matter; therefore, they should not discuss faith in Christ with other people. But genuine, biblical faith in Jesus Christ is a personal matter, not a private one. Think back to the day you professed faith in Jesus Christ. After thanking the Lord for the salvation he provided you, what was the first thing you wanted to do? Likely, you wanted to tell others about your decision and how they too could profess faith in Christ as Lord and Savior.

One weakness to this approach is that personal evangelists sometimes get bogged down in sharing their own story, and the conversation either gets sidetracked or never contains an explicit explanation of the gospel. To overcome this, you should have a three-part mental outline prepared: (1) what your life was like before Christ; (2) how you came to Christ; and (3) what your life has been like since coming to Christ. Try not to spend the majority of the time on your life before Christ or after Christ. Instead, focus on explaining how you heard about and came to Christ, while including an explicit gospel presentation.

This approach is ideal when you are sitting next to people on a plane. For example, you can ask them if they are coming home or going somewhere, make small talk, and ask what they do for a living. Typically, as the conversation progresses, they will ask you about yourself. At this point, you should share with them a little about your family and what you do and attempt to bridge the conversation into an opportunity to share your testimony, ultimately in order to share Christ.

The Storyteller: The Gospel as Story Evangelism

Those who approach evangelism as *storytellers* retell the metanarrative of redemption found throughout the Scriptures to share the gospel in the context of the Christian worldview. Generally, this approach to evangelism follows this outline:

1. How did it all begin? **Creation.**
2. What went wrong? **The Fall.**
3. Is there any hope? **Rescue.**
4. What will the future hold? **Restoration.**[7]

---

[7] The earliest forms of storying evangelism were used by cross-cultural missionaries among oral learning societies. While metanarrative approaches to sharing the gospel varied, the most well-known of them was the "From Creation to Christ" presentation. For example, see "Go Impact: Creation to Christ," accessed April 28, 2022, https://www.imb.org/wp-content/uploads/2021/10/go-impact -creation-to-christ.pdf.

During the twentieth century in the United States, W. A. Criswell used and modeled this kind of approach when he preached his famous sermon "The Scarlet Thread of the Bible," on December 31, 1961, from 7:30 p.m. that evening into the 1962 New Year. He later published it as the book *The Scarlet Thread through the Bible* (Nashville: Broadman, 1971).

This way of personally sharing the gospel was popularized early in the twenty-first century through a print and digital presentation, *The Story*, produced by a ministry called Spread Truth (www.spreadtruth.com). The four-part question and answer outline presented above is derived from *The Story*. Kevin DeYoung and Greg Gilbert explain this outline in greater detail in their book, *What Is the Mission of the Church?: Making Sense of Social Justice, Shalom, and the Great Commission* (Wheaton, IL: Crossway, 2011), 67–90.

This condensed framework summarizes the gospel story throughout the Old and New Testaments. In doing so, it answers popular questions people consider about life, evil, God, and death.

This metanarrative format of gospel presentation is only found periodically in the Bible (Acts 2:14–40; 3:11–26; 6:8–7:60; 13:13–41).[8] Of these occurrences, Acts 6:8–7:60 records the most exhaustive example. Stephen used this method by rehearsing the history of Israel. The metanarrative he presented differed in a few ways from the Creation-Fall-Rescue-Restoration framework popularly espoused today. Stephen began his preaching with Abraham rather than creation. Instead of explaining sin through Adam's and Eve's disobedience to God and how humanity inherited their nature, he repeatedly referenced the resistance of Israel's ancestors to God, and his hearers' complicity with them. Although storyteller evangelism appears within the Scriptures, personal evangelists in the New Testament overwhelmingly present distinct elements of the gospel and use previous biblical material to corroborate and authenticate the their message.

Personal evangelists should be aware of a couple of issues they may face when using a metanarrative evangelism approach. First, they should guard against reducing the Savior to only a portion of the gospel story. By including a greater amount of biblical content and explaining more detailed doctrinal themes when sharing the gospel, Christ's life, death, burial, and resurrection have may become a smaller component part of the presentation rather than the underlying and overarching climactic focus of what is shared.

Second, this approach can sometimes make it difficult for personal evangelists to reach the redemptive work of Christ in their presentations.

---

[8] Paul does seem to employ the use of metanarrative when he writes Romans. While Romans contains the gospel message, his purpose for writing this correspondence was not a purely evangelistic one (though it can be used and applied in this way), but rather to address the way the gospel affords unity between Jews and Gentiles in the context of Christian community.

Storyteller types of evangelism typically begin by presenting the biblical creation. Due to today's prominence of evolutionary theories concerning the origin of the earth and humanity, believers may face difficult and time-consuming questions that arise from introducing the Christian story of the beginning. If unbelievers' questions go unanswered or they remained unconvinced by the answers they receive, believers may never get a chance to advance the conversation forward to Christ.

In Western societies that are becoming increasingly more biblically illiterate, storyteller types of evangelism introduce their citizens to the larger scriptural narrative context of which they are unaware. This more comprehensive framework sets the gospel within a setting that hearers can both appreciate and understand. It also intuitively teaches and helps newly made disciples anticipate the need to read and study the Bible in order to grow in their understanding of God and his expectations of them.

The Inquisitor: Using Questions in Evangelism

The *inquisitor* asks questions that lead or leverage conversations to the point of directly sharing the gospel. Jesus best modeled this questioning approach in encounters like those he had with a group of Jews (John 5:46–47), the man born blind (John 9:35), Martha (John 11:25–26), and the Pharisees (Matt 22:41–45). Questions serve personal evangelists as transitions they can use to begin gospel conversations, as well as ways they can respond to objections unbelievers may raise so they can return to sharing the good news. Randy Newman's book *Questioning Evangelism* is an excellent resource for those interested in learning more about this approach.

A few potential problems can emerge from this approach. If the persons with whom you are sharing feel as though you are bombarding them with too many questions, it may cause them to become defensive. Additionally, if they have extroverted personalitites, asking a series of questions might inadvertently allow them to dominate the dialogue with responses or divert your intent for the conversation. Such occur-rences will likely leave you with little or no time to share the gospel due to time constraints.

To avoid these dangers, believers should avoid using general, open-ended questions. Their use of such queries, if necessary, should be to learn information that will assist them in either contextualizing or further clarifying the gospel. Personal evangelists should stick to a brief set of direct and deliberate questions. They should formulate a blueprint by which the questions they ask drive the conversation straight to the gos-pel. One way would be to ask unbelievers about the most important deci-sion they have ever made and use that subject to direct the dialogue to the personal evangelist's own conversion experience. They can also use questions to clarify unbelievers' objections to specific claims made by the gospel. By asking if their minds are genuinely open to consider faith in Christ, believers can gauge if their conversations should end for the time being or in what direction they should continue.

The Analogist: Conversational Evangelism

The *analogist* uses his or her environment, circumstances, situations, and current events to lead a conversation to the gospel. Examples include talking to your doctor about the Great Physician or connecting a tragic news story to evil or hopelessness in the world. Jesus used this approach generally when he evangelized through parables (e.g., Matt 13:1–23; 18:10–14; 21:33–45; 22:1–14; Mark 4:1–20; 12:1–12; Luke 15:8–10; 16:19–31; 18:9–14). He specifically used analogies when he discussed being born again with Nicodemus (John 3:1–10) and living water with the Samaritan woman at the well (John 4:7–15).

A few issues accompany this type of evangelism. Some analogies may sound like good connections in a believer's mind but fall short of the ideal when vocalized. A fellow church member and I once went to the hospital to visit our pastor, who had recently experienced a medical issue. Neither he nor I had made any plans to seek out an opportunity to share the gospel. Our focus was on our pastor and caring for him. Nevertheless, God had different plans for us that day.

We entered the hospital elevator to go to the floor of our pastor's room. As the doors of the elevator began to close, we heard a voice cry, "Please, hold the elevator for me!" Instinctively, I extended my arm to prevent the doors from closing. As the doors retracted, a mail carrier with the United States Postal Service stepped inside. We exchanged pleasantries, and she thanked us for allowing her to ride on the elevator with us.

At that very moment, the Holy Spirit prompted me to share the gospel with her. Because we were going to separate floors, I had little time to share the gospel with her and even less time to decide if I would share the gospel. Because I had predetermined that I would share the gospel whenever the Holy Spirit prompted me, I transitioned our brief conversation to the gospel with the first thought that came to my mind. I asked her, "So, you deliver messages to people for the post office, right?" She nodded her head in affirmation. I then said, "Well, I deliver messages to people for God, and I have one for you." My friend began laughing and exclaimed, "That is the cheesiest gospel transition I have ever heard." Because we had reached her floor, she politely exited the elevator. When the doors closed I replied to him, "Well, it was a lot better than my saying nothing at all!"

Another problem can accompany this way of evangelizing. Some seemingly harmless correlations Christians may make with the gospel could offend others. Without intending to do so, personal evangelists can sometimes choose an applicable metaphor about a person, place, or event that triggers an opposing personal, political, or economic viewpoint within unbelievers. Inadvertent situations like these may not only prevent believers from being able to share the gospel in those moments; they might also prevent unbelievers from ever wanting to hear it.

Nevertheless, the strength of this approach lies in its natural and conversational ability to bridge conversations to the gospel. Those who use analogies effectively to begin evangelistic presentations, illustrate truths about the good news, or clarify unbelievers' questions or misunderstandings

about Christ usually read widely and stay well-informed about world
and news events. They generally prefer making simple comparisons over
similarities requiring complicated, multilayered explanations and points
of connection. The more Christians initially observe or know about the
individuals with whom they share, the easier it will be for them to formulate gospel analogies.

The Server: Servanthood Evangelism

The *server* serves others through planned or spontaneous acts of service
to create an opportunity to evangelize others. Examples include servant-
hood evangelism, mercy ministries, and random acts of kindness.[9] This
approach demonstrates compassion and concern on behalf of the evangelist for the other person(s).

For years some believers have created a wedge between soul-winning
and service. Trueblood describes it this way: "It is common to hear some
speak scornfully of 'soul saving,' while others speak, with equal conde-
scension, of 'activism.' The clear answer is that both are needed and that
[until Christ returns] they will always be needed."[10] David Bosch observes
four attitudes relating to practice of social involvement and evangelistic
witness among evangelicals.[11] First, social involvement linked with evangelism forms a kind of holism that yields a *betrayal of the gospel*. Second,
social involvement serves as *the means to an end* for Christians to be able
to present the gospel. Third, social involvement is a noble but *optional*
Christian activity, whereas evangelism is a necessary one. Last, social

---

[9] Examples of this method include Steve Sjogren, *Conspiracy of Kindness*
(Ann Arbor, MI: Vine, 1993) and Alvin L. Reid and David A. Wheeler, *Servant
Evangelism* (Alpharetta, GA: NAMB, 1999).

[10] Trueblood, *The Validity of the Christian Mission*, 98 (see chap. 5, n. 21).

[11] David J. Bosch, *Witness to the World: The Christian Mission in Theological
Perspective* (Atlanta: John Knox, 1980), 202–3. In the sentences following, I have
summarized Bosch's four categories and use his categorical phrases, which are
indicated with italics.

involvement and evangelistic witness share a prioritistic relationship,[12] where the former is *secondary* and the latter is *primary*.

While personal evangelists must demonstrate genuine concern for unbelievers, this approach can potentially lead to the adoption of philosophies that hinder the practice of evangelism. For example, some servers will convince themselves that they must earn a right to evangelize a stranger. Attempting to earn a right to evangelize can foster a quid pro quo kind of evangelism, in which personal evangelists foster an expectation that those who receive their acts of service must listen to their gospel presentations or feel guilty for not doing so. Servers who adopt this philosophy and practice should remind themselves that the Lord Jesus has "earned" the right to command his followers to adopt the biblical philosophy and practice of evangelizing as many as possible, as soon as possible, with or without acts of service.

Over time, other well-meaning servers will be tempted to follow the path of social gospel advocates by confusing benevolence with evangelism or by promoting an unhealthy interdependence between gospel proclamation and mercy ministry. Believers have an obligation to practice both gospel proclamation and mercy ministry without the self-imposed guilt or expectation that they must do one in order to do the other. Jesus, who healed many infirmities and provided food for multitudes, stated that he came "to seek and to save the lost" (Luke 19:10).

If evangelism is relegated to nothing more than the practice of social services to those in need, then many people, including atheists, Muslims, Hindus, and Buddhists, evangelize. As they evangelize, Christians

---

[12] "Prioritistic relationship" refers to a particular evangelistic and missiological philosophy that David Hesselgrave explains "sustains the time-honored distinction between the primary mission of the church and secondary or supporting ministries. . . . The mission [of God] is primarily to make disciples of all nations. Other Christian ministries are good [and virtuous] but second and supportive [to the task of disciple-making]." Hesselgrave, *Paradigms in Conflict: 15 Key Questions in Christian Missions Today*, 2nd ed. (Grand Rapids: Kregel Academic, 2018), 109–10.

should practice compassion, and even meet physical needs when possible, but they should prioritize the practice of biblical evangelism, as they alone can offer the Bread of Life (John 6:31–35, 48, 50–51, 58). Elton Trueblood explains this sentiment best: "If we do not start with what is primary, we are not likely to achieve what is secondary, for this is a resultant. . . . The call to become fishers of men precedes the call to wash one another's feet."[13]

Servers will want to practice other evangelistic approaches as well. Otherwise, they will only evangelize those who have needs that they, themselves, can meet. Those using the server approach need to remember that Jesus also died to save those who have no discernible physical needs (e.g., the rich, teachers of the law, those who had no need for a physician), as well as those who have needs greater than they can meet.

The Networker: Relationship Evangelism

In their desire to be incarnational, *networkers* meet and befriend others with the intent to evangelize them. Relationships with unbelievers allow personal evangelists to discuss the gospel, demonstrate an authentic Christian lifestyle, and create a meaningful connection for subsequent discipleship if unbelievers profess faith in Christ. Some believers fail at building relationships with unbelievers in their evangelism, while others fail to be evangelistic in their existing relationships with unbelievers. The former fosters a "one and done" evangelism, whereas the latter yields a "some, but essentially none" kind of evangelism.

Some networkers will be tempted to delay evangelizing their new-found friends for fear of a negative effect on the relationships they seek to establish. D. J. Higgins penned a poem that captures the gravity of a Christian's failing to share the gospel with an unbelieving "friend":

---

[13] Trueblood, *The Validity of the Christian Mission*, 98 (see chap. 5, n. 21).

My, friend, I stand in judgment now
and feel that you're to blame somehow—
on earth, I walked with you day by day
and never did you point the way.

You knew the Lord in truth and glory,
but never did you tell the story.
My knowledge then was very dim,
you could have led me safe to Him.

Though we lived together on the earth,
you never told me of the Second Birth.
And now I stand here condemned,
because you failed to mention Him.

You taught me many things, that's true;
I called you friend, I trusted you.
But I learn now that it's too late,
you could have saved me from this state.

We walked and talked, by day, by night;
and yet you showed me not the Light.
You let me live and love and die,
you knew I'd never live on high.

Yes, I called you "friend" in life,
and trusted you through joy and strife.
And yet on coming to the end,
Now, I cannot call you "my friend."[14]

Relationships are essential in evangelism. Of all the relationships that evangelism entails, the most important relationship to be established

---

[14] Ray R. Morawski, *Leading People to Christ: Biblical Principles and Helpful Instructions for Personal Evangelism* (Santa Maria: Xulon, 2010), 7.

and prioritized is not between the personal evangelist and an unbeliever but between God and an unbeliever. Personal evangelists in the New Testament did not make friends with strangers in order to tell them about Christ after a period of time; rather, they shared Christ with strangers and, as a result, relationships were established.

Also, networkers should be careful to prepare new acquaintances to hear the gospel after a "sufficient" level of trust (however that can be measured) has been established.[15] Tommy Kiker has recounted on many occasions the story of a missionary who left America to live in another country. Almost immediately he made friends with one of the citizens; however, he assumed that his new friend was not ready to hear the gospel. After several months the missionary was reassigned and scheduled a meeting with his friend to say goodbye. The missionary looked deeply into the eyes of his friend and said, "I have bad news. The company for which I work has relocated me, so I will have to leave. Over the last several months I have grown to love you as a dear friend, so before I leave I want to share with you the most important thing I could ever share with you." The friend stopped the missionary and said, "If what you have to share is so important, then why didn't you share it with me earlier?"

Regrettably, attempts like this could lead would-be personal evangelists to emphasize relationship-building to the neglect of acknowledging both the Holy Spirit's preparing unbelievers' hearts to receive the gospel and the uncertainty of future encounters. For example, how can believers know to what extent the Holy Spirit has prepared others' hearts to receive the message of the gospel if they have not shared the gospel with them

---

[15] Don Everts referenced this presupposition when he wrote, "Not only are Christians called to 'love our neighbors,' but developing trusting friendships with our neighbors is an important precondition for having spiritual conversations. We have to gain a hearing before being able to share our faith . . . if trust is a prerequisite for spiritual conversations, we all need to consider what we can do to develop more trusting friendships with non-Christians." *The Reluctant Witness* (Downers Grove, IL: IVP, 2019), 69–71.

(cf. Matt 13:1–9, 18–23)? How can they be assured they have achieved a "sufficient" level of trust with their new acquaintances or friends so they can share the gospel with them? What if they never have a chance to meet them again, or if one or the other dies before a "sufficient" amount of trust is built for evangelism? While relationship-building has a place in evangelism, Networkers should not value it more than they do the preparatory work of the Holy Spirit in evangelism.

Networking evangelism also has its strengths. First, it provides unbelievers a context in which they can observe believers' words match their actions. Second, evangelism within relationships provides personal evangelists with multiple encounters in which to share the gospel with those they will likely see again. Sharing the gospel with those in relational networks over time also allows personal evangelists to seek and receive counsel from other experienced believers in how to respond in later encounters to the specific objections raised by their friends. Last, friendship evangelism provides a natural connection where the evangelist can assist new believers in the next steps of discipleship, specifically their friends' baptism and obedience to Christ's commands.

The Charging Bull: Confrontational Evangelism[16]

Sometimes Christians who practice what is referred to as *confrontational evangelism*—that is, evangelizing at particular points in time rather than over an extended period of time—are likened to a charging bull toward its target. These *charging bull* evangelists have the reputation for coming out of nowhere, rushing in on an unsuspecting stranger, and launching into an evangelistic presentation before a person can say, "Hello. My name is . . ." They prefer to immediately share the gospel and often bulldoze through bridges instead of building them. They rarely develop a

---

[16] Mittelberg referred to this approach as "truth-telling" in *Contagious Faith*, 127–44.

relationship before presenting the good news. They typically take control of such conversations and retain them as long as they can.

While we can applaud these personal evangelists for being very direct and intentional in evangelism, this approach often forces the conversation, lending itself to manipulation or hearers feeling pressured. When this happens, people will either change the subject or, worse, make a false profession of faith out of fear or ignorance just to get the "bull" to back off or go away. Personal evangelism occurs in the context of conversations, not monologues. Listeners will quickly tune out of one-sided conversations for lack of interest. Evangelists should present as much of the gospel as possible to their listeners; however, they should also encourage feedback so they can naturally address their listeners' specific situations, instead of sounding canned and forced.

Charging bulls also have the tendency to focus on their own ability to convince others to make a decision, rather than rely on the Holy Spirit to convince and convict them to repent and believe. They usually substitute Holy Spirit boldness and confidence with their extensive evangelism training certification, the breadth of apologetic facts and knowledge they have amassed, or their winsome, charismatic personality. While the Holy Spirit can use each of these qualities to make disciples through evangelism, he alone serves as the catalyst for effective evangelism.

Nevertheless, confrontational evangelism has a number of strengths to its credit. As mentioned previously, it ensures personal evangelists remain direct and intentional in their evangelism. This approach also conveys a clear expectation that those who hear the good news must either receive or reject it. And it guarantees that the gospel will be heard by more people much sooner than the previous six approaches. If practiced with correct motives by relying on the Holy Spirit in the context of a genuine conversation, confrontational evangelism closely resembles the bold presentations of the gospel practiced in the New Testament.

DISCUSSION AND REFLECTION QUESTIONS

1. Which of the evangelism methods and strategies discussed in this chapter do you frequently practice? What about them do you find helpful? While using them, have you experienced some of the difficulties the chapter identified? If so, how have you or how can you compensate for them?

2. Select at least one of this chapter's methods or strategies that you typically do not use when you evangelize. Why have you not used it? What new skills or changes in your evangelism could help you begin to incorporate it?

3. In the first exercise of chapter 5, you selected someone within your network of family, friends, and acquaintances for whose salvation you began to pray and with whom you planned to evangelize. Use the following exercise to assist you in sharing the gospel with that person.[17]

---

[17] Years ago, Kyle Worley, a former student, contacted me about a project he was compiling. He was composing a training program for the Village Church Institute. The training included an evangelism journal workbook. After asking for my input, he formulated the following tool I have found extremely helpful to assist networkers in their evangelism. Along with a few modifications, I have included it with his permission.

RELATIONSHIP EVANGELISM WORKSHEET

1. What is the name of the person for whose salvation you are praying and with whom you want to share the gospel?

2. In what ways has God burdened your heart for this person?

3. Where and in what situations do you normally meet with this person?

4. What are some things about which you have talked with him or her previously?

5. Do you know anything about his or her (a) spiritual background, (b) demeanor toward God, Christianity, the Bible, and other Christians, (c) interests, (d) family, (e) fears, and (f) personality that can help you as you formulate how to share the gospel?

Input the following information weekly as you attempt to win this person to Christ:

1. What are some specific ways I need God to help me evangelize this person?

2. What are some specific ways I can interact with this person this
    week to share the gospel?

3. What are some things I learned from this week's interaction(s)
    that can help me adjust how I share Christ with this person in
    the future? What questions or objections did this person offer for
    which I need to provide a response?

4. Who are some believers either God has laid on my heart or whom
    this person knows that can help me evangelize him or her?

PART 3

Implications for Evangelism

8

Evangelism as Communication
and Proclamation

E vangelism depends on God's proactive involvement before, during, and after its course. Nevertheless, he willingly invites and expects those within whom he dwells by faith in Jesus Christ to join him in the effort. His will and role in this process supersede the principles of communication theory, although some of its models can assist personal evangelists in visualizing how divine and human agencies collaborate in the process of evangelistic proclamation.

This chapter explores multiple facets of evangelism as a form of communication and proclamation. First, it will review and theologically assess the Engel Scale, the widely accepted diagram of the spiritual decision-making process during evangelism. Second, it will propose a new model of evangelistic communication that aims to represent the multidimensional aspects that influence and conceptualize evangelism. Third, it will discuss the dynamics of biblical contextualization. Fourth, the chapter will offer helpful tips for transitioning into gospel conversations. Last, it will present a model that provides Christians confidence to evangelize, along with a step-by-step tutorial of how to share the gospel and handle unbelievers' responses.

Measuring Receptivity in the Spiritual Decision-Making Process

Since the late twentieth century, evangelism and missions scholars have used a diagram known as the Engel Scale to visualize the spiritual decision-making process. Although they attribute the model to James F. Engel, Viggo Söggard actually first proposed a primitive format of it. Engel first published Söggard's scale, "The Spiritual Status of Man," in a 1973 edition of the *Church Growth Bulletin*.[1] After adding God's and the communicator's roles to the chart and revising the scale's grade designations, he produced the scale as it is now known in his book *What's Gone Wrong with the Harvest*. Charles Kraft and Peter Wagner then popularized its use within the academy.

The scale suggests three actors in the process of evangelism: *God*, the *communicator*, and *man*. For the sake of clarity, *communicator* will be referred to as *personal evangelist*, and *man* will be referred to as *unbeliever*. As the diagram demonstrates, each of these actors retains essential roles in the communication of the gospel.

God

According to the Engel Scale, God takes four actions in the process of evangelism. First, he provides general revelation by way of his creation of the world and endows humans with a conscience. Second, he convicts unbelievers of their sinful disobedience against him. Third, he

---

[1] James F. Engel, "Accountability for World Evangelization," *Church Growth Bulletin*, vol. ix, no. 6 (July 1973): 333.

FIGURE 2. The Engel Scale

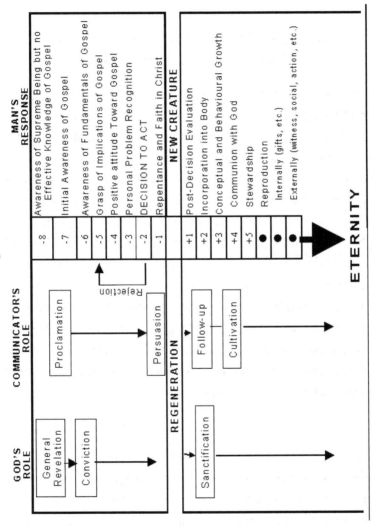

James F. Engel and Wilbert Norton, *What's Gone Wrong with the Harvest?* (Grand Rapids: Zondervan, 1975), 45. Copyright © 1975 by James F. Engel and Wilbert Norton. Used by permission of Zondervan. www.zondervan.com.

regenerates sinners into saints. Last, he sanctifies these new creations of Christ into eternity.

While it's helpful to acknowledge that God plays a role in the evangelism process, this illustration's portrayal of God's actions in evangelism and salvation fail to meet standard biblical and theological measures. Although God declares himself to unbelievers through general revelation, this diagram neglects to include his role in special revelation. The chart rightly denotes God's role in convicting unbelievers, but it errs by isolating the act of regeneration from God's direct function in salvation. In addition to misplacing regeneration, the Engel Scale minimizes God's salvific work to sanctification alone. By doing so, it fails to acknowledge his roles in the justification and glorification of believers from their conversion into eternity.

The Personal Evangelist

The scale displays four ways that personal evangelists contribute to the communication process in evangelism. First, they proclaim the gospel message to unbelievers. Next, they attempt to persuade sinners to receive Christ. Then they follow up to assist them in evaluating their faith decision and being incorporated into a local church. Last, the communicators take a nurturing role and cultivate the unbelievers-turned-disciples in Christian obedience.

The diagram offers two characterizations about the personal evangelist that create inadvertent confusion. The first one relates to persuasion's placement beside the "Man's Response" scale. It seems as if Engel designated persuasion to occur after unbelievers realize they have a decision to make. Yet the New Testament includes several examples of believers encouraging unbelievers to respond to the gospel before they realize they must accept or reject it. A number of these occur through Paul in his appeals to Jews and Greeks in the Corinthian synagogue (Acts 18:4–8), to the disciples of John in Ephesus (Acts 19:1–7), to those in the Ephesian synagogue (Acts 19:8–9), and to Agrippa (Acts 26:24–29).

The other designation is not so much inaccurate as it is ambiguous. Engel assigns the role of cultivating new disciples to the person who shares the gospel with them. In one sense, he is correct. The New Testament does not conceive of personal evangelists who reject their natural responsibility as disciple-makers to develop new believers spiritually. Nevertheless, the way in which he designates personal evangelists as cultivators begs the question: "Is the personal evangelist solely responsible for the new disciple's spiritual care, or do those who lead people to Christ fulfill this responsibility along with fellow believers in the context of a local church?" The sentiment undergirding Paul's rebuke about divisions within the Corinthian church (1 Cor 1:10–17; 3:1–11; 4:14–17), as well as the dynamic created when evangelists make disciples in locations where they cannot provide ongoing spiritual care, seem to support the latter option. Therefore, Engel's illustration obfuscates the matter.

The Unbeliever

Engel's illustration suggests unbelievers progress along a graded scale as they respond to God and the communicative actions of the personal evangelist. A person can move forward from point to point along this gradation system over time or in quick succession. The integrated process classifies unbelievers and operates in the following way:

> **-8 Classification**: As God reveals himself generally through creation and the individual's conscience, the unbeliever has an awareness of some supreme being, but no specific knowledge about the gospel.

> **-7 Classification**: Simultaneously while God is convicting, the personal evangelist is sharing, and the unbeliever becomes initially aware of the gospel.

-6 Classification: As God continues to convict, the personal evangelist persists to share, and the unbeliever understands the fundamental truths of the gospel.

-5 Classification: As God continues to convict, the personal evangelist persists to share, and the unbeliever grasps the implications of the gospel.

-4 Classification: As God continues to convict, the personal evangelist persists to share, and the unbeliever demonstrates a positive attitude about the gospel.

-3 Classification: As God continues to convict, the personal evangelist persists to share, and the unbeliever recognizes his or her need for the gospel.

-2 Classification: As God continues to convict, the personal evangelist persists to share, the unbeliever realizes he or she must either reject or accept the gospel.

If the unbeliever's decision is to reject the gospel, that he or she will return to the **-5** classification by default when confronted with sin and the gospel in the future. Any future progression will begin with that person being confronted with the implications of the gospel.

If the unbeliever's decision is to accept the gospel, he or she will progress to the **-1** classification.

-1 Classification: As God convicts, the personal evangelist persuades the unbeliever to repent and believe, at which point the person becomes a new creation in Christ.

+1 Classification: The personal evangelist counsels the new disciple in an evaluation of his or her decision, while God begins sanctifying the new disciple.

> The grading on the scale then increases as through eternity
> God sanctifies and the personal evangelist cultivates new
> believers as they are incorporated into a local church (+2) and
> grow conceptually and behaviorally (+3) in communion with
> God (+4), stewardship (+5), internal and external reproduction
> (+6), etc.

Two dilemmas arise from the scale's presentation of the unbeliever. The first relates to the legitimacy of believers' ability to gauge sinners' receptivity. Only God knows with certainty the thoughts and intents of any particular person. In fact, unsaved people, themselves, cannot know or trust their own minds and hearts. How then can personal evangelists discern with any amount of accuracy where unbelievers rank on the Engel Scale?

Second, Engel sequenced multiple actions he assigned to unbelievers in an incorrect order. As previously mentioned, unbelievers do not usually recognize they have a decision to make in regards to the gospel if believers fail to persuade them. Also, the chart positions repentance and faith prior to regeneration. Various theological systems differ on the order of salvation. While this *ordo salutis* accurately reflects the soteriology of Arminians, it does not coincide with that held by a majority of evangelicals. High and moderate Calvinists, along with Amyraldians, would position regeneration before repentance and faith. On the other hand, Molinists, Provisionalists, and some others would generally view these actions occurring almost simultaneously, yet prompted by God's preemptive operation. Engel's ordering of the conceptual and behavioral growth is also odd. The first thing a new Christian does after salvation is witness, yet he places evangelism as one of the last items on the list. Also, believers in the Baptist tradition enjoy communion with God while they await incorporation into the body. Although he likely did not intend to assign order to these particular activities, the fact he lists them beside a graded scale ultimately forces him to do so.

Observing the Evangelistic Communication Process

The biblical and theological issues raised by the Engel Scale evidence the need for another model. Proposing a new visual aid to **observe** the multiple dimensions of the evangelistic process, rather than continuing to rely on one that **measures** receptivity, avoids the complications noted earlier. Published after Engel's advancement of assessing gospel responsiveness, David Hesselgrave's "Perspectives from the Science of Communication" in *Communicating Christ Cross Culturally* and Mark McCloskey's "An Interpersonal Communication Model" serve as two valuable resources to better assist Christians in observing and interpreting the communication process in evangelism. The following diagram builds on the foundation of their work and provides a contemporary model of the communication process in evangelistic proclamation.

Similar to the Engel Scale, this model features three actors in the communication process of evangelism: the *triune God*, the *personal evangelist*, and the *other person*. But instead of chronicling and measuring receptivity from beginning to end, this diagram presents the factors that comprise a single episode of evangelistic proclamation. Such a tool provides personal evangelists with a multidimensional view of the active elements and operating influences occurring during evangelism.

The Triune God

As the outer rectangle of the model suggests, God the Father, the Son, and the Spirit superintend each and every evangelistic encounter. Their administration and control over evangelism is grounded in the scriptural truths that (1) God desires the salvation of every person (1 Tim 2:4; 2 Pet 3:9), (2) He has commanded his followers to make disciples of all nations (Matt 28:16–20; *Mark 16:15*; Luke 24:46–48; John 20:21; Acts 1:8; 4:19–20; 5:29; 13:47), and (3) each time the gospel is communicated, regardless of what motivates the one who shares it, and Christ is proclaimed, God actively oversees and accompanies every believer when they

FIGURE 3. A Proposed Model of the Communication Process in Evangelism

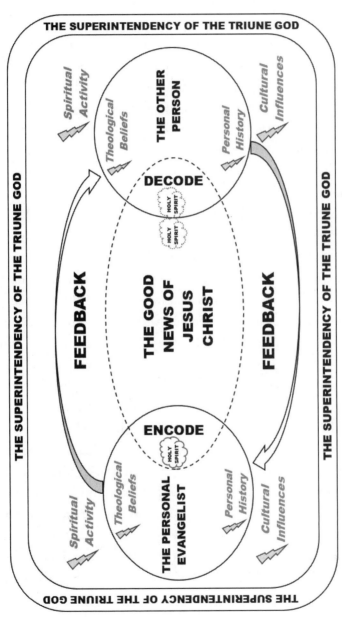

Although this particular chart is original to me, a number of different communication models and theories have contributed to my illustration of this particular model. Specifically, the following sources have influenced its design: David Hesselgrave, *Communicating Christ Cross-Culturally: An Introduction to Missionary Communication*, 2nd ed. (Grand Rapids: Zondervan, 1991), 39–54; McCloskey, *Tell It Often—Tell It Well*, 216–32 (see chap. 6, n. 3); and Claude E. Shannon and Warren Weaver, *The Mathematical Theory of Communication* (Urbana, IL: University of Illinois, 1949), 9.

present the gospel (Matt 28:20; Acts 18:9–10). God's superintendency assures Christians they are neither abandoned nor disobedient to God the Father whenever they tell someone else the good news.

In addition to being enveloped by the triune God, evangelistic presentations orbit around the saving message of God, the Son's life, death, burial, resurrection, and glorification. Illustrated with a dotted-line oval in the center of the diagram, the *good news of Jesus Christ* occupies the epicenter of evangelism. Christian presentations that neglect to incorporate and concentrate on the gospel, no matter how spiritual or sincere they may be, cannot be considered evangelism and will not save anyone.

Last, the Spirit of God is illustrated in the model by a cloud ($\bigcirc$). Because he indwells believers and divinely assists them with the very words they use to proclaim Christ, the Spirit of God is designated within the circle that indicates the *personal evangelist*, located on the left side of the model. Because the hearer could be either a believer or an unbeliever, the Spirit is denoted with dotted lines, positioned both outside (if an unbeliever) and inside (if a believer) the right circle labeled *other person*. Besides his activity in superintending the entire communication process along with the Father and Son, the Holy Spirit also helps personal evangelists to *encode* the gospel and the other person to *decode* it in order to preserve the message's fidelity. Mark McCloskey describes *encoding* as that activity in which believers "package and present the message in a manner that offers the best chance of reaching and influencing the listener."[2] *Decoding* refers to how the other person hears, comprehends, and understands the good news. As the diagram shows, the Holy Spirit leads, guides, and helps believers in what they say and how they say it when they evangelize (Matt 10:17–20; Mark 13:9–11; Luke 12:11–12; 21:12–15). It also exhibits the Holy Spirit's work in

---

[2] McCloskey, *Tell It Often—Tell It Well*, 218 (see chap. 6, n. 3).

convincing and convicting unbelievers as they hear and consider the claims made about Christ.

The Personal Evangelist

The triune God is the source of the gospel and sends those who proclaim it; however, in their role of communicating the gospel, the personal evangelist serves as the trans*mission*ary source of the gospel to unbelievers. As Paul reasoned, "And how can they hear without a preacher? And how can they preach unless they are sent" (Rom 10:14b–15a)? As the diagram demonstrates, God and the personal evangelist cooperate in evangelism (Isa 53:1; Rev 22:17), although throughout the process the latter is dependent on the former.

Enabled by the Spirit to encode the message, a believer shares the good news of Jesus with the other person. After the gospel is decoded, the other person generally responds to the personal evangelist with *feedback* (indicated by a curved arrow ⟲). Typically, their response will either restate what they have understood about the gospel or pose questions for further clarification. With the help of the Holy Spirit, the personal evangelist uses the decoded feedback received throughout the conversation to re-encode the gospel. The transmission of re-encoded explanations of the gospel, a form of feedback itself, continuously cycles from the sender to the recipient and vice versa with the aim that the personal evangelist will discern if the other person already possesses genuine faith in Christ or persuade him or her to repent and believe.

In addition to the Holy Spirit, believers are also influenced by numerous other factors. These include internal issues relating to their personal experiences and theological beliefs, as well as the external elements of cultural affluence and spiritual warfare. Each of these factors is depicted by a lightning bolt (⚡) inside and outside the circles that represent both the personal evangelist and the other person. In communication theory, these factors that affect and sometimes hinder, or distract from, the faithful transmission of the message and any resulting feedback are referred to as *noise*.

Personal History and Theological Beliefs

Concerning internal issues, the extent of personal evangelists' previous experience in evangelism can influence their practice of disciple-making, either positively or negatively. Little to no past experience in evangelism can illicit fear and tempt believers not to share. On the other hand, the more believers practice telling unbelievers about Christ, the more they gain confidence, familiarity with what to expect, and knowledge of how to respond to unbelievers' reactions. Also, Christians' theological beliefs affect if and how they evangelize. For more information, consult chapter 6 about the implications of believers' soteriology and how their doctrine affects the way they invite people to repent and believe.

Cultural Influences and Spiritual Activity

Regarding the external forces, some cultural influences and demonic spiritual activity have the potential to disrupt a personal evangelist's practice of evangelism. The culture in which they were reared has led them to form personal biases. A Christian's biases can generate overt or subconscious prejudices against other people. For example, a cultural bias may prevent a believer from initiating evangelism on the basis of another's ethnicity, economic status, or gender. Because the Father sent the Son to die for every person, there is no person with whom a personal evangelist should not share the gospel. A cultural bias can also lead a Christian to make assumptions about others that may or may not be true. For instance, believers in the "Bible Belt" intuitively surmise, many times wrongly, that just because people attend church that they are genuine Christians. When another's faith in Christ is merely assumed, evangelism will likely not happen. For these reasons, anyone who determines to share the gospel should be aware of and correct any such prejudices and assumptions formed by enculturation.

Satanic spiritual forces also attempt to counter the inner work of the Holy Spirit in believers when they evangelize. The tactics of the enemy to disrupt personal evangelists from proclaiming Christ vary in form and intensity. Demons regularly use discouragement, oppression, doubt, and distractions to prevent Christ from being shared with those they hold in their grasp. Nevertheless, believers should not despair "because the one who is in you is greater than the one who is in the world" (1 John 4:4b).

The Other Person

The individual who receives a personal evangelist's presentation of the gospel is designated in this model as the *other person*. A believer can never know whether or not another person is a genuine believer in Christ until after he or she has shared the complete gospel with that individual, and even then, only God definitely knows. After sharing it, the evangelist must biblically evaluate the response and decoded feedback he or she receives, and even then, absolute certainty is not possible. For this reason and because believers should evangelize strangers in addition to those they know, evangelism should not be restricted only to those the personal evangelist knows to be unbelievers. On the other hand, they should not feel obligated to evangelize those who demonstrate clear evidence of the fruit of the Spirit, because those people are very likely believers and need not be evangelized.

Personal History and Theological Beliefs

The other person's experiences and beliefs influence the communication process in evangelism. These factors affect the ability and extent to which he or she can decode and comprehend the gospel message. Whether or not the hearer has any past involvement with or exposure to Christianity can either positively or negatively affect his or her receptivity. Also, the religion with which the receiver identifies, if any, has a likelihood to predispose him or her to misinterpret the gospel vocabulary of the personal evangelist. For example, a Hindu may hear him or her explain, "Jesus is God," and understand from that declaration that Jesus is one of the thirty-three million gods they worship. Or, when sharing with a Muslim, the believer may appeal to a shared affirmation of Jesus's virgin birth to argue his full divinity and full humanity. But the believer's reasoning will likely be lost on the Muslim because Islam fails to link Mary's celibacy and Jesus's conception with his nature and the incarnation. Awareness of theological polysemy like these in the process of evangelistic communication should convince personal evangelists of the need to contextualize the gospel faithfully. A fuller treatment of biblical contextualization will follow this section.

Cultural Influences and Spiritual Activity

As with the personal evangelist, the other person's culture produces innate behaviors and customs that affect the communication process. In some cultures men and women freely engage in conversation; however, in other cultures this is viewed as taboo and dishonorable. Many contexts respect age over youth and consider it disrespectful for someone younger to evangelize an elder citizen. Personal evangelists should investigate these and other cultural mores when they evangelize cross-culturally.

Unbelievers are in bondage to Satan and his demons. The devil opposes any threat to his dominion; therefore, when Christians evangelize, he and his forces go on the offensive. While they may employ spiritual warfare by discouraging, oppressing, and distracting unbelievers when they are confronted with the gospel, God's adversaries sometimes resort to possessing them. Personal evangelists who encounter this phenomenon should not approach these situations as priests in Hollywood horror films, but rather with a total dependency on the Holy Spirit's leadership, using prayer, and in some cases, fasting, and insisting in the name of Jesus to speak with the unbeliever while proclaiming to them victory in Christ's death, burial, resurrection, and exaltation and calling for repentance and belief.[3]

Contextualized Bridges to the Gospel

Comprehending the language, culture, and beliefs of those whom personal evangelists evangelize is an important task. William Abraham writes:

> In taking the gospel to the world one must pay attention to the context of the hearer, making a careful study of the social and personal circumstances of the hearer or hearers. At times it may require specialist information about the nature of modern cities, or the character of a rural community, or the relation of persons to established Christian communities, and the like. This is especially important when the gospel is taken across significant cultural and linguistic borders. It requires great sensitivity and dexterity to fulfill Paul's policy of being "all things to all men." On the one side, the evangelist must proclaim the gospel with integrity and without compromise; on the other he or she must be willing and able to meet people where they are, drawing them into the orbit of the kingdom, taking up all that is valid, true, and God-given in the native culture.[4]

How much cultural expertise should personal evangelists possess before they evangelize? How up-to-date should they be on current trends and pop culture to communicate the gospel to those living in the world,

---

[3] Personal evangelists who want to learn more about dealing with spiritual warfare in evangelism can consult Merrill F. Unger, *Demons in the World Today: A Study of Occultism in the Light of God's Word* (Wheaton, IL: Tyndale, 1973); Rodger K. Bufford, *Counseling and the Demonic* (Dallas: Word, 1988); and William F. Cook III and Chuck Lawless, *Spiritual Warfare in the Storyline of Scripture: A Biblical, Theological, and Practical Approach* (Nashville: B&H, 2019).

[4] Abraham, *The Logic of Evangelism*, 172 (see chap. 5, n. 8).

whose lives are ever being conformed to the world? Sincere, inquiring evangelicals want to know.

A growing number of Bible scholars and writers have attempted to answer these questions by appealing to Paul's philosophical discourse on the Areopagus or Mars Hill in Acts 17:22–34. Among Greek Epicurean and Stoic philosophers, Paul recounted that his tour of the numerous temples and altars in Athens left him with the impression that they were very religious (17:22–23). On one such altar he found a dedicatory inscription "To an Unknown God" and gave them specifics about a deity they worshiped but did not know (17:23). Paul also quoted two poems, "Cretica" (cf. 17:28a) and "Phaenomena 5" (cf. 17:28b), composed by the pagan poets Epimenides and Aratus, respectively.

How did Paul preach the Christian gospel to curious, cultural Athenian philosophers, and what was their response? He identified an unknown divine being whom they worshiped but did not know, using it as a transition to proclaim a God they did not know—the Christian God who created everything in the world, determined the patterns for all the peoples of the world, and sent his righteous Son to die and be raised from the dead so that everyone everywhere might repent (17:24–31). When hearing about the resurrection of the dead, every person responded in one of three ways—many mocked Paul; others were intrigued and wanted a future conversation with him about Jesus and the resurrection; and some repented, believed, and joined him as he left (17:32–34).

Many Christian apologists contend that Paul's appeal to Greek philosophy, theology, architecture, and literature in his Areopagus speech serves as an impetus for contemporary Christians to become familiar with cultural mores in order to build a *comparative*, evangelistic bridge from culture to Christ.[5] In other words, believers should attempt to

---

[5] Some examples include Newman, *Unlikely Converts*, 34–36 (see chap. 5, n. 19); and Mittelberg, *Contagious Faith*, 108–10 (see chap. 7, n. 3). The *comparative bridge*, used as an evangelistic tool, is articulated by Alister McGrath in his chapter "Points of Contact," in *Intellectuals Don't Need God & Other Modern*

evangelize secular people by comparing similarities of their culture with Christ. Knowledge about pop culture certainly helps personal evangelists as they seek to contextualize the gospel to their hearers. Yet the philosophers did not invite Paul to preach Jesus and the resurrection atop the Areopagus because of the similarities he drew between their culture and his Christ. He was invited as a result of the curiosity created by his *contrastive*, evangelistic presentation to the Epicurean and Stoic philosophers in the marketplace (17:16–21).

Paul's familiarity with Athenian theology and its worshipful architecture was not the result of an eager, educational enculturation. Instead, the city's numerous idols and altars agitated him inwardly (17:16). In addition, the Epicureans and Stoics first heard the gospel in the market, not upon Mars Hill (17:18–20). D. A. Carson explains it this way: "[Paul] evangelizes day by day in the marketplace, targeting anyone who happens to be there. . . . He does not wait for an invitation to the Areopagus. He simply gets on with his evangelism, and the invitation to the Areopagus is the result."[6] Specifically, his articulation of the gospel prompted the philosophers to ask, "What is this ignorant show-off [lit., *seed picker*] trying to say? . . . . May we learn about this new teaching you are presenting?" (17:18–19). Their questions indicate that Paul's evangelistic contextualization of the gospel was not *comparative* in nature, but rather *contrastive*.[7]

Myths: Building Bridges to Faith Through Apologetics (Grand Rapids: Zondervan, 1993), 30–47.

[6] D. A. Carson, "Athens Revisited," in *Telling the Truth: Evangelizing Postmoderns*, ed. D. A. Carson (Grand Rapids: Zondervan, 2000), 391.

[7] David Hesselgrave codified the concepts of *comparative* and *contrastive* contextualization among evangelicals and suggested that while the comparative form should not be completely rejected, contrastive contextualization is preferred within evangelistic and missiological efforts. See "Christian Communication and Religious Pluralism," *Missiology: An International Review* 18, no. 2 (April 1990): 131–38.

Specifically, Michael Criner described and presented a critical explanation of comparative and contrastive contextualization in the context of Paul's

Instead of relating the Athenians' religious and cultural beliefs to the gospel, Paul was contrasting the gospel with their misunderstanding of the divine. His gospel proclamation centered emphatically on Jesus and his resurrection. Nevertheless, several of the philosophers accused him of being "a preacher of foreign deities"—Jesus and a divine female consort, Anastasia (the Greek word translated *resurrection*)—although he proclaimed only one God, Jesus, who was raised from the dead (17:18c).[8] These supposed "foreign deities" sounded so strange and unfamiliar to

---

evangelistic addresses in Acts. See *Text-Driven Contextualization: Biblical Principles for Fulfilling the Great Commission in the 21st Century* (Fort Worth: Seminary Hill, 2017), 103–42. Eckhard J. Schnabel observed these forms of contextualization particularly in Acts 17 when he identified the Greco-Roman "elements of contact" Paul contrasted with biblical "elements of contradiction" while preaching the gospel to the Athenian philosophers. Schnabel explained, "Paul's speech before the Council of the Areopagus includes points with which the philosophically informed audience can agree, but also points that would have provoked them." *Paul the Missionary: Realities, Strategies, and Methods* (Downers Grove, IL: IVP, 2008), 171. In addition, Bruce Ashford described these forms of contextualization with an emphasis on the *contrastive* form: "Although [Paul] began with points of contact, he did not end there. Over and again, Paul corrected pagan idolatry by showing how the Scriptures subvert and overthrow pagan idolatry as manifested in their literature, philosophy, and theology. . . . Although Paul began by using some categories familiar to the Athenians and answering some questions they likely would have raised, he followed through by also introducing them to biblical categories and answering questions that they had not raised," "The Gospel and Culture," in *Theology and Practice of Mission: God, the Church, and the Nations*, ed. Bruce Riley Ashford (Nashville: B&H Academic, 2011), 119.

[8] Although C. K. Barrett is skeptical of this interpretation in *A Critical and Exegetical Commentary on the Acts of the Apostles: Introduction and Commentary on Acts XV–XXVIII*, vol. 2, International Critical Commentary (London: T&T Clark, 1998), 830–31; David G. Peterson explains, "[Some of them] *remarked, 'He seems to be advocating foreign gods'*. The plural *xenōn daimoniōn* ('foreign divinities'), followed by the explanatory clause *because Paul was preaching the good news about Jesus and the resurrection*, suggests that they understood Paul to be preaching in polytheistic fashion about a god named Jesus (a masculine name in Greek) and his consort 'Resurrection' (*anastasis* is feminine in Greek)." in *The Acts of the Apostles*, The Pillar New Testament Commentary (Grand Rapids:

them, that out of curiosity, they invited Paul to explain more fully what he meant, as was their custom (17:20–21).

As the old adage states, "Christians are in the world, but not of it." While we are in the world, we will learn and acquire knowledge about the world, its beliefs, and customs. We can, and should, use some of what we learn to draw culture-to-Christ analogies for unbelievers who cannot comprehend the gospel. But believers should not feel the need to spend an eternity learning about this world, so they can point unbelievers to the Way to spend eternity in the world to come.

As Edward Rommen explains, "We are under great pressure to adapt the Gospel to its cultural surroundings. While there is a legitimate concern for contextualization, what most often happens in these cases is an outright capitulation of the Gospel to the principles of that culture."[9] Kevin DeYoung also warns, "Beware of having all contextualization, with no confrontation."[10] In other words, the practice of biblical evangelism is not primarily about what you know (of this world); it is who you know (the resurrected Jesus Christ). Preaching the gospel is as simple as telling others about Jesus and his resurrection from the dead and confronting them with their need to repent of their sins and believe in him.

Transitioning from a Conversation to a Gospel Presentation

Jeff Vanderstelt refers to the ability "to translate the world around [Christians] and the world inside of them through the lens of the gospel—the truths of God revealed in the person and work of Jesus" as

---

Eerdmans, 2009), 491. Peterson cites Gärtner, Longenecker, and Spencer, who also support this view.

[9] Rommen, *Get Real: On Evangelism in the Late Modern World*, 182 (see chap. 6, n. 16).

[10] Kevin DeYoung, Twitter post, October 26, 2013, 8:32 a.m., https://twitter .com/RevKevDeYoung/status/394094275702824960.

gospel fluency.[11] Achieving *gospel fluency* requires believers to experience *gospel immersion*. He describes *gospel immersion* as the process whereby believers actively participate within a gospel-speaking community whose members "bring the gospel to bear on one another's lives and on the lives of those who don't yet believe in Jesus."[12] According to Vanderstelt the process by which gospel immersion results in gospel fluency occurs by understanding that

> formal training alone does not make one fluent [in the gospel]. You become [gospel] fluent through immersion in a gospel-speaking community and through ongoing practice. You have to know it, regularly hear it, and practice proclaiming it. . . . Gospel fluency begins in you, gets worked out within community, and is expressed to a world that needs to hear about Jesus.[13]

Evangelistic fluency is the process of transitioning an initial or on-going dialogue into a gospel conversation where personal evangelists present the gospel. Getting to the gospel requires believers to listen for the spiritual cues the other person verbalizes when casually chatting. These indicators provide Christians prompts by which they can advance the discourse in an evangelistic direction to discuss spiritual matters. Spiritual conversations provide believers transitions to begin gospel conversations, which should include gospel presentations that culminate in issuing evangelistic invitations.

Personal evangelists should be careful of the ways and means they use to attempt to relate to unbelievers so they can share the gospel. Some leaders who rose to ministry prominence during the beginning of the twentieth century, and now who no longer hold influence, once suggested unconventional ways to introduce Christ to the lost. Some of these ways included the use of alcoholic beverages, coarse language, and

---

[11] Jeff Vanderstelt, *Gospel Fluency* (Wheaton, IL: Crossway, 2017), 41.

[12] Vanderstelt, 43–44.

[13] Vanderstelt, 43.

bait-and-switch bribes, just to name a few. Standing against this counsel, Pastor Greg Laurie, in a 2009 blog post, declared, "Let's not trade reverence for relevance."[14] True enough, but they also must not confuse what is reverent with what is relevant.

L. R. Scarborough advised, "Never seek a heavenly end with an earthly motive; never try to accomplish God's will with the devil's tools."[15] Sinful or less-than-sanctified lures must not be mistaken as gospel attractions for sinners. When fishing for men, do not expect a great catch by casting a rotten net. Instead, personal evangelists should use "lures" that do not detract attention from the gospel but rather lure people to the gospel. As C. E. Autrey suggested:

> The approach is to the successful witness what the lure is to the fisherman. The fisherman must have bait, and no fisherman would use the same lure each time he fishes. The situation, the type of fish, and the waters in which one is fishing will determine the bait. The skill with which he uses the lure enhances the prospects of success. The approach is the starting point. . . . The fisherman begins when he casts his lure into the waters. He does not walk up to the stream and splash the water and yell, "Look at me! I'm here," and then gracefully throw out the lure. Rather, he avoids drawing attention to himself, for he may frighten the fish away.[16]

Believers who find it difficult to transition a conversation into evangelism can consider asking someone, "Has anyone told you that Jesus loves you today?" If asked, most people will respond, "No," because most believers do not evangelize regularly. When they do, tell them something like, "I want to be the first one today to tell you he loves you. Although

---

[14] Greg Laurie, "Reverence or Relevance?," *Greg's Blog*, March 11, 2009, https://harvest.org/resources/gregs-blog/post/reverence-or-relevance/.

[15] Scarborough, *With Christ after the Lost*, 176 (see chap. 2, n. 9).

[16] C. E. Autrey, *You Can Win Souls* (Nashville: Broadman, 1961), 41–42.

you do not know me and I do not know you, the way I know he loves you is because the Bible says, 'But God proves his own love for us in that while we were still sinners, Christ died for us'" (Rom 5:8).

A missionary once shared with me about his meeting with Carl F. H. Henry during Henry's visit to Cameroon. While passing through a particular town, they encountered a female NGO worker. After exchanging cordial pleasantries, Henry asked her, "Friend, have you had the joy of knowing Jesus as your personal Savior?"

You may also choose to use Henry's question to transition into a gospel presentation. If you do, and the other person says yes to your question, ask the individual to share his or her conversion story. If the person says no, take that opportunity to present the gospel.

Toby DeHay has popularized another natural gospel transition. When he evangelizes, he asks people, "Have you heard any good news today?" As in the first example, most people reply, "No." When they do, he transitions to the gospel by saying, "Well, I want to be the first one to give you some good news today."[17]

Holidays like Christmas and Easter also provide Christians an instinctive way to begin a gospel presentation. Christmas observes Jesus's birth, and Easter emphasizes his resurrection. Asking someone a question like, "Do you know why we celebrate _____?" will easily allow you to direct such conversations toward Christ.

There are many techniques like these. Use any transition that feels natural to you and does not seem abrupt or cause awkwardness. Getting to the gospel during conversations is as easy as talking about anything else we insert into our daily conversations (e.g., sports, politics, world events, family celebrations, etc.). We have no difficulty beginning discussions that interest us. When applied to evangelism, introducing and including the gospel in our discussions with unbelievers is not so much

---

[17] See Toby DeHay, "Good News for You!," TobyDeHay.com, accessed May 2, 2022, https://tobydehay.com/good-news-for-you/.

a question of, "How do we do it?" so much as, "Do we want to do it?" As Autrey explained, "If one cares enough for an opening to speak to the lost, God will give him a chance, and almost any situation can be transformed into a proper atmosphere for witnessing for Christ."[18]

A Proposal for Evangelism Today

In 2002, Southeastern Baptist Theological Seminary New Testament and Greek professor David Beck used his sabbatical to address his concern that "[e]vangelism is often recognized as the heartbeat of the church, yet it is rarely the focus of serious research among biblical scholars."[19] Upon his return he gave a faculty lecture during a Southeastern chapel service on November 6, 2002. He asked faculty and students:

> How did people in the first century [evangelize] without attending an evangelism training seminar? Did Paul invent the FAITH outline, did Peter ever go through CWT, and did James write the Four Spiritual Laws booklet? . . . Why did none of the New Testament authors write and circulate an evangelism how-to manual? . . . It would seem that evangelism was not something planned or programmed by the early church. Yet consistently and constantly, "The Lord was adding to their number day by day those who were being saved [Acts 2:47]."[20]

He concluded that the early church does not appear "to have been trained in any special [evangelism] seminar. . . . Evangelism in the life of the early church was neither a plan, program, or [*sic*] particular presentation. Rather, it was the natural overflow of hearts filled with Jesus."[21]

---

[18] Autrey, 8.

[19] David R. Beck, "Evangelism in Luke-Acts: More Than an Outreach Program," *Faith & Mission* 20, no. 2 (Spring 2003): 85.

[20] Beck, 86.

[21] Beck, 101–2.

Since the mid-twentieth century, evangelicals have equipped and trained believers to evangelize by memorizing a scripted gospel message and then articulating it. But many people have found it hard to memorize these outlines verbatim. They find it even more difficult to recite what they have memorized in the middle of a conversation with an unbeliever. The pressure they feel in the moment, combined with not having been taught how to answer spontaneous questions, has resulted in believers feeling more frustrated over evangelism than they are faithful in doing it.

How might today's believers return to less programmatic gospel presentations that emanate from "the natural overflow of hearts filled with Jesus?" Can our evangelism sound less forced and more focused; less scripted and more scriptural; and less confusing and more clarified when instructing unbelievers how to respond to the Spirit's conviction and the gospel's call? Perhaps such a transition would occur if our evangelism were to shift from reciting our latest memorized gospel outline to recalling the gospel we first heard in order to believe. This is the same gospel unbelievers must hear if they will ever be forgiven of their sins. We can recover evangelism that focuses on the gospel message we already know instead of a newly structured format by addressing the following four questions:

(1) What Are the Gospel Essentials?

What content must personal evangelists communicate to share the entire gospel with unbelievers? Does they have to recite the entire Old and New Testaments before they can share the gospel? Of course not! While believers should feel the freedom to share as much of the biblical narrative as they desire, they can share the gospel concisely.

Anyone who knows enough of the gospel to have heard it, believed it, and been saved by it knows enough of the gospel to share it. Conversely, those who doesn't know enough of the gospel to share it should ask themselves whether or not they have ever heard and believed enough of the gospel to have been saved by it in the first place. Major Dalton remarks, "If the gospel is really simple enough that a child can understand it, then it must also be simple enough that an adult can explain it."[22] To explain the gospel simply and faithfully, recall the gospel message you heard and believed. At its core, it likely included the reality and consequences of sin; the truth that the God-man Jesus Christ died for your sins, was buried, and raised on the third day; and an invitation to repent of your sins, believe in Jesus Christ and his death, burial, and resurrection for your salvation, and verbally confess, "Jesus is Lord." Although your recollection of the gospel's core elements may be worded or enumerated differently, find encouragement that you already know the gospel and can share it naturally with unbelievers who need to hear it.

The New Testament contains well-known summaries of the gospel Jesus and Paul preached. Mark recorded Jesus's gospel: "After John was arrested, Jesus went to Galilee, proclaiming the good news of God: 'The time is fulfilled, and the kingdom of God has come near. Repent and believe the good news!'" (Mark 1:14–15). Paul also recounted his summary of the gospel in a correspondence he wrote to the Corinthians: "For I passed on to you as most important what I also received: that Christ died for our sins according to the Scriptures, that he was buried, [and] that he was raised on the third day according to the Scriptures" (1 Cor 15:3–4). Although both Jesus and Paul likely communicated more than what the Bible records they said, these summaries of the gospel faithfully convey what unbelievers must hear in order to be saved. In fact, Paul stated in verse 15:3a that the essential content of the good news that he shared with the Corinthians, found in 15:3b–4, was what was communicated to him when he believed the gospel. Therefore, the message that someone shared with you, which you now believe, is the same essential content you can share with others so they might believe.

---

[22] Major Dalton, Twitter post, June 12, 2014, 7:17 p.m., https://twitter.com /majorhdalton/status/477243259815616512.

(2) What Scriptures Will I Use to Communicate These Essentials?

Which Scriptures communicate these essentials you heard and believed? The New Testament presents two reasons why the Scriptures must be incorporated in our gospel presentations. First, hearing the Word of Christ is prerequisite for biblical faith. Paul wrote, "So faith comes from what is heard, and what is heard comes through the message about Christ" (Rom 10:17). Second, evangelistic proclamations in the New Testament overwhelmingly incorporate the Scriptures (e.g., Luke 24:14–32; Acts 2:14–41; 3:11–26; 4:1–12; 7; 8:4, 35; 13:13–49; 16:25–32; 17:10–13; 18:5, 28; 20:27; 26:22–23; 28:23–27).

Likely you can call to mind verses, which in their immediate context and with their intended meaning, communicate the gospel essentials you heard and believed. For example, Rom 3:23 communicates the consequences and reality of sin; 1 Cor 15:3–4 conveys the truth that the God-man Jesus Christ died for your sins, was buried, and raised on the third day; and Rom 10:9 conveys the gospel's invitation to repent of your sins, believe in Jesus Christ and his death, burial, and resurrection for your salvation, and verbally confess, "Jesus is Lord." With the Spirit's help, select a verse that communicates each of the gospel essentials you have already identified. Now incorporate these verses into your evangelistic presentation of those gospel essentials. Feel free to use any presentation of the gospel that is both biblically accurate and easy to share. But remind yourself that the power of God for salvation resides in the Scriptures, not the script you have memorized.

(3) How Will I Instruct a Willing Hearer to Repent, Believe, and Confess?

Some Christians believe that the most nerve-racking aspect about evangelism comes at the beginning of the process—starting a gospel conversation with another person. Yet another aspect of evangelism can be just as, if not more, terrifying—helping the person receive Christ. When personal evangelists are convinced unbelievers genuinely desire to repent, believe, and confess, they should consider asking them to have their first-ever conversation with God. Usually, unbelievers do not know how to speak to God, so first suggest they say in their own words through prayer the reason they came to God. Generally, personal evangelists are listening for some sign of the Holy Spirit's conviction of their sins and their repentance by hearing them admit their sinfulness and need for God's forgiveness.

If they verbalize repentance for their sins, then invite them to tell God, in their own words, what they have understood from your conversation about the good news that alone provides forgiveness for their sins and makes them right with God. Listen for them to reference the essence of the gospel—Jesus's righteous life, sacrificial death, burial, and glorious resurrection as the means for their salvation. If their response agrees that salvation is by grace alone, through faith alone, in Christ alone, then instruct them to confess their repentance and faith in the God-man, Jesus Christ, as their Lord and Savior by stating, "Jesus is Lord."

Last, after they confess the lordship of Christ by calling on the name of the Lord in accordance with the Scriptures, invite them to thank God in their own words for what they understand he has done for them through repentance and faith in Jesus Christ. New believers will thank God for his forgiveness, presence, mercy, and grace, although probably not in those words. More than likely, they will use language such as, "Thank you for removing the weight of my sin," "Thank you for this peace you have given me," or something similar.

An Overview of Personal Evangelism

Intentionality in evangelism is not simply knowing that believers should evangelize; rather, it is making a plan to evangelize consistently and then executing it. One simple approach personal evangelists can use as they intentionally seek to evangelize unbelievers includes the following principles:

(1) Begin in Prayer

Personal evangelists who do not pray will almost certainly fail in evangelism before they even begin. During their quiet times, periodically during each day, and before they gather for planned times of evangelism, believers should pray for God's Spirit to precede their witness and to empower their witness for Jesus with boldness. Praying for these requests will not guarantee that everyone who hears the gospel will respond in faith, nor does it mean that believers will not experience spiritual attacks; however, failure to pray in preparation for evangelism essentially forfeits the blessings of God and leads to spiritual vulnerability.

(2) Identify and Use Points of Contact

Personal evangelists will find no shortage of people who need to hear the gospel; however, those who find trouble identifying someone with whom they will share the gospel should use their existing points of contact. They will likely identify someone with whom they regularly interface and whom they already know (e.g., unbelieving family, friends, and neighbors). In addition, they can approach people such as their restaurant server, hair stylist, dentist, or even solicitors who visit their homes.

Some who desire to evangelize decide to do so only if God will provide them with opportunities. By "opportunities" they mean someone coming to them and asking them what they must to do be saved. Rarely, if ever, will these willing personal evangelists get these "opportunities." Therefore, they should consider evangelistic opportunities from God as those people with whom they come into contact and about whose spiritual states with Christ they do not know.

(3) Articulate a Transition Statement

Once personal evangelists have identified points of contact for evangelism, they should engage those people in conversation. Because God is the creator of all things, evangelists should anticipate and listen for topics that arise in the conversation to transition to the gospel. Some examples of these transitions include the following: (1) Discussions about an earthly father can lead to discussions about the heavenly Father's love as demonstrated by sending Jesus Christ to die for everyone's sins. (2) Information about important life events can lead to personal evangelistic testimonies about how they came to Christ. (3) Concerns about impending death or the uncertainty of life can lead to conversations about how believing in the gospel provides the only way for people to go heaven. (4) Details about others' weekend activities can lead to dialogues about believers' Sunday worship of God and ultimately to the gospel.

(4) Present the Gospel

Personal evangelists who want to evangelize in natural and extemporaneous ways will want to ensure they present the core elements of the gospel. First, they must convey the reality and consequences of sin in the lives of their hearers. Second, they must declare how the life, death, burial, and resurrection of Jesus Christ alone serve as the provision for everyone to be reconciled to God. Last, they must explain that reconciliation with God through Jesus can only occur if they will repent of their sins and believe in Jesus Christ alone for salvation.

(5) Encourage Questions for Clarification

After personal evangelists give a complete presentation of the gospel, they should ask their hearers one or more of the following questions: "Do you understand what I have shared with you?" "Do you have any questions about what I have shared with you?" "Have you ever made this kind of decision?"

To the last question, if they respond, "Yes," then ask them to share with you when this decision was made and to provide some of the details of how they received Christ. If you hear something in their response that convinces you they have experienced a biblical conversion, then encourage them to share the good news with someone else, just as you have done.

(6) Invite Your Hearers to Receive Christ

If those with whom you share the gospel claim they have already received Christ but do not articulate a biblical conversion experience, explain to them how their experience falls short according to Scripture. Then inquire whether or not they understand the difference between it and the Bible's teaching about repentance and faith. If their response indicates they do not, refer to 2 Cor 13:5, which says, "Test yourselves to see if you are in the faith. Examine yourselves. Or do you yourselves not recognize that Jesus Christ is in you?—unless you fail the test." Ask them, "In what specific ways do your speech, actions, and desires provide evidence that you pass the test to demonstrate Jesus lives within you?" If they cannot provide any, then extend to them an invitation to receive Jesus through repentance and faith.

If unbelievers respond negatively to a gospel invitation, ask them, "May I ask what is preventing you from making this decision today?" Many of those with whom personal evangelists share the gospel will decline to repent and believe. In these cases, personal evangelists should, with complete sincerity and devoid of any manipulation, ask them to reconsider this decision. If they still reject the offer of the gospel, then the evangelist should offer a gospel tract that includes the contact information of the believer's local church.[23]

On the other hand, if recipients of the gospel message indicate they would like to repent and believe, then summarize the gospel and emphasize the demands of the gospel. Ask what specific life changes

---

[23] A personal evangelist should consider creating an email address and registering for a Google Voice number (http://voice.google.com) instead of using a personal email address and phone number. The new contact information will provide an intermediary step of security and privacy.

this decision will require them to make. Depending on the response you receive, do the following:

a. If they, under the conviction of the Holy Spirit, desire to repent and believe, then instruct them to call on the Lord for salvation (Rom 10:13) in repentance and faith. Remind them that Jesus, not prayer, saves; but that salvation is received by calling on the name of the Lord in repentance and faith. Encourage them to express their (1) sinfulness before God; (2) need for salvation through Jesus Christ alone; (3) confession of Jesus as Lord; and (4) gratitude for God's grace through prayer. If they need help praying, instruct them to pray the previous four aspects (taking time after each one) in their own words, rather than having them repeat your words after you.

b. If the unbelievers previously misunderstood what they were being asked to do and are not prepared to repent and believe, then encourage them to give more thought to what you have shared, and provide them with a gospel tract that includes follow-up contact information.

c. If they say they understand and want to make this decision, but you have doubts, then reemphasize the high demands of the gospel. If they then reconsider the decision to repent and believe, follow up with discerning questions to determine how, or if, the Holy Spirit is working the kind of conviction that leads to repentance. If upon hearing the high demands of the gospel, and under the conviction of the Holy Spirit, the unbelievers remain steadfast in their desire to repent and believe, then explain how they can call on the Lord for salvation, using the instructions detailed above in (a).

If you are confident in the gospel for your salvation, then be confident in that same gospel to share it. The same gospel you heard, and by which you were saved, is the same gospel someone else needs to hear so they may be saved.

DISCUSSION AND REFLECTION QUESTIONS

1. Do you find it more helpful to visualize the communication pro-
    cess in evangelism through the model that attempts to measure
    receptivity or the one that allows you to observe its multiple
    dimensions? Explain the reasons you prefer one over the other.

2. What (a) past experiences in evangelism, or lack thereof, as well
    as any (b) personal biases you have identified, if any, have you
    learned inhibit your practice of evangelism? In what ways can
    you intentionally address these obstacles so you evangelize more
    confidently, consistently, and collectively?

3. Do you disregard or recognize the dynamic of spiritual warfare
    when you evangelize? If you ignore it, in what specific ways will
    you acknowledge it without allowing it to illicit an unhealthy
    fear? If you give attention to it, in what ways do you guard your-
    self from being fascinated by it to the point you are more pre-
    occupied with chasing after the devil than you are with seeking
    after the lost?

4. When you contextualize the gospel in a cross-cultural environ-
    ment, do you generally prefer to use comparative or contrastive
    contextualization? Provide biblical evidence for your preferred
    way of contextualizing. Also, explain how your use of contextual-
    ization avoids both syncretism and confusion.

5. What are some of the ways you have found most helpful to
    transition naturally from a casual conversation to a gospel
    presentation?

9

Evangelism in the Local Church

Other than the triune God's power and work in evangelism, no greater agency is more instrumental to mobilizing, practicing, and conserving the results of evangelism than local New Testament churches. God enables local churches to advance the gospel by their proclamation of it, and in doing so, evangelism contributes to their vitality and stability. As Karl Barth declares, "Certainly a Church which is not as such an evangelising Church is either not yet or no longer the Church, or only a dead Church, itself standing in supreme need of renewal by evangelisation."[1] This chapter investigates common misconceptions concerning evangelism within local churches and then suggests recommendations for their evangelistic effectiveness.

---

[1] Karl Barth, *Church Dogmatics IV.3.2: The Doctrine of Reconciliation*, ed. G. W. Bromiley and T. F. Torrance, trans. G. W. Bromiley (1961; repr., London: T&T Clark, 2004), 874.

Addressing Common Church-Related
Misconceptions about Evangelism

Chapter 1 surveyed eight misnomers Christians attribute to evangelism. Similarly, the evangelism operation in local churches has been misconceived by some pastors and parishioners. Consider five of the most prominent misunderstandings concerning congregational evangelism:

Misconception 1: Grace-Gifted Evangelists and/or Ministers of a Church Are Its Sole Evangelistic Agents

Some pastors have convinced themselves that only those endowed with the grace-gift of evangelist should evangelize. As chapter 1 explained, evangelism is not a spiritual gift. Although every pastor may not be a grace-gifted evangelist, each one has an obligation to be a Spirit-empowered personal evangelist. Related to that misconception, a number of Christians also believe evangelism is a task belonging only to pastors, preachers, ministers, and evangelists. But evangelism is not a job reserved for so-called Christian professionals. It is required of each and every person who professes to be a Christian. Randy Newman affirms the necessity of every congregational member's participation in evangelism by positing an extremely perceptive rhetorical question: "Note the importance of the church in evangelism. The concept of *body evangelism* can't be overstressed. If people need to hear multiple presentations from numerous voices and see the gospel lived out in a variety of ways, what better [way is there] for that to occur than [by] a local church?"[2]

The democratization of evangelism among all members of first-century churches, and not a minor subset of them, contributed to the rapid spread of Christianity. As John R. Mott explains:

The disciple discussed with his teacher and fellow students the Christian truth which had laid powerful hold upon him. The

---

[2] Newman, *Unlikely Converts*, 54 (see chap. 5, n. 19).

slave who had fallen under the spell of the One who had come to proclaim release to captives could not refrain from pointing to the Great Deliverer. Wherever the Christian disciples scattered, the evidences multiplied of Christianity as a leaven working quietly for the conversion of one household after another. It is this commending by life and by word the reality and wonder-working of the Living Lord on the part of the rank and file of His disciples within the sphere of their daily calling that best explains the penetration of Roman society with the world conquering Gospel.[3]

Elton Trueblood concurs, specifying those during the first century who were spreading the gospel with missionary zeal: "All were of the laity in the sense that all were nonprofessional, but all were ministers [of the gospel] in the sense that all ministered. Given their faith in Christ, no other situation was possible and the result was that their contagious influence finally penetrated the whole of the ancient world."[4]

J. E. Conant wrote a classic evangelism book that he entitled *Every-Member Evangelism*. In it, he urged churches to aim for the full participation of their members in the work of evangelism. Today, congregations should seek this same goal as they evangelize for at least two reasons. First, it was the evangelistic approach of the early churches. Second, the professionalization of evangelism by Christians in their congregations confines the reach and results of the gospel. Trueblood warns, "When we think of religion as the professional responsibility of . . . clergymen . . . the major harm lies in the consequent minimizing of the religious responsibility of *other* men and women. The harm of too much localizing of religious responsibility in a few—however dedicated they may be—is that it gives the rank and file a freedom from responsibility which they ought not to

---

[3] John R. Mott, *Liberating the Lay Forces of Christianity* (New York: Macmillan, 1932), 2–3.

[4] Elton Trueblood, *Your Other Vocation* (New York: Harper & Brothers, 1952), 43.

be able to enjoy."[5] If denominational leaders, evangelists, pastors, and congregations adopt and advance a professionalized evangelism, Trueblood's warnings will be realized. As a result, the professionalization of evangelism will impede the overall participation of congregants in evangelism.

Misconception 2: Church Activities and/or Events Comprise Evangelism

Some churches equate church activities with evangelism.[6] This misunderstanding can come in various forms. For example, in *Evangelism after Christendom*, Bryan Stone promotes an evangelism so inextricably identified with ecclesiology that evangelistic witness itself embodies the essence of a church. He posits that "the most evangelistic thing the church can do today is to be the church—to be formed imaginatively by the Holy Spirit through core practices such as worship, forgiveness, hospitality, and economic sharing into a distinctive people in the world, a new social option, the body of Christ."[7] He contrasts his proposal with what he describes as an "ecclesiology that currently underwrites the contemporary practice of evangelism—at least that which predominates in North America—[which] is at best an ecclesiology in which the church is . . . instrumentalized in the service of 'reaching' or 'winning' non-Christians."[8] In arguing for the former to displace the latter, Stone audaciously admits, "One of the enormous challenges of Christian evangelism today is that in order to learn once again to bear faithful and embodied witness to the Spirit's creative 'social work,' it may have to reject as

---

[5] Trueblood, *The Company of the Committed*, 9 (see chap. 1, n. 8).

[6] C. E. Autrey articulated this evangelistic mischaracterization in his *Basic Evangelism*, 26–27 (see chap. 1, n. 3).

[7] Bryan Stone, *Evangelism after Christendom: The Theology and Practice of Christian Witness* (Grand Rapids: Brazos, 2007), 15.

[8] Stone, 16.

heretical the pervasive characterization of salvation as 'a personal relationship with Jesus.'"[9] Ecumenical churches resonate with Stone's evangelism proposition, and many of them advocate a form of it. His problem, and the problem of many ecumenical churches, is that they conceive of evangelism in terms of ecclesiological practice rather than a concept that yields an ecclesiological essence.

While evangelical churches historically have resisted the extreme version found in the mainline churches, growing numbers of them have embraced their own version of this problem. They conceive of evangelism as any and every activity or event that occurs in their churches. While churches and believers should do everything they do with an eye toward evangelism, the sad reality is that they do not. Because churches and believers do lots of different kinds of things, they convince themselves that their activities constitute evangelism, even if they haven't shared the gospel in the course of all they are doing. They believe when they have a potluck meal and many unbelievers attend, they have evangelized. Some have convinced themselves that because many guests visit their churches on a particular Sunday morning, evangelism has occurred. Still others think they have evangelized because they have offered a ministry (e.g., vacation Bible school, a financial workshop, a marriage enrichment weekend, a food pantry, or a clothes closet) to the community. While all these endeavors and situations are commendable and can be outlets to evangelize, those who think anything and everything they do is evangelism must realize that if the gospel of Jesus Christ is not verbally proclaimed and offered to those in attendance, then an event, not evangelism, has taken place.

Misconception 3: Transfer Growth Equals Evangelistic Growth

Other well-meaning church members encourage a member from another church to unite with their church. They call this "evangelism" when really

---

[9] Stone, 17.

it is "sheep-stealing." This practice proves unhealthy and essentially becomes a kind of spiritual cannibalism. C. H. Spurgeon rebuked this practice in lecturing to his students. He said:

> We do not regard it to be soul-winning to steal members out of churches already established, and train them to utter our peculiar Shibboleth: we aim rather at bringing souls to Christ than at making converts to our synagogue. There are sheep-stealers abroad, concerning whom I will say nothing except that they are not "brethren," or, at least, they do not act in a brotherly fashion. To their own Master they must stand or fall. We count it utter meanness to build up our own house with the ruins of our neighbours' mansions; we infinitely prefer to quarry for ourselves.[10]

Anglican pastor and professor, Michael Niebauer, seemed to echo London's most famous Baptist more than a century later, writing:

> The contemporary problem is simply that numerical growth isn't the same as conversion growth. Church growth is not the same thing as evangelism. You can grow a church or a ministry numerically and not bring one lost soul into the kingdom. . . . The fastest way to grow a church is usually through appeals to people who are already following Jesus. It's intuitive: The people looking for churches are already Christians. Those who are far from Christ ignore our advertisements, our events, and our seeker-friendly sermons. . . . We shouldn't think ourselves gifted evangelists or as having "cracked the code" of evangelism when the bulk of our new members are a product of ecclesial migration. At the same time, we shouldn't necessarily equate a lack of explosive growth with a failure to evangelize. . . . We can't control

---

[10] Spurgeon, *The Soul-Winner*, 9 (see chap. 1, n. 30).

who shows up to our church, but we can control whether or not we do evangelism. We must evaluate the things we actually control—our dutifulness in engaging lost people, our steadfastness in prayer and fasting for them, and our diligence in working to present the gospel clearly."[11]

Spurgeon's and Niebauer's justified rebukes evoke a different and disturbing metaphor to describe this practice—"Christian cannibalism"—due to the scandalous picture of congregations that appear to "feed" on sister churches' members to fill themselves. Returning to the more subdued analogy; however, believers should remember that instead of "stealing sheep" who already belong to God, his people need to seek after sheep the thief has stolen (cf. John 10:1–16).

Although every church should encourage an inviting and accepting atmosphere for believers who are searching for a church, a welcoming spirit toward believers on its own merits does not constitute evangelism. Churches and believers do not evangelize believers, they evangelize unbelievers. Furthermore, *evangelism* is not inviting already established believers to become members of a church, although such an invitation is encouraged if personal evangelists find believers who are not actively involved in a Bible-believing church. Rather, *evangelism* is inviting unbelievers to respond to the good news of Jesus Christ through repentance and faith by becoming disciples of Jesus Christ, professing their newfound faith through believer's baptism, and being taught obedience to all the commands of Christ, primarily in the local church into which they will baptized and to which they will belong.

---

[11] Michael Niebauer, "Don't Mistake Transfer Growth for Evangelism," Gospel Coalition, March 13, 2019, https://www.thegospelcoalition.org/article/mistake-transfer-growth-evangelism.

Misconception 4: Merely Inviting Someone to Church Constitutes Evangelism[12]

Some Christians attempting to evangelize merely invite unbelievers to attend their churches. While church members should invite unbelievers to their churches, any invitation to attend a service that does not also invite unbelievers to receive Christ cannot be considered evangelism. What about unbelievers who never accept the invitation to attend church in order to hear the gospel? Or what about those unbelievers who intend to come to church but suddenly die before Sunday comes? To evangelize unbelievers, personal evangelists must present the entire gospel and invite them to receive Jesus as their Savior and Lord.

As discussed previously, this misconception of congregational evangelism also has a tendency to blend with professionalized evangelism. Some church members invite unbelievers to church, operating under the assumption that their pastor will share the gospel in his sermon and they are only required to bring non-Christians to the worship service. Yet what if unbelievers accompany them, but the pastor fails to present the gospel in his sermon? Furthermore, what if a special presentation is made by a visiting speaker or the church's musicians and singers, and the gospel is not explicitly given? If a Sunday morning sermon is the only time members of a church's community have an opportunity to hear the gospel, then that church likely neither has nor ever will reach all its community with a gospel witness.

Misconception 5: People Need to Belong before They Believe

The thesis "belonging comes before believing" was first coined by Professor Robin Gill. His student, John Finney, conducted studies to

---

[12] C. E. Autrey articulated this mischaracterization of evangelism in *Basic Evangelism*, 27–28 (see chap. 1, n. 3).

test this proposition and believed he sustained it.[13] In *The Celtic Way of Evangelism*, George G. Hunter III used Finney's research findings to popularize this philosophy within the Church Growth Movement, writing, "For [Gill's and Finney's] reasons, evangelism is now about 'helping people to belong so that they can believe.'"[14] In 2018 Bryan Stone updated and expanded upon Finney's previous study to understand how people come to faith. He concludes:

> Those who are first-timers to a faith tradition are likely to take one to three years. For a significant number, the journey is even longer than that, and several persons claimed the process is ongoing, if not lifelong. For faith communities interested in ministries of invitation, outreach, and inclusion, that means the emphasis should be placed on accompaniment, formation, and education rather than solely on tactics to get people in the door. In contrast to some traditional religious approaches that emphasize conversion, and make incorporation and assimilation secondary, it is abundantly clear from our study that people *belong before they believe* rather than *believing* [sic] *before they belong.*[15]

Initially influenced by centuries-old Celtic evangelization, these scholars observed a form of proselytizing focused on unbelievers' sense of and need for belonging. They seemingly preferred it over believers' responsibility and urgency to spread the good news and call for a response.

Although this phenomenon might be observed between the fifth and tenth centuries on the British Isles, we will be hard-pressed to locate it in the first century within the Roman world. Instead, "believing before belonging" is observed from the first century until today. Randy Newman

---

[13] See John Finney, *Finding Faith Today: How Does It Happen* (London: British and Foreign Bible Society, 1992), 46–47.

[14] George G. Hunter III, *The Celtic Way of Evangelism: How Christianity Can Reach the West . . . Again* (Nashville: Abington, 2000), 55.

[15] Bryan P. Stone, *Finding Faith Today* (Eugene: Cascade, 2018), 213.

articulates the danger with practicing the "belong before they believe" misconception:

> I appreciate the sentiment behind this statement, and I agree that people more often identify with a church or Christian fellowship before they cross from unbelief to belief. But . . . there's a world of difference between identifying with a group of Christians and belonging to Christ. Let's not blur the line between being objects of God's wrath and being saved from that wrath. If we do, we'll distort the urgent nature of the gospel's demands for repentance and faith.[16]

Churches and Christians must be friendly, approachable, sympathetic, inviting, and exhibit any other adjectival disposition when they evangelize. Nevertheless, they should not concede the conviction of the Spirit and evangelistic persuasion to a process of faith acclimation when unbelievers' souls are on the line. As Jesus taught Nicodemus, who indicated his belonging qualified as his belief, "The wind blows where it pleases, and you hear its sound, but you don't know where it comes from or where it is going. So it is with everyone born of the Spirit" (John 3:8).

Suggestions for Effective Congregational Evangelism

Congregations that fail to evaluate the state of their evangelism and make frequent, necessary adjustments will find its practice plateauing or declining. Thom Rainer suggests churches ask themselves the following ten questions to assess their evangelism and formulate a plan to address any deficiencies:

1. Are members more concerned about the lost than their own preferences and comfort?
2. Is the church led to pray for lost persons?

---

[16] Newman, *Unlikely Converts*, 57–58 (see chap. 5, n. 19).

3. Are church members open to reaching people who don't look or act like them?

4. Do conflicts and critics zap the evangelistic energy of the church?

5. Do small groups and Sunday school classes seek to reach lost persons within their groups?

6. Is the leadership of the church evangelistic?

7. Do the sermons regularly communicate the gospel?

8. Are there ministries in the church that encourage members to be involved in evangelistic outreach and lifestyle?

9. Have programs become ends in themselves rather than means to reach people?

10. Is there any process of accountability for members to be more evangelistic?[17]

My book *Mobilize to Evangelize* provides detailed evaluation tools to help pastors and their churches track their congregations' evangelistic effectiveness over five years and identify the similarities and differences in the evangelism philosophies and practices of pastors, ministry staff members, or lay leaders (depending on the size of the church) in order to develop a congregational evangelistic strategy.[18] Whether or not a church uses available tools to determine or measure the extent of their evangelistic effectiveness, the following suggestions can be adopted by any church with minimal, or no, increase in spending.

---

[17] See Matt Queen, *Mobilize to Evangelize: The Pastor and Effective Congregational Evangelism* (Fort Worth: Seminary Hill Press, 2018).

[18] Thom Rainer, "Ten Questions to Diagnose the Evangelistic Health of Your Church," August 22, 2012, https://archive.thomrainer.com/2012/08/ten _questions_to_diagnose_the_evangelistic_health_of_your_church.

Proclaim the Gospel through the Ordinances

Outside the corporate proclamation of the Word, congregations have no more natural medium for sharing the gospel than through the church ordinances—baptism and the Lord's Supper. Many pastors and ministers spend more time making preparations for filling the baptistery with water, securing robes or ordering shirts for baptismal candidates to wear, ordering the bread and juice, placing the elements in trays, and designating who will serve which row of seats than they do developing how they will clearly proclaim the gospel through the ordinances. Though unintentional, this common routine resembles times when Jewish worshipers and the Levitical priesthood were more concerned with the details of the sacrifices than with the meaning behind them. Throughout Hebrews the writer makes clear that Jesus's death for sins was the ultimate fulfillment of all the Old Testament sacrifices. When they administrate the ordinances in their churches, pastors should not neglect the obvious connection of baptism to the death, burial, and resurrection of Christ, and the Lord's Supper to the death of Christ for sins. Although many do include these presentations, they should also consider intentionally contemplating, as well as discussing with their ministry staff, fresh ways to present the gospel during these celebrations to avoid monotony.

Evaluate the Church's Evangelistic History and Profile

The evangelistic history and profile of a church serves as a valuable tool to measure and assess its effectiveness. One common way a congregation can evaluate its ministry of spreading the gospel is to observe its annual number of baptisms over five to ten years. An even more valuable metric tracks the church's annual baptism-to-membership ratios over that same period of time. This ratio divides the number of the church's members by the number of the church's baptisms for a given year.[19] When this quo-

---

[19] Many pastors and churches prefer to use their worship attendance instead of their membership in calculating this ratio. Generally they do so because the

tient is calculated, it reveals the number of members required to see one person baptized. Lower ratios are preferred because they depict greater evangelistic effectiveness among the total number of members.

Thom Rainer suggests using this metric to measure evangelistic effectiveness as opposed to total baptisms for several reasons. First, the annual report of baptisms may overstate conversion due to re-baptisms, as well as those of new church members with alien baptisms from other denominations, who submit to believer's baptism by immersion. Second, Rainer claims this metric reveals the number of church members necessary to make a disciple of one person, which "allows [for] a more accurate assessment of evangelistic effectiveness year by year" than total baptisms do.[20] To acquire an accurate number of the new believers each year, and to gauge the number of members active in evangelism, the baptism-to-membership ratio is preferred.

Calculating the baptism-to-membership ratio gives churches a chronicle of their evangelistic activity. It allows them to recall the outreaches, training, expectations, and events that produced a low-ratio year, so they can plan future such events with the hope that God similarly blesses. They can also recollect other initiatives or occurrences that may have negatively affected evangelistic activity in a high-ratio year. By identifying them, congregations can either adjust or avoid these

---

former is usually smaller than the latter, resulting in a more favorable ratio. This preference, however, should be avoided because church membership accurately represents those baptized believers who are in covenant relationship with the congregation. Because of the nature of church covenants, they are expected to fulfill the covenantal expectations of the congregation, which includes disciple-making. Every person who attends worship is not necessarily saved nor a member, meaning they have no obligation to covenant expectations. Therefore, if they are not liable to make disciples alongside members of the churches they attend until they enter such a covenantal agreement, then these people should not be included in a formula that measures activity they have not actually performed.

[20] Thom S. Rainer, "A Resurgence Not Yet Fulfilled: Evangelistic Effectiveness in the Southern Baptist Convention since 1979," in Lawless and Greenway, *The Great Commission Resurgence*, 33, 36 (see chap. 6, n. 47).

detracting factors in the future. Last, patterns that emerge from the data can help pastors and church leaders set and promote goals to lower the ratio through more fervent prayer and increased congregational involvement.

Set, Promote, and Measure Evangelistic Expectations

Outside the work of the Holy Spirit, a church's evangelistic success or failure is directly tied to its pastor's effectiveness in both setting and executing ministry expectations and goals. C. B. Hogue writes, "The most influential voice in the life of the church comes from the pulpit. Several times each week, the pastor has an opportunity to share his vision of the church and its mission. As the acknowledged leader . . . the pastor can profoundly shape the ministry of his congregation. . . . If he stresses growth, growth occurs."[21]

Congregations reflect their pastors. They value the things their pastors value. If church members never see or hear about their pastors evangelizing, their pastors will rarely, if ever, see or hear of their congregants doing it either. As Chuck Lawless observes, "I've never seen an evangelistic church *not* led by an evangelistic pastor." In it he also suggests eight essential ways and reasons pastors can lead their churches evangelistically: "(1) The pastor who preaches every Sunday sets the agenda for the church. . . . (2) The pastor has the best opportunity to keep the challenge of evangelism in front of the people. . . . (3) The pastor can be an evangelistic role model, even from the pulpit. . . . (4) The pastor can set the example of getting connected with non-believers. . . . (5) The pastor has opportunity to tell stories of evangelism. . . . (6) The pastor can often enlist enthusiastic disciples to train. . . . (7) The pastor can hold other pastors and staff members

---

[21] C. B. Hogue, *I Want My Church to Grow* (Nashville: B&H, 1977), 66.

accountable for evangelism. . . . (8) The pastor can teach and empha-size the ordinance of baptism."[22]

Charles Roesel, former pastor of First Baptist Church of Leesburg, Florida, is known for saying, "People do not tend to drift toward evan-gelism, but drift away from it. Leaders must continually call the mem-bers back to evangelism." If pastors do not habitually communicate their weekly evangelistic expectations of themselves, their staff, and their churches, their congregations and staffs will assume they do not have such expectations. Pastors can express their evangelistic expectations to their congregations in a number of ways, including (1) proposing a weekly number of intentional gospel conversations they should aim to have; (2) expecting members to attend a weekly, monthly, or quarterly outreach event of the church; and (3) encouraging members to adopt Charles Stewart's witnessing principles, referenced in chapter 1.

Once a pastor has determined his specific evangelistic expectations for every member of the church, how might he effectively articulate them? For starters, he should not assume all his congregants are aware he has such expectations. Probably not everyone in a church knows them; and if his people do not know them, they are not likely to evangelize consistently.

A pastor whose church understands and meets his evangelistic expectations does so because he frequently reiterates them and encour-ages the same of his staff and lay leadership. When a pastor believes his promotion of evangelism to be monotonous, his staff or lay leaders are just beginning to listen. When they join in the pastor's promotion to the point they believe it has become routine, the congregation is just begin-ning to listen. The more a pastor and his staff and lay leaders broadcast the goal for every church member to evangelize, the more people hear it and the more he can expect them to do it.

---

[22] Chuck Lawless, "8 Reasons the Pastor Matters Most in a Church's Evangelistic Efforts," accessed on April 5, 2021, http://chucklawless.com /2017/06/8–reasons-the-pastor-matters-most-in-a-churchs-evangelistic-efforts.

Consistently Celebrate and Acknowledge the Practices of Evangelism by the Congregation

Churches replicate what they celebrate. A pastor should identify the members of his church who evangelize in order to promote evangelism within the congregation. Church members respond to their pastor's encouragement. Pastors should ask their members to keep them informed about their personal soul-winning activities. When congregants do, their pastors should consider sharing brief, anonymous testimonies from the pulpit of how members are actively sharing the gospel, and send a brief note or email periodically to appreciate them for their faithful evangelism.

During his staff meetings, the pastor should include time for him and the staff to share about recent witnessing encounters. He should encourage those he senses are struggling in the spiritual discipline of evangelism, while also celebrating and acknowledging their increased ability and frequency in sharing the gospel.

Traditionally, Southern Baptist Sunday school class members would report if they attended class, studied for their lesson, brought their Bible to class, invited someone to class, and shared the gospel each week. While churches have probably abandoned using that kind of reporting tool anymore, think of ways your church and Sunday school class members can report their weekly or monthly evangelistic activity. Some include reporting through a church management software tool, emailing, or texting. Celebrate the church's or the class's total number of gospel presentations each week corporately by using a display, reporting during the announcements, or publicizing in a newsletter.

Prepare, Plan, and Extend Public, Evangelistic Invitations in Worship Services and Events

The inherent nature of both the Scriptures and the gospel elicits a response on the part of those who hear it. If preachers are asked how long they spend studying for their weekly sermon(s), most will be quick to provide the number of hours they have read, researched, crafted illustrations, and composed their sermon outlines or formats. Nevertheless, if they are asked whether they spent any of that time crafting the public invitation of the sermon, very few would say yes. Many would explain they did not because they do not issue appeals for the audience to respond. The remaining others would likely indicate they did not because they use the same invitation each week.

Effective text-driven and expositional preachers who call sinners to salvation should not tack on generic and repetitive invitations to the ends of their sermons. Rather, their calls for sinners to repent and believe Christ should naturally flow from the text's own application.[23] Stephen Rummage offers several examples of how to identify gospel invitations in the texts preachers exposit:

> Connect your invitation to a central truth of your sermon. Instead of giving the same invitation each time you preach, look for key areas in your preaching text that lend themselves to a Gospel presentation. If you are preaching on giving, connect the invitation to God's sacrificial generosity in giving His Son. If you are preaching on family relationships, invite the listener to enter God's family through faith in Christ. Employing a central truth from the text in your invitation will add variety to your appeal and create greater unity in your message.[24]

He also provides a helpful template to create clear invitations to receive Christ by means of what has been traditionally referred to as an *altar call*:

> The evangelistic invitation should include two basic elements: a simple explanation of how to trust in Jesus for salvation and

---

[23] Queen, "Seeking the Lost and Perishing," 151 (see chap. 3, n. 16).
[24] Stephen Rummage, "FIRST PERSON: Five Reasons to Give an Invitation," January 3, 2020, https://www.baptistpress.com/resource-library/news /first-person-five-reasons-to-give-an-invitation.

practical instructions for what you are asking the listener to do. Make the steps clear and tell what will happen when the listener takes those steps. If you are extending a "come forward" type of invitation, you might say something like, "I'm inviting you to step out from your seat and to walk down one of these aisles. A minister will meet you here at the front. Just tell him, 'I want to follow Jesus today.' He will introduce you to a decision counselor who will help you take your next steps with the Lord." Whatever you are asking people to do in response, be prepared to communicate clearly.[25]

Public appeals for people to respond to the gospel can take other forms too. These include, but are not limited to, response cards, text messaging, counseling rooms, silent prayers in the pews, so-called "spontaneous" calls for baptism, delayed response meetings, etc.

No matter what method(s) pastors use to provide people a way to respond to the preached Word, they should be sure to give them at least one avenue by which they can be counseled about a decision they feel led to make. A personal example illustrates the importance of offering some form of public invitation in worship services. On August 15, 2021, a young woman who had been visiting a local Baptist church in Lewisville, Texas, approached the pastor and me after the morning worship service and asked the most unanticipated of questions: "Pastor Donald, why do you ask people to come forward every week?" She continued, "My boyfriend and I have been attending this church since Easter, and every week you ask people to come forward to speak to one of the pastors. Today the guest evangelist did the same thing. It makes us both feel uncomfortable. In fact, as soon as it happens each week, it bothers my boyfriend so much he walks out of the service and goes to sit in our car."

All of the sudden, the pastor was called away to attend to another situation. Leaving me to respond to her, I explained, "We believe that

---

[25] Rummage, "Five Reasons to Give an Invitation."

when this church meets to worship God, he calls people through the preaching of his Word to respond to him. Some of those he speaks to are first-time guests, and others are regular attenders. Because people need help knowing how to respond to God's call upon them, and because there is not a spiritual hotline for them to call, this church's pastor makes himself available to assist those God is calling to obey him." The answer not only satisfied her curiosity; it made sense to her.

She went to the car to recount my response to her boyfriend, who returned inside to speak to me. I took that opportunity to share the gospel with him. Over the period of at least an hour, he asked me questions he had always had about the gospel and the Christian God. Although he did not come to faith in Christ that day, he did tell me before he left that everything now made sense, and he was going to go home and consider what he had heard. I have spoken with him by phone several times since that day, and he has now received Christ! If it had not been for a public invitation, he may never have had the kind of extended conversation he had that day to get answers to his questions about the gospel.

Identify and Use Grace-Gifted Evangelists

As previously discussed in chapter 1, Christ's gift of evangelists to his churches are gifts of his grace to equip and encourage them to evangelize. Biblical, grace-gifted evangelists do not do local churches' evangelism for them; rather they equip them to share the gospel. As I state elsewhere:

> Churches that desire the total participation of their membership in evangelism will employ a vocational or voluntary staff evangelist for the purpose of equipping and encouraging evangelism. In churches that do so, pastors must overcome any temptation to abdicate their evangelistic leadership among the congregation to the evangelist. No matter how much charisma, giftedness, and respect staff evangelists may possess, congregations ultimately follow the headship and example of their lead pastors. Thus,

even as all believers are responsible for reaching the lost, the pastor must model that obedience for those with whom he serves. The most effective and consistent churches who seek the lost and perishing utilize ministry teams that include pastors who champion evangelism and employ the assistance of staff evangelists who equip and encourage evangelism under the direction of their shepherd.[26]

Some of the ways churches can employ evangelists include, but are not limited to, allowing them (1) to teach during evangelism trainings, (2) to make preparations for the church's evangelistic outreaches, (3) to preach or present the gospel at some special services or events, (4) to present the church's evangelistic activity celebration report, and (5) to serve as an evangelism coach to those in the congregation who desire to develop into consistent and experienced personal evangelists.

Regularly Provide Evangelism Training

Many churches have not provided any evangelism training for years, if ever. By offering it regularly, pastors will intuitively communicate their expectation that members evangelize. Churches that do provide it are likely to offer some form of instruction annually, yet church members typically attend the training either to meet or appease their pastors' wishes, then set what they learn aside until they attend the following year's training. It's advisable to offer training more often, such as biannually or quarterly, to motivate members to retain what they have learned.

Pastors can provide evangelism instruction in many different ways. Some training comes in the form of a kit that includes video tutorials, listening guides, props, and theme-based sermon outlines. Others provide a script for learners to memorize, while others build confidence by

---

[26] Queen, "Seeking the Lost and Perishing," 148 (see chap. 3, n. 16).

convincing them they already know the basics of the gospel message and encourage them to put it into practice.

Evangelism training can also take the more personal form of an apprenticeship. The pastor, grace-gifted evangelist(s), and those with evangelism experience select willing church members to mentor in personal evangelism. Consistent and intentional evangelism does not begin with everyone at once; rather, it begins when one or more of these evangelistic individuals invest in a few people to multiply the process. C. H. Spurgeon advised how a pastor should enlist his people to evangelize:

> Sometimes, the very best plan would be to call all the members of the church together, tell them what you would like to see, and plead earnestly with them that each one should become for God a soul-winner. Say to them, "I do not want to be your pastor simply that I may preach to you; but I long to see souls saved, and to see those who are saved seeking to win others for the Lord Jesus Christ." . . . Then, if that should not succeed, God may lead you to *begin with one or two.*
>
> There is usually some "choice young man" in each congregation; and as you notice deeper spirituality in him than in the rest of the members, you might say to him, "Will you come down to my house on such-and-such an evening that we may have a little prayer together?" You can gradually increase the number to two or three, godly young men if possible. . . . Having secured their sympathy, you might say to them, "Now we will try if we cannot influence the whole church; we will begin with our fellow-members before we go to the outsiders. . . ."
>
> . . . Your work, brethren, is to set your church on fire somehow. You may do it by speaking to the whole of the members, or you may do it by speaking to the few choice spirits, but you must do it somehow.[27]

---

[27] Spurgeon, *The Soul-Winner*, 99–100 (see chap. 1, n. 30).

Such an evangelistic apprenticeship would incorporate the following steps:

- You evangelize, the apprentice observes, then you discuss any questions.
- You evangelize, the apprentice assists you in evangelizing, then you discuss how your student felt about it.
- The apprentice evangelizes, you observe, then together you review the strengths and weaknesses.
- The apprentice identifies another willing church member with whom to take through this process, you do the same, and together you compare notes.

This model of evangelism training represents an ideal form of disciple-making, in which evangelism and discipleship operate synchronously together in perpetuity. Mature Christians evangelize unbelievers to make disciples, while teaching other believers to share the gospel, that they too reproduce disciples and train them to evangelize *ad infinitum*.

Leverage Sunday School or Small Groups for Evangelism

Sunday school classes or small groups provide opportunities for evangelism in at least two ways. First, pastors should communicate an expectation to the teachers that they explain the gospel in each lesson. Some unbelieving guests may feel more comfortable asking questions or responding to the gospel in a small group atmosphere than they do in a worship service. Pastors should brainstorm different ways to convey this requirement to teachers and how they can reinforce it over time. Education ministers or Sunday school directors can help publicize and measure the results among the teachers.

Second, churches should practice *open enrollment* in their Sunday school or small groups, if they don't already do so, meaning that classes enroll people at any place and at any time, so long as the person agrees to be enrolled. Numerous classes and groups enroll people only after they have attended a set number of times, and they will un-enroll people who have not attended in a while. Usually this type of enrollment places the onus on each enrolled member's commitment to the class.

Open enrollment shifts the responsibility of class commitment to enrolled members. Therefore, class members invite local family, neighbors, friends, coworkers, and new acquaintances to join their class, and so obligate themselves to minister to and reach these enrollees with the gospel. Most of these newly enrolled members will be inactive in church, or dechurched altogether. The class can minister to them weekly by contacting them to pray, inviting them to attend class and worship on Sunday, and asking them to social functions and fellowship events. Enrolled members will not be removed from the roll unless they request it, or until the class makes a conscious decision to no longer reach out to them. This intentional strategy to gain prospects and connect with them consistently also provides teachers with a mandate to share the gospel weekly, as the groups will no longer consist of only believing church members.

Community-Oriented Evangelism

Churches will not reach their communities with the gospel if they are not intentional in sharing the gospel with those who live in their immediate area. Those that employ strategies that include home evangelism can reach a greater number of people. Many churches limit the practice of their evangelism to their Sunday worship service and periodic evangelistic events; however, believers almost always outnumber unbelievers at these venues. These churches also target individuals to the exclusion of targeting households.

Some approaches churches can use to reach greater numbers of people with the gospel in their communities include personal evangelism in family-oriented environments like parks and local community sporting events, evangelism booths at town festivals, evangelistic block parties, door-to-door evangelism, and evangelistic home Bible studies. Evangelism in these locations and in these ways has the potential of reaching many people with the gospel. For example, when they go to the park, gym, pool, ball field, or walking track, believers should speak about the gospel with those they meet.

Churches can also gain permission in neighborhoods and housing complexes to have block parties or holiday festivals. The food, games, and music generally attract people and provide opportunities to discuss the gospel. Also, the relaxed and informal nature of these gatherings gives believers ample time to share the gospel throughout the event, without feeling the need to rush from person to person to present the good news. These get-togethers generally have a time when the activities end, so people can hear a message from the event host. This is an ideal time for the pastor or someone who has experience sharing the gospel in public settings to do so.

Door-to-door evangelism offers congregations an excellent opportunity to interact with their neighbors and provide materials about their services and activities. When strangers visit someone's house, the homeowner expects the visitor to explain the purpose of the visit. For this reason, teams who evangelize this way should not feel obligated to conduct long surveys or gain the tenant's trust through a lengthy introduction. Instead, they should courteously say something like: "Hello, our names are _____ and from _____ Church. We are in the neighborhood today getting to know our neighbors and letting them know that we and God care about them, so we have come to tell you God loves you." Instead of asking to share the gospel with the owner, naturally progress from the introduction and say something like, "The Bible says. . . ." and present the gospel and ask if the person would like to receive God's forgiveness.

Longer-term methods, like hosting unbelieving neighbors for Bible studies, provide churches with the information and structure to follow up with interested unbelievers and new believers through continued evangelism, ministry, and discipleship. Evangelistic home Bible studies create the perfect venue for unbelievers to dialogue at length about their questions concerning the gospel. The intimacy within these settings can foster an environment in which unbelievers share their needs and life concerns with the believing hosts. As long as the unbelievers' confidentiality is respected, churches can use this information to minister to their needs while also sharing the gospel with them. The trust believers build through this form of home evangelism increases the likelihood that new believers will want to get involved in their hosts' churches.

When practicing home evangelism at unbelievers' houses or at locations where households are gathered, believers should intentionally target the entire family. While salvation through Jesus must be accepted individually, contemporary evangelism often underestimates, or even ignores, the role of an unbeliever's household. The extent to which people's households understand and believe the gospel can either benefit or impede evangelistic effectiveness. Believers who practice door-to-door evangelism find that a significant number of people who come to the door claim to be Christians. When residents respond this way to the spiritually diagnostic questions, the personal evangelists should ask if members of the household are home with whom they can share the gospel. Sometimes when unbelievers hear the gospel from believers outside the home, it helps to reinforce the gospel witness of their believing household members. At other times, door-to-door evangelists may be the answer to believing household members' prayers for the salvation of the unbelieving family members.

Offer Members Multiple Layers of Evangelism

When he served as pastor of Northeast Houston Baptist Church, Nathan Lino expected that all his congregants be engaged and active in some form of sharing the gospel. He envisioned that the church could offer multiple evangelism venues so that as many members as possible would corporately participate. He believed their involvement in structured forms of collaborative evangelism would naturally lead them to begin practicing personal evangelism.

After he and his staff decided on and prepared the methods they would offer, he launched what he referred to as *evangelism layers* to the church. He explained to them:

Organic personal evangelism is the ideal evangelism strategy as it seems to be the teaching of Matthew 28:19—"as you go." But the reality is that the vast majority of believers do not practice organic personal evangelism unless they are first encouraged and trained through organized public evangelism. Organized public evangelism is the catalyst for organic personal evangelism—those who participate in organized public evangelism with the church family begin organic personal evangelism in their own spheres of influence. So, it is essential for church leadership to organize public evangelism opportunities for the church family.[28]

He then offered the following seven options from which every member could choose: (1) Evangelistic Praying, (2) Cold Call Evangelism, (3) Warm Call Evangelism, (4) Mercy Ministry, (5) Big Event Evangelism, (6) Harvest Sunday, and (7) Evangelism Training.

FIGURE 4. Layers in Evangelism

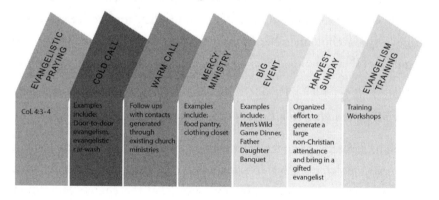

Every congregant was expected to be involved in at least one of these layers; however, they could practice more than one. In fact, Lino wanted as many members as possible ultimately involved in many, if not all, of

---

[28] Nathan Lino, "Layers of Evangelism," unpublished document (Humble, TX: Northeast Houston Baptist Church), 2019.

the evangelism layers. After he launched this initiative, he informed those joining the church in their new members' classes that they were expected to choose at least one layer through which they would evangelize, with the hope they would get involved in more than one.

Whether or not pastors choose any or all of the evangelism layers Northeast Houston Baptist Church has prioritized, they would do well to identify some that naturally fit with their churches' contexts, personalities, and already existing evangelistic ministries. No "one way" exists by which believers must evangelize. Otherwise, large subsections of believers would likely never share the gospel. But if churches provide multiple venues and methods by which they can participate in the evangelistic enterprise, more will get involved.

DISCUSSION AND REFLECTION QUESTIONS

1. What is the most common misconception related to congregational evangelism that you have heard, whether one referenced in this chapter or another? How would you seek to correct it if it was predominantly held among your church's membership?

2. Of the suggestions this chapter offered to promote effective congregational evangelism:
   a. select one, if applicable, that your church practices. In what way(s) does it encourage the practice of evangelism within the church? In what way(s) could it be improved to stimulate more members to share more of the gospel, more of the time?
   b. select one that you believe your pastor and church might be willing to adopt. What steps would need to be taken to initiate it within the congregation?

3. Who in your church could you train as an evangelistic apprentice like the one described in this chapter? How would you invite this person to do this? Where would you go to evangelize? How would you train your apprentice to present the gospel? How long would you propose this apprenticeship last?

10

Evangelism That
Makes Disciples

This book has endeavored to explore and explain biblical evangelism as an essential component in the disciple-making process.
This understanding requires that believers share the gospel with this
end in mind, rather than conceive of evangelism as merely an end unto
itself. This chapter begins by surveying the ways Christians have comprehended the relationship between evangelism and discipleship over the
last century. Next, it will identify essential attributes of Christian disciples. It then presents a tutorial to guide personal evangelists in conducting evangelistic follow-up with new believers. It also addresses the
implications of false professions of faith resulting from believers' disciple-
making efforts. The chapter concludes by discussing the necessity for and
the role of the practice of evangelism in Christian homes.

Understanding the Relationship between Evangelism and Discipleship

Christians generally view the relationship between evangelism and discipleship in one of three ways: as *conflicted enemies, conjoined twins,* or *cooperative friends.*

Evangelism and Discipleship as Conflicted Enemies

In 1936 C. H. Dodd introduced *The Apostolic Preaching and Its Developments* by asserting a stark differentiation between evangelism and discipleship. He claims:

> The New Testament writers draw a clear distinction between preaching and teaching. The distinction is preserved alike in Gospels, Acts, Epistles, and Apocalypse, and must be considered characteristic of early Christian usage in general. Teaching (*didaskein*) is in a large majority of cases ethical instruction. Occasionally it seems to include what we should call apologetic, that is, the reasoned commendation of Christianity to persons interested but not yet convinced. Sometimes, especially in the Johannine writings, it includes the exposition of theological doctrine. Preaching, on the other hand, is the public proclamation of Christianity to the non-Christian world.
>
> . . . The verb [*keryssein*] "to preach" frequently has for its object "the Gospel." Indeed the connection of ideas is so close that *keryssein* by itself can be used as a virtual equivalent for *evangelizesthai*, "to evangelize," or "to preach the Gospel." It would not be too much to say that wherever "preaching" is spoken of, it always carries with it the implication of "good tidings" proclaimed.
>
> For the early Church, then, to preach the Gospel was by no means the same thing as to deliver moral instruction or exhortation. While the Church was concerned to hand on the

teaching of the Lord, it was not by this that it made converts. It was by *kērygma*, says Paul, not by *didache*, that it pleased God to save men.[1]

Dodd's understanding of the relationship between evangelism (which he called "preaching") and discipleship (which he called "teaching") was one of bifurcation. His views pervaded throughout Western Christianity throughout the remainder of the twentieth century.

This conceptual separation between evangelism and discipleship led some believers to favor evangelism over discipleship, while others preferred discipleship to evangelism. Advocates of evangelism looked suspiciously on those who advanced discipleship, and vice versa. Although disciple-making persisted during the twentieth century, this particular model saw scores of converts who failed to progress to the next steps of the disciple-making process. In addition, numerous disciples focused on studying the implications of the gospel without actually sharing it.

Evangelism and Discipleship as Conjoined Twins

In his classic text *The Master Plan of Evangelism*, Robert Coleman observed eight principles he believed marked Jesus's strategy of evangelism: "(1) Selection; (2) Association; (3) Consecration; (4) Impartation; (5) Demonstration; (6) Delegation; (7) Supervision; and (8) Reproduction."[2] Jesus's strategy to make disciples of those who would become his apostles was an extended one, taking place over about three years.

Here is a summary of this strategy: People were Jesus's method of saving the world, so he *selected* twelve men who were willing to be his learners. He *associated* with them by spending time teaching and living among them. Their affiliation with him necessitated they *consecrate*

---

[1] Dodd, *The Apostolic Preaching and Its Developments*, 7–8 (see chap. 4, n. 53).

[2] Robert Coleman, *The Master Plan of Evangelism* (1963; repr., Grand Rapids: Revell, 1993), vii.

themselves to obey him. As a result, Jesus *imparted* to them his peace, joy, keys to the kingdom, abundant life, and ultimately, his Spirit. He *demonstrated* to them how to act, react, and live their lives. He also *delegated* specific tasks for them to accomplish, over which he *supervised*. His plan consummated in expecting them to *reproduce* what he had taught them in others. The intent of Jesus's model, he observed, was to lead his disciples to progress from the first principle to the last.

Coleman's book resonated with many Christians who found frustration with the division between evangelism and discipleship. This protracted method aligned with the incremental form of evangelism. It emphasized teaching but not to the exclusion of proclamation. In some ways, this new model so blended the disciplines of proclaiming and teaching that discerning a distinction between them proved difficult.

Evangelism and Discipleship as Cooperative Friends

Hal Poe explored a way to resolve the relationship between evangelism and discipleship in an essay he wrote to honor his doctoral supervisor, Lewis Drummond. He posits, "Any resolution of the relationship between evangelism and discipleship must come from the gospel message itself. The difficulties in Christian practice cannot be solved by altering the gospel in its demands, rather the gospel ought to contain the clue for the solution. Simply stated, evangelism means proclaiming the gospel. Simply stated, discipleship means following Jesus."[3] He continued by discussing how the gospel connects evangelism and discipleship. Instead of integrating these two disciplines like Coleman, or bifurcating them, as did Dodd, Poe concentrated on sharing the good news in such a way that those who hear it naturally and intuitively anticipate the demands

---

[3] Harry L. Poe, "Evangelism and Discipleship," in *Evangelism in the Twenty-First Century: The Critical Issues*, ed. Thom S. Rainer (Wheaton, IL: Harold Shaw, 1989), 137.

of discipleship required of those who receive its message. He concludes, "By presenting salvation as only a transaction whereby we obtain eternal life, we limit the extent to which discipleship can occur. We present the gospel as though nothing else remains to experience, instead of as the prelude Jesus described to Nathaniel: 'You shall see greater things than that' (John 1:50b, RSV). With a faulty view of salvation, Christians have no basis for pursuing Christ."[4]

This model of the correlation between evangelism and discipleship avoids both a break between and a blurring of each other. Instead, this understanding preserves the distinctions of both disciplines, as the gospel sustains an interdependency between the two. Just as two sides comprise one coin, evangelism and discipleship, when linked together by the gospel, result in Great Commission disciple-making.

Biblical Marks of Christian Disciples

Not every person who claims to have received Christ is a genuine Christian. In order to authenticate such claims, those who are made disciples through evangelism should soon after begin to exhibit evidence that they are *converted, committed, congregational, confessional,* and *commissioned.* The mere expression of these five attributes does not save disciples; rather they provide indicatory evidence that they likely have been saved. Therefore, they assist personal evangelists and churches as a kind of rubric, along with the fruit of the Spirit and visible signs of repentance, by which they can evaluate and assess the authenticity of those who profess faith in Christ.

Converted

The fundamental mark of Christian disciples is their conversion. This experience involves unbelievers turning away from their sin through

---

[4] Poe, 141.

repentance, while also turning to Christ in faith. The idea that conversion is a journey rather than a destination has garnered support among some evangelicals since the early twenty-first century. Although the evangelization of unbelievers may take place over a period of time, they are converted at a particular point in time. At that moment, those who repent and believe will confess, "Jesus is Lord," as an initial profession of their faith.

Committed

This biblically prescribed articulation of Christ's lordship is more than words; it necessitates new believers' commitment to it. New disciples will find the demands of Christian discipleship in the gospel they have both heard and believed. After unbelievers become Christ's disciples, they should be baptized and taught to obey his commands. Their baptism initiates and incorporates them into the body of Christ through membership in a local congregation of believers (cf. Acts 2:41; 1 Cor 12:13).

Congregational

God does not save individuals so that they practice their faith in isolation from others. On the contrary, he saves them to bring them into a community of faith with others—a local body of believers known as a church. As John Stott so keenly observes from Acts 2, "The Lord did not add them to the church without saving them, and he did not save them without adding them to the church. Salvation and church membership went together; they still do."[5] The members of local churches should teach newly baptized disciples obedience to the gospel's demands. Together they provoke one another to good works, consistently gather together to

---

[5] John Stott, *The Living Church: Convictions of a Lifelong Pastor* (Downers Grove, IL: InterVarsity, 2007), 32.

learn about and worship Christ, and encourage one another as they await his return (Heb 10:24–25).

Confessional

As a condition of their membership, disciples enter a covenant with all the members of the church. This embodies a statement of faith they agree to affirm and a biblically ethical code to which they will adhere. Church members hold one another accountable for their beliefs, as well as their actions. The confessional statement the church has adopted conveys the theological doctrines one must believe in order to be a Christian, as well as a member. Southern Baptist churches almost unanimously use *The Baptist Faith and Message* as their statement of faith and their message.[6]

Commissioned

The confessional faith held by disciples is inextricably tied to the message they proclaim. Although a statement of faith encompasses more than the gospel, it does include the message of salvation. Members of local churches are commissioned by the Lord and their congregations to present the gospel in order to make disciples. For this reason, they bear responsibility both to Christ and to their church to share as much of the gospel with as many as possible anywhere possible.

Evangelism as Disciple-Making

When Christians think of disciple-making, they immediately recall the Great Commission. Interestingly, the accounts of the commission found in Matthew 28:19–20 and John 20:21 do not include the word *evangelism*—it is only implied. In addition, the versions of it in *Mark*

---

[6] See *Baptist Faith & Message 2000*, https://bfm.sbc.net/bfm2000.

16:15; Luke 24:46–48; and Acts 1:8 convey preaching the gospel without specifically mentioning *discipleship* or one of its derivatives. Does the fact that some Great Commission passages include *evangelism* and not *discipleship*, while another includes *discipleship* and does not mention *evangelism*, mean that biblical disciple-making is limited to one or the other, or neither one of them?

Both evangelism and discipleship are necessary for biblical disciple-making to occur. Where, then, in the Scriptures are both of them explicitly mentioned? Luke included them both in Acts 14:21a when he wrote, "They . . . preached the gospel in that town and made many disciples." Through their preaching the gospel (referring to a form of evangelism) in Derbe, Paul and Barnabas made disciples (implying from their custom that they baptized and taught them to obey Christ's commands).

Due to its interdependent association with the gospel, biblical disciple-making requires both evangelism and discipleship. If they fail to operate together in symbiotic unison, both become something foreign to New Testament disciple-making. As Billie Hanks, Jr., explains, "Personal evangelism will not produce multiplication in isolation from effective follow-up. In other words, personal witnessing and personal follow-up must be seen as interlocking parts of a comprehensive and intentional discipling process."[7] Additionally, if the gospel does not prompt and stimulate believers' practice of evangelism and discipleship, both will devolve into insignificance. As Sammy Rhodes warned in a now-deleted, March 15, 2014, tweet, "[The g]reatest obstacle to evangelism [is] assuming the gospel has been heard [by unbelievers]. [The g]reatest obstacle to discipleship [is] assuming the gospel has been remembered [by believers]."

---

[7] Billie Hanks Jr. "The Secret of Effective Follow-Up," in *Evangelism for a Changing World*, ed. Timothy Beougher and Alvin Reid (Wheaton, IL: Harold Shaw, 1995), 170.

The desired result of biblical evangelism is not for a believer to merely lead an unbeliever who desires forgiveness of sins to repeat a prayer to God. Rather, it is for a believer to make a disciple, by way of the repentance and belief of unbelievers, who then profess faith in Christ through baptism by immersion and are taught to obey all his commands. C. E. Autrey rightly asserted in 1966 at the World Congress on Evangelism in Berlin, Germany: "The goal of evangelism is for the evangelized to become the evangelizer." Instead of practicing the Great Commission, believers who evangelize without intending to make baptized, Christ-obeying disciples are making some "great omissions." As Scarborough explains, "The evangelism that stops at conversion and public profession is lop-sided, wasteful and indeed hurtful."[8] Therefore, disciple-makers must evangelize in such a way that new believers will be baptized and be taught obedience to Christ's commands.

The gospel that personal evangelists share informs the disciples that they make. Those who hear the gospel should be able to conceptualize becoming disciples based on how they have heard the gospel's content and call explained to them. Because many Christians wrongly assume unbelievers have the same spiritual vocabulary, make the same intuitive conclusions, and understand all the same things they do, they can confuse their hearers when sharing the gospel.

A prime example of the unintentional confusion they create occurs when personal evangelists sound as if they are prescribing "works salvation," which they soundly reject, in their initial instruction to new believers. Recall a time you heard or invited unbelievers to receive Christ by saying something like, "All you have to do is call on the Lord by praying this prayer" (cf. Rom 10:13). Then, immediately after unbelievers pray and ask God to forgive them, they are told, "Now you must be baptized, read the Bible, pray to God every day, and put away any known sin." New believers in Christ may be thinking either, "I thought all I had to do was

---

[8] Scarborough, *With Christ after the Lost*, 168 (see chap. 2, n. 9).

pray, and now there is a lot more to do," or, "I thought I was forgiven of my sins when I asked God for it, but now it sounds like I have to do much more to be forgiven." The following warnings will help to avoid confusing unbelievers:

1. If personal evangelists fail to include in their gospel presentations natural prompts to which they refer new disciples, the immediate, post-conversion, discipleship instruction they give may sound like arbitrary rules they have devised and not commands of Christ.

2. If personal evangelists tell unbelievers about Jesus's death on the cross for their sins and omit his resurrection from the dead, they risk sounding like they are asking them to believe in a dead man, rather than the risen God-man.

3. If personal evangelists tell unbelievers about Jesus's death on the cross for their sins and his resurrection from the dead, yet omit his burial, they naively assume any disciples they make will intuitively make the connection between the gospel and baptism.

4. If, while presenting the gospel, personal evangelists accentuate life in the here and now, with little to no regard for life in the hereafter, any resulting disciples will likely attempt to transform earth into heaven instead of anticipating God's new heaven and new earth.

5. If personal evangelists accentuate life in the hereafter to the exclusion of life in the present in their gospel presentations, any resulting disciples will likely be too heavenly minded to be much earthly good.

To avoid these inadvertent perceptions, believers should articulate the gospel in such a way that naturally connects to the initial instruction they provide. In other words, their gospel presentations should anticipate their expectations of the new disciples. The content of the gospel message personal evangelists proclaim will become the template for the discipleship that new believers will practice. Consider three natural evangelism-to-discipleship bridges found in the gospel:

Include Christ's Death, Burial, and Resurrection When You Evangelize So You Can Naturally Instruct a New Disciple to Be Baptized

Just because baptism is not necessary for an unbeliever to be saved does not mean that baptism is not necessary for a believer who has been saved. Numerous gospel presentations focus on Christ's death for sins to the exclusion of mentioning his burial and resurrection. The inclusion of all three events (cf. 1 Cor 15:3–4) affords a direct connection between evangelism and discipleship. One such way includes telling the new believer:

> A moment ago, I shared with you how Jesus died for your sins, was buried, and was raised from the dead. The Bible prescribes for you to profess your faith in what I have shared with you by presenting yourself for believer's baptism by immersion. When you are laid back into the water, you are professing you believe that Jesus died for your sins and he was buried. Then, as you are lifted from the water, you are professing your belief in his resurrection from the dead.

Including Christ's death, burial, and resurrection in gospel presentations provides new believers with a context for believer's baptism that is lost to them if they hear only about his death for their sins. When communicating these three truths to sinners, consider illustrating them by raising your arm straight up vertically when you talk about Jesus's death, then dropping it horizontal to the ground when you refer to his burial. Then, when you mention his resurrection, raise it back to the original vertical position. Providing that illustration when sharing the gospel will help new believers quickly recall the core elements of the good news and

visualize the biblical meaning of the baptism Christ commands them to
undergo (Rom 6:1–12; Col 2:12–14).

Use Scripture When You Evangelize So You Can Naturally Instruct a New Disciple to Read the Bible

Incorporating the Scriptures when you present the gospel will help you
advise new believers to read their Bible. For example, you can say something like this:

> Do you remember the Scriptures I shared with you that explained
> who Jesus is and what he did for you? Do you also remember that
> passage that instructed you to repent and believe? God wants you
> to learn more about him and his expectations for you now that
> you are his child. You will find this information in the Bible.

Personal evangelists should ask new believers if they own a Bible. If not,
they should provide one. If they do own one, ask if it's written in a way
they can understand. If not, give them one, preferably with a translation
that adheres to formal or optimal equivalency.

Suggest a place to begin reading, such as the Gospels of John or
Mark. Then show them where the book you suggest is located in the
Bible and mark it with a bookmark or ribbon. Instruct them to read at
least a few verses, if not an entire section, of the Bible daily. Advise them
to ask God to help them understand that day's text before they begin
reading it. After they read the passage, counsel them to ask themselves
what it taught them about God and how to live their life. They may find
it helpful to write their answers, as well as any questions the reading
raised, in a journal and discuss it with you or another mature Christian
in their church.

Invite Your Hearers to Confess "Jesus Is Lord" So You Can Naturally Instruct a New Disciple to Pray and to Put Away Any Known Sins

As personal evangelists articulate the provision made available by the gospel for unbelievers to be justified, they must also inform them of its implications while they are being sanctified. As chapter 5 stated, the use of a prayer to convey a sinner's contrition before God, as well as a means by which they can verbally confess that Jesus is Lord, proves helpful in connecting evangelism and discipleship. Convey such a connection by explaining:

> Just a moment ago, you had your first conversation with God. The Bible refers to this conversation with God as "prayer." God wants you to continue to communicate with him in this way. Also, you confessed to God in that prayer you believe that Jesus is Lord. What things are you now doing that you know you need to stop in order to submit to Jesus's rule and reign in your life; and what things are you not doing for Christ that you need to begin?

When some new disciples hear that God wants to continue to converse with them, they may assume that God wants them to repeat a version of the prayer they prayed to confess Jesus's lordship. To avoid this, provide them with an easy outline to help them get started. A sample could include the following prompts: (1) praise God for who he is; (2) thank God for what he has done; (3) ask God to help you and others; (4) request guidance as you read your Bible and make life choices; and (5) confess daily disobedience in your life and ask for his forgiveness.

In addition to instructing them in prayer, ask them how you can help them make the necessary changes in their life that would align their speech, thoughts, and actions with their profession that Jesus is Lord. Discuss with them how they intend to make these necessary changes. If the person is someone you know, who avoids discussing a behavior you know needs to change, lovingly ask how you can pray for that particular behavior. Also share a difficult adjustment you had to make to honor Jesus's lordship and how you conformed to his will.

Do False Professions of Faith Disqualify Evangelistic Disciple-Makers and Their Methods?

Inevitably, personal evangelists will share the gospel with unbelievers who indicate they want to become Christ's disciples and who initially appear to repent and believe. Nevertheless, they may never follow through with being baptized or being taught obedience to Christ. Or they may be baptized and begin to attend the church to which they now belong, but abruptly stop and cut off communication. Did the disciple-maker necessarily do something wrong? Should that person automatically assume the blame? Does this outcome mean that he or she should stop evangelizing out of fear it might happen again?

The answer to these questions is a resounding "No!" If the disciple-maker shared the gospel and instructed the other person in Great Commission discipleship, then those thoughts should not be entertained. Of course, personal evangelists can always improve their practice of evangelism, and no one ever does it perfectly. But as chapter 1 explained—if believers cannot take credit when people accept Christ, they also cannot take the blame when unbelievers reject Christ.

The fruit of the indwelling Spirit of God is the faith *shibboleth* of any person who has genuinely repented of sins, believed in Christ alone, and confessed, "Jesus is Lord" (cf. 2 Cor 13:5; Gal 5:22–23). If those who disciple-makers appear to lead to Christ do not follow through with the instruction they received, they also are not likely exhibiting the fruit of the Spirit. While personal evangelists feel a deep sense of hurt over those who falsely profess faith in Christ, it is unavoidable in disciple-making. It has happened to every professor of evangelism, pastor, and Christian who has ever consistently shared the gospel. It happened to John the beloved (1 John 2:19), Philip the evangelist (Acts 8:13–25), Paul the apostle in the churches with which he corresponded (cf. 1 Corinthians and Galatians), and it happened to Jesus Christ, the Son of God (Matt 26:14–16, 21–25; Mark 14:10–11, 18, 20–21; Luke 22:48–51; John 6:22–71; 8:13–59; 13:18, 26–27; 17:11–12; 18:2–3). In fact, Jesus described this phenomenon (Matt 13:1–9, 18–23, 24–30, 36–43; Mark 4:1–9, 13–20; Luke 8:4–8, 11–15).

In addition to the fruit of his Spirit, the Lord has provided another test by which those who have professed faith in Christ but do not exhibit a sanctifying life can be evaluated. In Matt 18:15–20, Jesus instructed his disciples in what is known as church discipline. Those who sin should be approached by those who have been sinned against. This meeting is not to enact retribution upon sinning ones but rather to restore them spiritually. They should be confronted, in love, with their sins and encouraged to repent. If this approach is exhausted, those sinned against should bring a witness to confront the sinning ones lovingly for the purpose of restoration. If this effort fails, then sinning ones are to be brought before the church. The church then pleads with the erring ones to repent. If this attempt is met with immediate resistance, then those who persist in their sins are removed from the membership and treated like outsiders. By treating them like outsiders, the members of the church should then seek to evangelize them.

An example of the confrontation of a newly baptized "disciple" with activity inconsistent with his profession of faith can be found in Acts 8:9–24. Simon the sorcerer heard Philip the evangelist preach the gospel. Simon indicated that he believed what he heard. Philip baptized him, after which Simon accompanied him everywhere he went around the town. When Peter and John traveled to Samaria after the church in Jerusalem heard about God's work there among the people, Simon went with them. They prayed and laid hands on the Samaritan believers, who then received the Holy Spirit. Simon then demonstrated that his profession of faith was false by offering money to the apostles to "buy" their power for himself to imbue the Spirit on others. Notice that Peter and John did not lay a guilt trip on Philip for evangelizing and baptizing Simon. They did not critique and chastise his methods. Instead, they disciplined Simon by informing him that he had no part with the matter, because his heart was not right with God. Peter went so far as to say that Simon's silver would perish just as he would. Although Simon feared what Peter said and asked for prayer, Luke did not indicate whether or not he repented and believed afterward.

The Scriptures referenced in this section instruct churches and believers on how to deal with those who falsely profess faith in Christ. First, biblically faithful personal evangelists should not be ridiculed or criticized when this situation occurs. Of course, every believer can be lovingly critiqued and advised about their practice of evangelism; however, if they are disciple-making in accordance with biblical instructions and examples, they and their methods should not be attacked by fellow believers. Second, disciple-makers who adhere to biblical principles should not impose guilt upon themselves for these occurrences. All Christians who evangelize will unfortunately see people falsely profess faith in Christ. This does not mean they should not do their due diligence in evangelism and discipleship. They should take comfort, knowing they are not the only ones who have experienced the hurt and pain they feel. Last, instead of abandoning newly baptized members who no longer exhibit spiritual fruitfulness, their churches have a responsibility to discipline them for the purpose of restoring them. Practicing church discipline on them assumes they may be believers needing help submitting to the lordship of Jesus Christ. Only after they come to the point of rejecting the entire church's rebuke and exhortation to them can the church know with certainty that they never belonged to the faith. In these cases, the church should intentionally try to win them to faith in Christ.

Disciple-Making in the Home

As this book has discussed, believers must make disciples in their churches, neighborhoods, workplaces, and third spaces. They should also make them on the go and around the world. Yet while they are going, they cannot neglect the disciple-making opportunities they have in their homes.

When preaching a sermon on heaven, D. L. Moody urged the fathers and mothers in attendance, "If we have made sure that our own names are written in heaven, the next most important thing is to be sure that our children's names are there."[9] Over a century and a half later, some Christian leaders echo this sentiment. For example, Chuck Lawless suggests, "Parents are to be the primary gospel witnesses in their children's lives. The God who gave birth to children through their parents expects their parents to be instrumental in leading them to their second birth."[10]

Nevertheless, as referenced in the preface, the twenty-first century's decline in evangelism by Christians across the board has taken its toll on numerous families with a rich Christian heritage. In the Southern Baptist context, baptism trends among young adults, youth, and children since the 1970s have precipitously declined.[11] As believers neglect

---

[9] D. L. Moody, "Heaven: Part I," in *Twelve Select Sermons* (Chicago: Revell, 1881), 135.

[10] Chuck Lawless, "My Concern about Much Evangelism Training, and 8 Reasons We Must Equip Parents to Evangelize Their Children," October 11, 2021, https://chucklawless.com/2021/10/my-concern-about-much-evangelism -training-and-8-reasons-we-must-equip-parents-to-evangelize-their-children/.

[11] Historically, Southern Baptists have reaped their greatest evangelistic harvest among children and teenagers, so this trend is both alarming and disturbing. Evidence of this decline can be seen in Bill Day's unpublished research through New Orleans Baptist Theological Seminary's Leavell Center for Evangelism and Church Health. In it, he reported: "I chose the period from the year before the highest number of baptisms in the SBC [1971] to 2014. It is interesting that the group with the lowest baptisms in 1972 (adults) have now become the highest group. It is also interesting that while baptisms of children and youth were having their steepest decline (1971–75), young adults and adults were having a period of growth. However, from 1975 to 1978, all four groups experienced major decline. It is a great concern to me that the baptisms of young adults have declined from 102,260 in 1980 to 51,192 in 2014 (a 67.5% decrease), the baptisms of youth have declined from 137,667 in 1972 to 71,457 in 2014 (a 48.1% decrease), and children's baptisms have declined from 159,770 in 1972 to 89,775 (a 43.8% decrease). Only adult baptisms have exceeded their 1972 total,

to make disciples in their homes and from among their children and grandchildren, which should be natural and disarming for them, they become less likely to evangelize people they know less intimately outside their homes. While a number of factors have contributed to this outcome, Lawless identifies one key reason for this trend: "Parents who have been trained to evangelize and disciple their children will be more comfortable doing so. One of the reasons [so many in our churches] expect pastors to evangelize their children and their church to disciple them is [because] we haven't trained them or held them accountable to the task. By our lack of training, we've let them off the hook."[12] Richard Ross, Southwestern Seminary professor of student ministry, has written extensively on this topic. Parents, grandparents, pastors, and churches interested in turning this tide would benefit from his insights.

For my part as I conclude this book, I would like to share how my wife, Hope, and I have practiced disciple-making in our home with our two daughters, Madison and Matia. Of all the types of evangelism we practice, Hope and I very much enjoy sharing the gospel door to door. When each of the girls was old enough to accompany us in her stroller, we took her evangelizing. We endeavored to provide opportunity after opportunity for both of them to hear the gospel, and they did.

As each of them grew and learned how to speak, we taught them to introduce our family when occupants of the homes we visited came to the door. They would say something like, "Hello, I am Madison/Matia. This is my mommy, and this is my daddy. Can we tell you about Jesus?" Every time, without fail, that we had one of the girls introduce us, Hope and I were able to share the entire gospel with the tenants and invite them to receive Christ. Every time a resident heard the gospel, our daughters also heard it. Together, Hope and I prayed that God would

---

going from 66,324 to 92,877 (a 40% increase)." Cited in Queen, *Mobilize to Evangelize*, 49 (see chap. 1, n. 20).

[12] Lawless, "My Concern about Much Evangelism Training, and 8 Reasons We Must Equip Parents to Evangelize Their Children."

use this way of saturating our children with the gospel to convict them of their sins, so one day in the future they would repent and believe. We also knew that taking them evangelizing with us was setting an example for them of what Christians were supposed to do. The more they heard the gospel shared and defended by their parents, as well as rejected or accepted by unbelievers, the more they would be prepared to evangelize if God saved them.

Thanks be to God, both of our girls met the Lord in their childhood. They walk with him daily. They are active in sharing their faith in Christ with others. In fact, their ability to evangelize in their childhood, and now into adolescence, has encouraged adults I know to begin proclaiming the gospel—convicted that if children can do it, they can too.

Two particular memories about the girls and evangelism stand out in my mind. First, I distinctly remember being surprised one day when Matia made her typical introduction at a door. The woman who lived in the house we visited said, "Yes, I will hear what you have to say." As I took a step forward to begin to tell her about Jesus, the lady put her hand up to stop me and said, "I will listen—if she tells me!" When she pointed to Matia, I was conflicted. While she had heard the gospel numerous times, she was not a believer, so she really had no business sharing the gospel. But if we said, "No," we would have lost an opportunity for this woman to hear the good news. I quickly reasoned that I would allow her to say whatever she would, and then I would follow up by presenting the gospel.

For a four-year-old who was unregenerate, Matia did a great job conveying the gospel as best as she understood it. When she finished, I said to the lady, "Ma'am, please allow me to fill in some of the gaps in what she said," and then told her about Christ, calling her to repent and believe. Although the lady did not receive Christ, Hope and I were able to gauge Matia's understanding of the gospel. While she did not share the gospel again until after she was saved, as she does quite frequently now, her attempt at evangelism helped Hope and me when we shared Christ with her at home.

Second, I remember having a conversation with a fellow believer about evangelism and how few people practice it. Madison, who had since become a believer, was with me listening intently. During the conversation, I lamented to my friend, "I do not want my girls to join the norm in Christianity and never share the gospel." Mild-mannered and quiet-spirited Madison quickly interrupted us and said, "Wait a minute, Daddy. Are you saying that it is not normal for Christians to share the gospel regularly?"

Both of these memories provide parents and grandparents, and other family members for that matter, three reasons why they should ensure that of all the places they make disciples, they do so at home. First, taking unsaved children in your family with you when you evangelize ensures they are exposed to the gospel multiple times. Second, lost children in your home who accompany you when you evangelize see how much the gospel means to you and how much it should mean to them one day when they receive it. Last, finding ways to hear your children recount to you the gospel they have heard from you will help you know exactly what they are understanding and not understanding about it. This information will assist you as you share the gospel with them one-on-one.

DISCUSSION AND REFLECTION QUESTIONS

1. Before reading this chapter, how did you understand the relationship between evangelism and discipleship? Did you believe them to be like conflicted enemies, conjoined twins, or cooperative friends? Has your perception changed? If so, why?

2. What do you consider to be the identifying marks of a genuine disciple of Jesus Christ?

3. How can you incorporate the three evangelism-to-discipleship bridges in your presentations of the gospel, as well as your instruction to new believers concerning discipleship? Have you identified any other bridges in the way you make disciples?

4. How do you deal with those you have personally evangelized and who have falsely professed faith in Christ? How do you treat or speak about others who have that experience? How does your church take steps to restore and reclaim those who may have falsely professed faith in Christ? If your church does not practice church discipline, what might be some ways it could begin to do so?

5. If you have children and/or grandchildren, do you have an intentional plan to make disciples of them? If not, what are some steps you can take to begin to enact such a plan? How can you encourage other Christian parents and grandparents to make disciples in their homes?

SUBJECT INDEX

SCRIPTURE INDEX

Mark

Luke